React Anti-Patterns

Build efficient and maintainable React applications
with test-driven development and refactoring

Juntao Qiu

BIRMINGHAM—MUMBAI

React Anti-Patterns

Copyright © 2023 Packt Publishing

Group Product Manager: Rohit Rajkumar
Publishing Product Manager: Jane D'Souza
Senior Editor: Hayden Edwards
Technical Editor: K Bimala Singha
Copy Editor: Safis Editing
Project Coordinator: Aishwarya Mohan
Proofreader: Safis Editing
Indexer: Subalakshmi Govindhan
Production Designer: Shankar Kalbhor
Marketing Coordinators: Namita Velgekar and Nivedita Pandey

First published: January 2024

Production reference: 1071223

Published by
Packt Publishing Ltd.
Grosvenor House
11 St Paul's Square
Birmingham
B3 1RB, UK

ISBN 978-1-80512-397-2

www.packtpub.com

To my loving wife, Mansi, and joyful daughter, Luna – your laughter was my daily respite, and your support allowed me the time at my desk to bring this book to fruition. While the pages reflect my work, they also echo your sacrifice and love. Thank you.

– Juntao

Contributors

About the author

Juntao Qiu is an accomplished software developer with over 15 years of industry experience, dedicated to helping others write better code. With a strong passion for crafting maintainable and high-quality code, he has become a trusted resource in the industry. As an author, Juntao has shared his expertise through influential books such as *Maintainable React* (2022) and *Test-Driven Development with React and TypeScript – Second Edition* (2023).

He orchestrates a blend of code snippets, illustrations, and before and after comparisons to unravel intricate concepts, making them accessible to fellow developers. His insightful blog posts at `https://juntao.substack.com/` and educational videos on YouTube (`https://www.youtube.com/@icodeit.juntao`) are a testament to his commitment to sharing knowledge and fostering a deeper understanding of coding practices within the developer community.

I am immensely thankful to my Atlassian teammates, Alex Reardon, Daniel Del Core, Michael Dougall, and many others. Many of the design patterns elucidated in this book germinated from our collective intellect while engrossed in Atlassian Design System components. A special shoutout to Tom Gasson, with whom I had an enriching time developing an internal system; our dialogues, particularly on React Context, have been significantly enlightening.

I also extend my appreciation to James Sinclair and Jason Sheehy for our enlightening discussions on TDD within our current monorepo. A special thank you goes to Vanessa Goah and Mirela Tomicic, who were instrumental during my recent onboarding. Their willingness to engage with my inquiries and provide clarity amid the myriad documents and conventions significantly accelerated my adaptation to the new project and enriched my understanding of the patterns embedded within the code base – a treasure trove of ideas discussed in this book.

My heartfelt appreciation goes to my former colleagues at Thoughtworks. Martin Fowler, your guidance has been a beacon, refining my focus and teaching me the essence of audience-centric writing. I am grateful to Xiaojun Ren for the stimulating design discussions, which were often accompanied by our serene strolls through the chilly suburbs of Melbourne. Thanks to Andy Marks and Cam Jackson for their meticulous reviews and insightful suggestions on technical nuances and linguistic improvements. The consultancy nature of the work at Thoughtworks provided a fertile ground to cross-pollinate ideas with various teams and individuals, an experience I hold dear.

A big thank you to my editor, Hayden Edwards, whose professional editing suggestions were instrumental in enhancing the narrative flow of this book. The journey from a manuscript to a published book is indeed a collaborative venture, and the unseen yet pivotal contributions from the team behind the scenes have been invaluable. Your expertise and dedication have breathed life into this work, and for that, I am profoundly grateful.

About the reviewers

Dennis Persson is a Swedish full stack web and mobile developer with over 10 years of expertise and a master of science degree in computer science and engineering. His academic journey includes a noteworthy tenure at Linköping University, where he imparted knowledge in more than a dozen courses, including both theoretical and practical applications of cutting-edge technologies.

Parallel to his current role as an application developer, Dennis manages a tech blog, providing insights into the evolving tech landscape. This unique combination of academic depth, practical expertise, and knowledge-sharing positions Dennis as a driving force at the intersection of education and industry innovation.

Krishnan Raghavan is an IT professional with over 20 years of experience in the areas of software development and delivery excellence across multiple domains and technologies, ranging from C++, Java, and Python to Angular, Golang, and data warehousing.

When not working, Krishnan likes to spend time with his wife and daughter, reading fiction and nonfiction as well as technical books, and participating in hackathons. Krishnan tries to give back to the community by being part of the GDG Pune volunteer group, helping the team to organize events.

Table of Contents

Part 1: Introducing the Fundamentals

1

2

3

4

Part 2: Embracing Testing Techniques

5

6

Exploring Common Refactoring Techniques 103

7

Introducing Test-Driven Development with React 119

Part 3: Unveiling Business Logic and Design Patterns

8

Exploring Data Management in React 147

9

Applying Design Principles in React   165

10

Diving Deep into Composition Patterns   187

Part 4: Engaging in Practical Implementation

11

Introducing Layered Architecture in React   217

12

Implementing an End-To-End Project   247

13

Recapping Anti-Pattern Principles   285

Preface

Building frontend applications is challenging, especially when constructing large ones, and the difficulty escalates without proper guidance. Unfortunately, many React-based applications fall into this scenario due to the library's UI-centric nature, leaving developers to navigate the other complexities of frontend development on their own. There are numerous other considerations such as asynchronous network requests, accessibility, performance, and state management, to name a few. These factors contribute to the complexity of frontend applications. As the scale of the application grows, maintaining the code becomes an arduous task. Adding new features requires considerably more time than it first appears, and identifying defects (and then fixing them) is equally challenging, if not more so.

However, these challenges are surmountable. We can learn to identify common anti-patterns that cause problems, then employ established patterns, design principles, and practices to address and rectify these issues. History teaches us that solutions derived in one field often find relevance in others, especially when it comes to fundamental design principles such as the Single Responsibility Principle, the Dependency Inversion Principle, and Don't Repeat Yourself. These principles guided the construction of UNIX systems back in the 1970s and Java Swing applications in the 1990s, and they remain valid today. They will undoubtedly continue to be pertinent for future frameworks and libraries.

This book seeks to delve into these problems and examine how established patterns and practices can mitigate the challenges of building large applications. We'll see how design principles and design patterns can simplify the design, making the code easier to understand, modify, and maintain in the long run. Through this exploration, readers will gain a deeper understanding of how to navigate the multifaceted world of frontend development with React, ensuring their applications are both robust and maintainable.

Who this book is for

This book is for React developers who are interested in improving the maintainability and efficiency of their code. Whether you're just starting out or have some experience under your belt, there's something here for you. It's beneficial to have a basic understanding of React, but the book aims to guide you through the concepts in a straightforward manner.

The focus is on identifying common anti-patterns and addressing them with established design principles and patterns. Through practical examples and a step-by-step approach, you'll learn how to simplify your code for better understanding, easier modifications, and long-term maintenance.

What this book covers

In *Chapter 1, Introducing React Anti-Patterns*, you'll get a closer look at the hurdles of building user interfaces, handling state management, addressing "unhappy paths," and identifying common anti-patterns in React.

In *Chapter 2, Understanding React Essentials*, you will delve into the basics of React covering static components, props, UI breakdown, state management, the rendering process, and common React Hooks to lay a solid foundation for subsequent chapters.

In *Chapter 3, Organizing Your React Application*, you will learn about different types of project structures in React, exploring their advantages, drawbacks, and practical applications.

In *Chapter 4, Designing your React Components*, you will learn to identify common anti-patterns in React component design and explore fundamental design principles including the Single Responsibility Principle and Don't Repeat Yourself to improve component structure.

In *Chapter 5, Testing in React*, you will learn about the significance of software testing, explore various types of tests such as unit, integration, and end-to-end testing, and get acquainted with popular testing tools including Cypress and Jest, setting a strong foundation for complex testing scenarios in React applications.

In *Chapter 6, Exploring Common Refactoring Techniques*, you will learn about the essence of refactoring and delve into various refactoring techniques, such as Rename Variable, Extract Variable, and Replace Loop with Pipeline, to enhance code maintainability and readability.

In *Chapter 7, Introducing Test-Driven Development with React*, you'll learn the core principles of test-driven development through a practical example, while building various features of a pizza store's menu page in a React application.

In *Chapter 8, Exploring Data Management in React*, you'll delve into the common challenges of state management in React, such as business logic leaks and prop drilling, and explore solutions including employing an Anti-Corruption Layer and utilizing the React context API to enhance code maintainability and user experience.

In *Chapter 9, Applying Design Principles in React*, you'll revisit the Single Responsibility Principle, embrace the Dependency Inversion Principle, and understand the application of Command and Query Responsibility Segregation in React to fortify your knowledge of key design principles to aid you in mastering React.

In *Chapter 10, Diving Deep into Composition Patterns*, you'll delve into composition through higher-order components and custom Hooks, and explore the headless component pattern. You'll gain an appreciation of composition techniques for creating scalable, maintainable, and user-friendly UIs in React.

In *Chapter 11, Introducing Layered Architecture in React*, you'll explore Layered Architecture, delve into Application Concern Layers, define data models, and learn strategy patterns through a practical example, understanding their significance for large-scale applications.

In *Chapter 12, Implementing an End-To-End Project*, you'll traverse the complete process of developing a weather application, from understanding requirements to implementing features such as City Search and Add To Favourite, while ensuring the code remains maintainable, understandable, and extensible.

In *Chapter 13, Recapping Anti-Pattern Principles*, we'll take a concise look back at common anti-patterns, React design patterns, and fundamental principles, and recap the techniques and practices discussed earlier in the book, providing a succinct refresher before you continue applying these insights to your own projects.

To get the most out of this book

To delve deeply into this book, having a text editor at hand is crucial; choices such as Visual Studio Code or Vim are commendable, but any other editor of your preference will serve well. An alternative is a full-featured **Integrated Development Environment** (IDE) such as WebStorm or IntelliJ, which, while not mandatory, could significantly ramp up your efficiency.

A command-line interface is another requisite; for Mac or Linux users, the setup is already in place, but Windows users might need to make an installation—Windows Terminal is a good choice, providing a modern terminal and command-line experience. Preparing these tools in advance will ensure a seamless journey as you traverse through the content of this book.

Software/hardware covered in the book	Operating system requirements
React 16+	Windows, macOS, or Linux
TypeScript 4.9.5	
Visual Studio Code or WebStorm	
Terminal/Window Terminal (for Windows users)	

Download the example code files

You can download the example code files for this book from GitHub at `https://github.com/PacktPublishing/React-Anti-Patterns/`. If there's an update to the code, it will be updated in the GitHub repository.

We also have other code bundles from our rich catalog of books and videos available at `https://github.com/PacktPublishing/`. Check them out!

Conventions used

There are a number of text conventions used throughout this book.

`Code in text`: Indicates code words in text, database table names, folder names, filenames, file extensions, pathnames, dummy URLs, user input, and Twitter handles. Here is an example: "We can then pass the desired `heading` and `summary` to the `Article` component."

A block of code is set as follows:

```
<Article
  heading="Think in components"
  summary="It's important to change your mindset when coding with
React."
/>
```

When we wish to draw your attention to a particular part of a code block, the relevant lines or items are set in bold:

```
<article>
  <h3>Think in components</h3>
  <p>It's important to change your mindset when coding with React.</p>
</article>
```

Any command-line input or output is written as follows:

```
$ mkdir css
$ cd css
```

Bold: Indicates a new term, an important word, or words that you see onscreen. For instance, words in menus or dialog boxes appear in **bold**. Here is an example: "Select **System info** from the **Administration** panel."

> Tips or important notes
> Appear like this.

Get in touch

Feedback from our readers is always welcome.

General feedback: If you have questions about any aspect of this book, email us at `customercare@packtpub.com` and mention the book title in the subject of your message.

Errata: Although we have taken every care to ensure the accuracy of our content, mistakes do happen. If you have found a mistake in this book, we would be grateful if you would report this to us. Please visit `www.packtpub.com/support/errata` and fill in the form.

Piracy: If you come across any illegal copies of our works in any form on the internet, we would be grateful if you would provide us with the location address or website name. Please contact us at `copyright@packt.com` with a link to the material.

If you are interested in becoming an author: If there is a topic that you have expertise in and you are interested in either writing or contributing to a book, please visit `authors.packtpub.com`.

Share Your Thoughts

Once you've read *React Anti-Patterns*, we'd love to hear your thoughts! Scan the QR code below to go straight to the Amazon review page for this book and share your feedback.

https://packt.link/r/1-805-12397-1

Your review is important to us and the tech community and will help us make sure we're delivering excellent quality content.

Download a free PDF copy of this book

Thanks for purchasing this book!

Do you like to read on the go but are unable to carry your print books everywhere?

Is your eBook purchase not compatible with the device of your choice?

Don't worry, now with every Packt book you get a DRM-free PDF version of that book at no cost.

Read anywhere, any place, on any device. Search, copy, and paste code from your favorite technical books directly into your application.

The perks don't stop there, you can get exclusive access to discounts, newsletters, and great free content in your inbox daily

Follow these simple steps to get the benefits:

1. Scan the QR code or visit the link below

https://packt.link/free-ebook/9781805123972

2. Submit your proof of purchase
3. That's it! We'll send your free PDF and other benefits to your email directly

Part 1: Introducing the Fundamentals

In the first part of this book, you will set foot into the realm of React by exploring its core essentials and understanding how to efficiently structure your application. This part will aid in building a strong foundation, crucial to navigate through the more complex aspects of React that are discussed in the following parts.

This part contains the following chapters:

- *Chapter 1, Introducing React Anti-Patterns*
- *Chapter 2, Understanding React Essentials*
- *Chapter 3, Organizing Your React Application*
- *Chapter 4, Designing Your React Components*

Introducing React Anti-Patterns

This book dives deep into the realm of React anti-patterns. An anti-pattern is not necessarily a technical error – the code often functions properly at first – but although it may initially seem correct, as the code base expands, these anti-patterns can become problematic.

As we navigate through the book, we'll scrutinize code samples that might not embody best practices; some could be intricate to decipher, and others, tough to modify or extend. While certain pieces of code may suffice for smaller tasks, they falter when scaled up. Moreover, we'll venture into time-tested patterns and principles from the expansive software world, seamlessly weaving them into our frontend discourse.

I aim for practicality. The code illustrations originate either from past projects or commonplace domains such as a shopping cart and a user profile component, minimizing your need to decipher domain jargon. For a holistic view, the concluding chapters showcase detailed, end-to-end examples, furnishing a more organized and immersive experience.

Specifically, in this introductory chapter, we'll address the intricacies of constructing advanced React applications, highlighting how state management and asynchronous operations can obfuscate code clarity. We'll enumerate prevalent anti-patterns and offer a glimpse into the remedial strategies detailed later in the book.

In this chapter, we will cover the following topics:

- Understanding the difficulty of building UIs
- Understanding the state management
- Exploring "unhappy paths"
- Exploring common anti-patterns in React

Technical requirements

A GitHub repository has been created to host all the code we discuss in the book. For this chapter, you can find the code at `https://github.com/PacktPublishing/React-Anti-Patterns/tree/main/code/src/ch1`.

Understanding the difficulty of building UIs

Unless you're building a straightforward, document-like web page — for example, a basic article without advanced UI elements such as search boxes or modals — the built-in languages offered by web browsers are generally insufficient. *Figure 1.1* shows an example of a website using **HTML** (**HyperText Markup Language**):

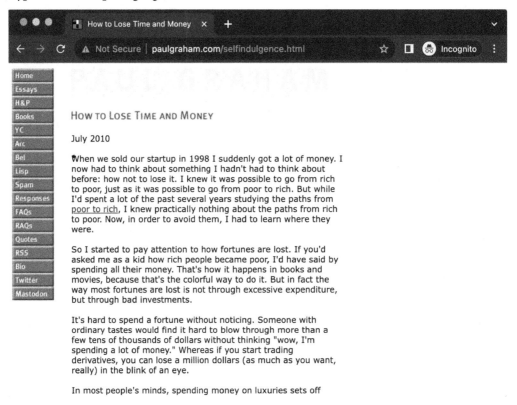

Figure 1.1: A simple HTML document website

However nowadays, most applications are more complicated and contain more elements than what this language was originally designed for.

The disparity between the language of the web and the UI experiences that people encounter daily is substantial. Whether it's a ticket booking platform, a project management tool, or an image gallery, modern web UIs are intricate and native web languages don't readily support them. You can go the extra mile to "simulate" UI components such as accordions, toggle switches, or interactive cards, but fundamentally, you're still working with what amounts to a document, not a genuine UI component.

In an ideal world, building a UI would resemble working with a visual UI designer. Tools such as C++ Builder or Delphi, or more modern alternatives such as Figma, let you drag and drop components onto a canvas that then renders seamlessly on any screen. This isn't the case with web development. For instance, to create a custom search input, you'll need to wrap it in additional elements, fine-tune colors, adjust padding and fonts, and perhaps add an icon for user guidance. Creating an auto-suggestion list that appears right under the search box, matching its width exactly, is often far more labor-intensive than one might initially think.

As shown in *Figure 1.2*, a web page can be super complicated and look nothing like a document on the surface, although the building blocks of the page are still pure HTML:

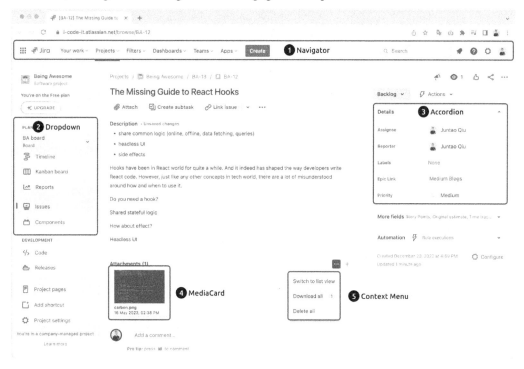

Figure 1.2: Jira issue view

This screenshot shows the issue view of Jira, a popular web-based project management tool used to track, prioritize, and coordinate tasks and projects. An issue view contains many details such as the issue's title, description, attachments, comments, and linked issues. It also contains many elements a user can interact with, such as an **Assign to me** button, the ability to change the priority of the issue, add a comment, and so on.

For such a UI, you might expect there to be a navigator component, a drop-down list, an accordion, and so on. And seemingly, they are there, as labeled in *Figure 1.2*. But they are not actually components. Instead, developers have worked hard to *simulate* these with HTML, CSS, and JavaScript.

Now that we've glanced over the language mismatch issue in web UI development, it might be helpful to delve into what's under the surface – the different states we need to manage in frontend applications. This will provide a taste of the challenges that lie ahead and shed light on why introducing patterns is a key step toward addressing them.

Understanding the state management

Managing the state in modern frontend development is a complex task. Nearly every application has to retrieve data from a remote server via a network – we can call this data **remote states**. Remote state originates from an external source, typically a backend server or API. This is in contrast to local state, which is generated and managed entirely within the frontend application itself.

There are many dark sides of remote states, making the frontend development difficult if you don't pay close attention to them. Here, I'll just list a few obvious considerations:

- *Asynchronous nature*: Fetching data from a remote source is usually an asynchronous operation. This adds complexity in terms of timing, especially when you have to synchronize multiple pieces of remote data.

- *Error handling*: Connections to remote sources might fail or the server might return errors. Properly managing these scenarios for a smooth user experience can be challenging.

- *Loading states*: While waiting for data to arrive from a remote source, the application needs to handle "loading" states effectively. This usually involves showing loading indicators or fallback UIs (when the requesting component isn't available, we use a default one temporarily).

- *Consistency*: Keeping the frontend state in sync with the backend can be difficult, especially in real-time applications or those that involve multiple users altering the same piece of data.

- *Caching*: Storing some remote state locally can improve performance but bring its own challenges, such as invalidation and staleness. In other words, if the remote data is altered by others, we need a mechanism to receive updates or perform a refetch to update our local state, which introduces a lot of complexity.

- *Updates and optimistic UI*: When a user makes a change, you can update the UI optimistically assuming the server call will succeed. But if it doesn't, you'll need a way to roll back those changes in your frontend state.

And those are only some of the challenges of remote states.

When the data is stored and accessible immediately in the frontend, you basically think in a linear way. This means you access and manipulate data in a straightforward sequence, one operation following another, leading to a clear and direct flow of logic. This way of thinking aligns well with the synchronous nature of the code, making the development process intuitive and easier to follow.

Let's compare how much more code we'll need for rendering static data with remote data. Think about a famous quotes application that displays a list of quotes on the page.

To render the passed-in quotes list, you can map the data into JSX elements, like so:

```
function Quotes(quotes: string[]) {
  return (
    <ul>
      {quotes.map((quote, index) => <li key={index}>{quote}</li>)}
    </ul>
  );
}
```

> **Note**
>
> We're using index as the key here, which is fine for static quotes. However, it's generally best to avoid this practice. Using indices can lead to rendering issues in dynamic lists in real-world scenarios.

If the quotes are from a remote server, the code will turn into something like the following:

```
import React, { useState, useEffect } from 'react';

function Quotes() {
  const [quotes, setQuotes] = useState<string[]>([]);

  useEffect(() => {
    fetch('https://quote-service.com/quotes')
      .then(response => response.json())
      .then(data => setQuotes(data));
  }, []);

  return (
    <ul>
      {quotes.map((quote, index) => <li key={index}>{quote}</li>)}
    </ul>
  );
}

export default Quotes;
```

In this React component, we use `useState` to create a quotes state variable, initially set as an empty array. The `useEffect` Hook fetches quotes from a remote server when the component mounts. It then updates the quotes state with the fetched data. Finally, the component renders a list of quotes, iterating through the `quotes` array.

Don't worry, there's no need to sweat about the details for now; we'll delve into them in the next chapter on React essentials.

The previous code example shows the ideal scenario, but in reality, asynchronous calls come with their own challenges. We have to think about what to display while data is being fetched and how to handle various error scenarios, such as network issues or resource unavailability. These added complexities can make the code lengthier and more difficult to grasp.

For instance, while fetching data, we temporarily transition into a loading state, and should anything go awry, we shift to an error state:

```
function Quotes() {
  const [quotes, setQuotes] = useState<string[]>([]);
  const [isLoading, setIsLoading] = useState<boolean>(false);
  const [error, setError] = useState<Error | null>(null);

  useEffect(() => {
    setIsLoading(true);

    fetch('https://quote-service.com/quotes')
      .then(response => {
        if (!response.ok) {
          throw new Error('Failed to fetch quotes');
        }
        return response.json();
      })
      .then(data => {
        setQuotes(data);
      })
      .catch(err => {
        setError(err.message);
      })
      .finally(() => {
        setIsLoading(false);
      });
  }, []);

  return (
    <div>
      {isLoading && <p>Loading...</p>}
```

```
      {error && <p>Error: {error}</p>}
      <ul>
        {quotes.map((quote, index) => <li key={index}>{quote}</li>)}
      </ul>
    </div>
  );
}
```

The code uses useState to manage three pieces of state: quotes for storing the quotes, isLoading for tracking the loading status, and error for any fetch errors.

The useEffect Hook triggers the fetch operation. If the fetch is successful, the quotes are displayed and isLoading is set to false. If an error occurs, an error message is displayed and isLoading is again set to false.

As you can observe, the portion of the component dedicated to actual rendering is quite small (i.e., the JSX code inside return). In contrast, managing the state consumes nearly two-thirds of the function's body.

But that's just one aspect of the state management. There's also the matter of managing local state, which means the state only needs to be maintained inside a component. For example, as demonstrated in *Figure 1.3*, an accordion component needs to track whether it's expanded or collapsed – when you click the triangle on the header, it toggles the list panel:

Figure 1.3: An expandable section

Using a third-party state management library such as Redux or MobX can be beneficial when your application reaches a level of complexity that makes state tracking difficult. However, using a third-party state management library isn't without its caveats (learning curve, best practices in a particular library, migration efforts, etc.) and should be considered carefully. That's why many developers are leaning toward using React's built-in Context API for state management.

Another significant complexity in modern frontend applications that often goes unnoticed by many developers, yet is akin to an iceberg that warrants closer attention, is "unhappy paths." Let's look at these next.

Exploring "unhappy paths"

When it comes to UI development, our primary focus is often on the "happy path" – the optimal user journey where everything goes as planned. However, neglecting the "unhappy paths" can make your UI far more complicated than you might initially think. Here are some scenarios that could lead to unhappy paths and consequently complicate your UI development efforts.

Errors thrown from other components

Imagine that you're using a third-party component or even another team's component within your application. If that component throws an error, it could potentially break your UI or lead to unexpected behaviors that you have to account for. This can involve adding conditional logic or error boundaries to handle these errors gracefully, making your UI more complex than initially anticipated.

For example, in a `MenuItem` component that renders an item's data, let's see what happens when we try accessing something that doesn't exist in the passed-in prop `item` (in this case, we're looking for the aptly named `item.something.doesnt.exist`):

```
const MenuItem = ({
  item,
  onItemClick,
}: {
  item: MenuItemType;
  onItemClick: (item: MenuItemType) => void;
}) => {
  const information = item.something.doesnt.exist;

  return (
    <li key={item.name}>
      <h3>{item.name}</h3>
      <p>{item.description}</p>
      <button onClick={() => onItemClick(item)}>Add to Cart</button>
    </li>
  );
};
```

The `MenuItem` component receives an `item` object and an `onItemClick` function as props. It displays the item's name and description, as well as including an **Add to Cart** button. When the button is clicked, the `onItemClick` function is called with the item as an argument.

This code attempts to access a non-existing property, `item.something.doesnt.exist`, which will cause a runtime error. As demonstrated in *Figure 1.4*, the application stopped working after the backend service returned some unexpected data:

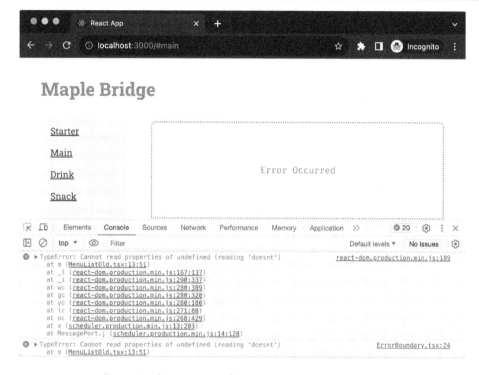

Figure 1.4: A component-thrown exception during render

This can cause the whole application to crash if we don't isolate the error into an **error boundary**, as we can see in *Figure 1.4* – the menus are not displayed, but the category and page titles remain functional; the area affected, which I've outlined with a red dotted line, is where the menus were supposed to appear. Error boundaries in React are a feature that allows you to catch JavaScript errors that occur in child components, log those errors, and display a fallback UI instead of letting the whole app crash. Error boundaries catch errors during rendering, in life cycle methods, and in constructors of the whole tree below them.

In real-world projects, your UI might depend on various microservices or APIs for fetching data. If any of these downstream systems are down, your UI has to account for it. You'll need to design fallbacks, loading indicators, or friendly error messages that guide the user on what to do next. Handling these scenarios effectively often involves both frontend and backend logic, thus adding another layer of complexity to your UI development tasks.

Learning the unexpected user behavior

No matter how perfectly you design your UI, users will always find ways to use your system in manners you didn't anticipate. Whether they input special characters in text fields, try to submit forms too quickly, or use browser extensions that interfere with your site, you have to design your UI to handle these edge cases. This means implementing additional validation, checks, and safeguards that can complicate your UI code base.

Let's examine a basic `Form` component to understand the considerations for user input. While this single-field form might require additional logic in the `handleChange` method, it's important to note that most forms typically consist of several fields (which means there will be more unexpected user behavior we need to consider):

```
import React, { ChangeEvent, useState } from "react";

const Form = () => {
  const [value, setValue] = useState<string>("");

  const handleChange = (event: ChangeEvent<HTMLInputElement>) => {
    const inputValue = event.target.value;
    const sanitizedValue = inputValue.replace(/[^\w\s]/gi, "");
    setValue(sanitizedValue);
  };

  return (
    <div>
      <form>
        <label>
          Input without special characters:
          <input type="text" value={value} onChange={handleChange} />
        </label>
      </form>
    </div>
  );
};

export default Form;
```

This `Form` component consists of a single text input field that restricts input to alphanumeric characters and spaces. It uses a `value` state variable to store the input field's value. The `handleChange` function, triggered on each input change, removes any non-alphanumeric characters from the user's input before updating the state with the sanitized value.

Understanding and effectively managing these unhappy paths are critical to creating a robust, resilient, and user-friendly interface. Not only do they make your application more reliable, but they also contribute to a more comprehensive and well-thought-out user experience.

I believe you should now have a clearer insight into the challenges of building modern frontend applications in React. Tackling these hurdles isn't straightforward, particularly since React doesn't offer a definitive guide on which approach to adopt, how to structure your code base, manage states, or ensure code readability (and by extension, ease of maintenance in the long run), or how established patterns can be of aid, among other concerns. This lack of guidance often leads developers to create solutions that might work in the short term but could be riddled with anti-patterns.

Exploring common anti-patterns in React

Within the realm of software development, we often encounter practices and approaches that, at first glance, appear to offer a beneficial solution to a particular problem. These practices, labeled as **anti-patterns**, may provide immediate relief or a seemingly quick fix, but they often hide underlying issues. Over time, reliance on these anti-patterns can lead to greater complexities, inefficiencies, or even the very issues they were thought to resolve.

Recognizing and understanding these anti-patterns is crucial for developers, as it enables them to anticipate potential pitfalls and steer clear of solutions that may be counterproductive in the long run. In the upcoming sections, we'll highlight common anti-patterns accompanied by code examples. We'll address each anti-pattern and outline potential solutions. However, we won't delve deeply here since entire chapters are dedicated to discussing these topics in detail.

Props drilling

In complex React applications, managing state and ensuring that every component has access to the data it needs can become challenging. This is often observed in the form of **props drilling**, where props are passed from a parent component through multiple intermediary components before they reach the child component that actually needs them.

For instance, consider a `SearchableList`, `List`, and a `ListItem` hierarchy – a `SearchableList` component contains a `List` component, and `List` contains multiple instances of `ListItem`:

```
function SearchableList({ items, onItemClick }) {
  return (
    <div className="searchable-list">
      {/* Potentially some search functionality here */}
      <List items={items} onItemClick={onItemClick} />
    </div>
  );
}

function List({ items, onItemClick }) {
  return (
    <ul className="list">
      {items.map(item => (
        <ListItem key={item.id} data={item} onItemClick={onItemClick}
        />
      ))}
    </ul>
  );
}

function ListItem({ data, onItemClick }) {
```

```
    return (
      <li className="list-item" onClick={() => onItemClick(data.id)}>
        {data.name}
      </li>
    );
  }
```

In this setup, the `onItemClick` prop is drilled from `SearchableList` through `List` and finally to `ListItem`. Though the `List` component doesn't use this prop, it has to pass it down to `ListItem`.

This approach can lead to increased complexity and reduced maintainability. When multiple props are passed down through various components, understanding the flow of data and debugging can become difficult.

A potential solution to avoid props drilling in React is by leveraging the Context API. It provides a way to share values (data and functions) between components without having to explicitly pass props through every level of the component tree.

In-component data transformation

The component-centric approach in React is all about breaking up tasks and concerns into manageable chunks, enhancing maintainability. One recurrent misstep, however, is when developers introduce complex data transformation logic directly within components.

It's common, especially when dealing with external APIs or backends, to receive data in a shape or format that isn't ideal for the frontend. Instead of adjusting this data at a higher level, or in a utility function, the transformation is defined inside the component.

Consider the following scenario:

```
function UserProfile({ userId }) {
  const [user, setUser] = useState(null);

  useEffect(() => {
    fetch(`/api/users/${userId}`)
      .then(response => response.json())
      .then(data => {
        // Transforming data right inside the component
        const transformedUser = {
          name: `${data.firstName} ${data.lastName}`,
          age: data.age,
          address: `${data.addressLine1}, ${data.city}, ${data.
          country}`
        };
        setUser(transformedUser);
```

```
    });
  }, [userId]);

  return (
    <div>
      {user && (
        <>
          <p>Name: {user.name}</p>
          <p>Age: {user.age}</p>
          <p>Address: {user.address}</p>
        </>
      )}
    </div>
  );
}
```

The `UserProfile` function component retrieves and displays a user's profile based on the provided prop `userId`. Once the remote `data` is fetched, it's transformed within the component itself to create a structured user profile. This transformed data consists of the user's full name (a combination of first and last name), age, and a formatted address.

By directly embedding the transformation, we encounter a few issues:

- *Lack of clarity*: Combining data fetching, transformation, and rendering tasks within a single component makes it harder to pinpoint the component's exact purpose

- *Reduced reusability*: Should another component require the same or a similar transformation, we'd be duplicating logic

- *Testing challenges*: Testing this component now requires considering the transformation logic, making tests more convoluted

To combat this anti-pattern, it's advised to separate data transformation from the component. This can be achieved using utility functions or custom Hooks, thus ensuring a cleaner and more modular design. By externalizing these transformations, components remain focused on rendering and business logic stays centralized, making for a far more maintainable code base.

Complicated logic in views

The beauty of modern frontend frameworks, including React, is the distinct separation of concerns. By design, components should be oblivious to the intricacies of business logic, focusing instead on presentation. However, a recurrent pitfall that developers encounter is the infusion of business logic within view components. This not only disrupts the clean separation but also bloats components and makes them harder to test and reuse.

Consider a simple example. Imagine a component that is meant to display a list of items fetched from an API. Each item has a price, but we want to display items above a certain threshold price:

```
function PriceListView({ items }) {
  // Business logic within the view
  const filterExpensiveItems = (items) => {
    return items.filter(item => item.price > 100);
  }

  const expensiveItems = filterExpensiveItems(items);

  return (
    <div>
      {expensiveItems.map(item => (
        <div key={item.id}>
          {item.name}: ${item.price}
        </div>
      ))}
    </div>
  );
}
```

Here, the `filterExpensiveItems` function, a piece of business logic, resides directly within the view component. The component is now tasked with not just presenting data but also processing it.

This approach can become problematic:

- *Reusability*: If another component requires a similar filter, the logic would need to be duplicated

- *Testing*: Unit testing becomes more complex as you're not just testing the rendering, but also the business logic

- *Maintenance*: As the application grows and more logic is added, this component can become unwieldy and harder to maintain

To ensure our components remain reusable and easy to maintain, it's wise to embrace the **separation of concerns** principle. This principle states that each module or function in software should have responsibility over a single part of the application's functionality. By separating the business logic from the presentation layer and adopting a **layered architecture**, we can ensure each part of our code handles its own specific responsibility, leading to a more modular and maintainable code base.

Lack of tests

Imagine building a shopping cart component for an online store. The cart is crucial as it handles item additions, removals, and total price calculations. As straightforward as it may seem, it embodies various moving parts and logic interconnections. Without tests, you leave the door open for future problems, such as incorrect pricing, items not being added or removed correctly, or even security vulnerabilities.

Consider this simplistic version of a shopping cart:

```
function ShoppingCart() {
  const [items, setItems] = useState([]);

  const addItem = (item) => {
    setItems([...items, item]);
  };

  const removeItem = (itemId) => {
    setItems(items.filter(item => item.id !== itemId));
  };

  const calculateTotal = () => {
    return items.reduce((total, item) => total + item.price, 0);
  };

  return (
    <div>
      {/* Render items and controls for adding/removing */}
      <p>Total: ${calculateTotal()}</p>
    </div>
  );
}
```

While this shopping cart's logic appears straightforward, potential pitfalls are lurking. What if an item gets added multiple times erroneously, or prices change dynamically, or discounts are applied? Without tests, these scenarios might not be evident until a user encounters them, which could be detrimental to the business.

Enter **test-driven development** (**TDD**). TDD emphasizes writing tests before the actual component or logic. For our ShoppingCart component, it means having tests verifying that items are correctly added or removed, total calculations are adjusted appropriately, and edge cases, such as handling discounts, are managed. Only after these tests are in place should the actual component logic be implemented. TDD is more than just catching errors early; it champions well-structured, maintainable code.

For the ShoppingCart component, adopting TDD would necessitate tests ensuring items get added or removed as expected, totals are correctly computed, and edge cases are tackled seamlessly. This way, as the application grows, the foundational TDD tests ensure each modification or addition maintains the application's integrity and correctness.

Duplicated code

It's a familiar sight in many code bases – chunks of identical or very similar code scattered across different parts of the application. Duplicated code not only bloats the code base but also introduces potential points of failure. When a bug is detected or an enhancement is needed, every instance of the duplicated code may need to be altered, leading to an increased likelihood of introducing errors.

Let's consider two components in which the same filtering logic is repeated:

```
function AdminList(props) {
  const filteredUsers = props.users.filter(user => user.isAdmin);
  return <List items={filteredUsers} />;
}

function ActiveList(props) {
  const filteredUsers = props.users.filter(user => user.isActive);
  return <List items={filteredUsers} />;
}
```

The **DRY (don't repeat yourself) principle** comes to the rescue here. By centralizing common logic into utility functions or **higher-order components (HOCs)**, the code becomes more maintainable and readable, and less prone to errors. For this example, we could abstract the filtering logic and reuse it, ensuring a singular source of truth and easier updates.

Long component with too much responsibility

React encourages the creation of modular, reusable components. However, as features get added, a component can quickly grow in size and responsibility, turning into an unwieldy behemoth. A long component that manages various tasks becomes difficult to maintain, understand, and test.

Imagine an `OrderContainer` component that has a huge prop list that includes a lot of different aspects of the responsibilities:

```
const OrderContainer = ({
  testID,
  orderData,
  basketError,
  addCoupon,
  voucherSelected,
  validationErrors,
  clearErrors,
  removeLine,
  editLine,
  hideOrderButton,
  hideEditButton,
```

```
  loading,
}: OrderContainerProps) => {
  //..
}
```

Such a component violates the **single-responsibility principle** (**SRP**), which advocates that a component should fulfill only one function. By taking on multiple roles, it becomes more complex and less maintainable. We need to analyze the core responsibility of the `OrderContainer` component and separate the supporting logic into other smaller, focused components or utilize Hooks for logic separation.

> **Note**
>
> These listed anti-patterns have different variations, and we'll discuss the solutions correspondingly in the following chapters. Apart from that, there are also some more generic design principles and design patterns we'll discuss in the book, as well as some proven engineering practices, such as refactoring and TDD.

Unveiling our approach to demolishing anti-patterns

When it comes to addressing prevalent anti-patterns, an arsenal of design patterns comes to the fore. Techniques such as **render props**, HOCs, and **Hooks** are instrumental in augmenting component capabilities without deviating from their primary roles, while leveraging foundational patterns such as layered architecture and separation of concerns ensures a streamlined code base, demarcating logic, data, and presentation in a coherent manner. Such practices don't just elevate the sustainability of React apps but also lay the groundwork for effective teamwork among developers.

Meanwhile, **interface-oriented programming**, at its core, zeroes in on tailoring software centered around the interactions occurring between software modules, predominantly via interfaces. Such a modus operandi fosters agility, rendering software modules not only more coherent but also amenable to alterations. The **headless components** paradigm, on the other hand, embodies components that, while devoid of direct rendering duties, are entrusted with the management of state or logic. These components pass the baton to their consuming counterparts for UI rendering, thus championing adaptability and reusability.

By gaining a firm grasp on these design patterns and deploying them judiciously, we're positioned to circumvent prevalent missteps, thereby uplifting the stature of our React applications.

Plus, within the coding ecosystem, the twin pillars of TDD and consistent refactoring emerge as formidable tools to accentuate code quality. TDD, with its clarion call of test-before-code, furnishes an immediate feedback loop for potential discrepancies. Hand-in-hand with TDD, the ethos of persistent refactoring ensures that code is perpetually optimized and honed. Such methodologies not only set the benchmark for code excellence but also instill adaptability to forthcoming changes.

As we navigate the realm of refactoring, it's pivotal to delve into the essence of these techniques, discerning their intricacies and optimal application points. Harnessing these refactoring avenues promises to bolster your code's clarity, sustainability, and overarching efficiency. This is something that we'll be doing throughout the book!

Summary

In this chapter, we explored the challenges of UI development from its complexities to state management issues. We also discussed the common anti-patterns due to the nature of its complexity, and briefly introduced our approach that combines best practices and effective testing strategies. This sets the foundation for more efficient and robust frontend development.

In the upcoming chapter, we'll dive deep into React essentials, giving you the tools and knowledge you need to master this powerful library. Stay tuned!

2
Understanding React Essentials

Welcome to this fundamental chapter of our React essentials guide! This chapter serves as a solid foundation for your journey into the exciting world of React development. We will delve into the fundamental concepts of React and provide you with the essential knowledge needed to kickstart your React projects with confidence.

In this chapter, we will explore how to think in components, a crucial mindset for building reusable and modular **user interfaces** (**UIs**). You will learn the art of breaking your application down into smaller, self-contained components, enabling you to create maintainable and scalable code bases. By understanding this fundamental concept, you will be equipped with the skills to architect robust and flexible React applications.

Additionally, we will introduce you to the most commonly used Hooks in React, such as `useState`, `useEffect`, and more. These Hooks are powerful tools that allow you to manage state, handle side effects, and tap into React's lifecycle methods within functional components. By mastering these Hooks, you will have the ability to create dynamic and interactive UIs effortlessly.

By the end of this chapter, you will be well prepared to explore more advanced topics and tackle real-world React challenges in the subsequent chapters of our guide. So, buckle up and get ready to embark on an exciting journey into the world of React.

So, in this chapter, we will cover the following topics:

- Understanding static components in React
- Creating components with props
- Breaking down UIs into components
- Managing internal state in React
- Understanding the rendering process
- Exploring common React Hooks

Technical requirements

A GitHub repository has been created to host all the code we discuss in the book. For this chapter, you can find it under `https://github.com/PacktPublishing/React-Anti-Patterns/tree/main/code/src/ch2`.

Understanding static components in React

React applications are built on components. A **component** can range from a simple function returning an HTML snippet to a more complex one that interacts with network requests, dynamically generates HTML tags, and even auto-refreshes based on backend service changes.

Let's start with a basic scenario and define a **static component**. In React, a static component (also known as presentational components or dumb components) refers to a component that doesn't have any state and doesn't interact with the data or handle any events. It is a component that only renders the UI based on the props it receives. Here's an example:

```
const StaticArticle = () => {
  return (
    <article>
      <h3>Think in components</h3>
      <p>It's important to change your mindset when coding with
      React.</p>
    </article>
  );
};
```

This static component closely resembles the corresponding HTML snippet, which uses the `<article>` tag to structure content with a title and a paragraph:

```
<article>
  <h3>Think in components</h3>
  <p>It's important to change your mindset when coding with React.</p>
</article>
```

While encapsulating static HTML in a component is useful, there may be a need for the component to represent different articles, not just a specific one. Just as we pass parameters to a function to make it more versatile, we can pass parameters into a component to make it useful in different contexts. That can be done with props, which we will discuss in the next section.

Creating components with props

In React, components can receive input in the form of properties, which are commonly referred to as props. **Props** allow us to pass data from a parent component to its child components. This mechanism enables components to be reusable and adaptable, as they can receive different sets of props to customize their behavior and appearance.

Props are essentially JavaScript objects containing key-value pairs, where the keys represent the prop names and the values contain the corresponding data. These props can include various types of data, such as strings, numbers, Booleans, or even functions.

By passing props to a component, we can control its rendering and behavior dynamically. This allows us to create flexible and composable components that can be easily composed together to build complex UIs.

Now, let's move beyond a static component and see how we can make it more generic by using props. Suppose we want to display a list of blog posts, each with a heading and a summary. In HTML, we would manually write the HTML fragments. However, with React components, we can dynamically generate these HTML fragments using JavaScript.

First, let's start with the basic structure:

```
type ArticleType = {
  heading: string;
  summary: string;
};

const Article = ({ heading, summary }: ArticleType) => {
  return (
    <article>
      <h3>{heading}</h3>
      <p>{summary}</p>
    </article>
  );
};
```

We can then pass the desired `heading` and `summary` values to the `Article` component:

```
<Article
  heading="Think in components"
  summary="It's important to change your mindset when coding with
React."
/>
```

Or, we could define another `Article` component:

```
<Article
  heading="Define custom hooks"
  summary="Hooks are a great way to share state logic."
/>
```

By using props, we can pass different values to the `heading` and `summary` props when we use the `Article` component. This makes the component versatile and reusable, as it can be used to display various articles with different titles and summaries based on the provided props.

Props are a fundamental concept in React that allows us to customize and configure components, making them dynamic and adaptable to different data or requirements.

A component can have any number of props, although it's recommended to keep them to a manageable amount, preferably no more than five or six. This helps maintain clarity and understandability, as having too many props can make the component harder to comprehend and extend.

Breaking down UIs into components

Let's examine a more complex UI and explore how to break it down into components and implement them separately. In this example, we will use a weather application:

Figure 2.1: A weather application

The entire application can be defined as a `WeatherApplication` component, which includes several subcomponents:

```
const WeatherApplication = () => {
  return (
    <>
      <Heading title="Weather" />
      <SearchBox />
```

```
      <Notification />
      <WeatherList />
    </>
  );
};
```

Each subcomponent can perform various tasks, such as fetching data from a remote server, conditionally rendering a drop-down list, or auto-refreshing periodically.

For example, a `SearchBox` component might have the following structure:

```
const SearchBox = () => {
  return (
    <div className="search-box">
      <input type="text" />
      <button>Search</button>
      <div className="search-results" />
    </div>
  );
};
```

The `search-results` section will only appear when data is fetched from the search query.

On the other hand, a `Weather` component could be more straightforward, rendering whatever is passed to it:

```
type WeatherType = {
  cityName: string;
  temperature: number;
  weather: string;
};

const Weather = ({ cityName, temperature, weather }: WeatherType) => {
  return (
    <div>
      <span>{cityName}</span>
      <span>{temperature}</span>
      <span>{weather}</span>
    </div>
  );
};
```

When implementing components in real-world scenarios, it is crucial to pay attention to styling and refine the HTML structure with meticulous detail. Additionally, components should effectively manage their own state, ensuring consistency and responsiveness across renders.

By grasping the concept of components and their proper structuring in React, you gain the ability to construct dynamic and reusable UI elements that contribute to the overall functionality and organization of your application.

As you advance in your React development journey, don't forget to polish the visual presentation through styling and consider efficient state management techniques to enhance the performance and interactivity of your components.

A complete `Weather` component could be something like this:

```
type Weather = {
  main: string;
  temperature: number;
}

type WeatherType = {
  name: string;
  weather: Weather;
}

export function WeatherCard({ name, weather }: WeatherType) {
  return (
    <div className={`weather-container ${weather.main}`}>
      <h3>{name}</h3>
      <div className="details">
        <p className="temperature">{weather.temperature}</p>
        <div className="weather">
          <span className="weather-category">{weather.main}</span>
        </div>
      </div>
    </div>
  );
}
```

The code snippet defines two types: `Weather` and `WeatherType`. The `Weather` type represents the weather data with two properties: `main` (string) and `temperature` (number). The `WeatherType` type represents the structure of the weather data for a specific location, with a name property (string) for the location name and a `weather` property of the `Weather` type.

The `WeatherCard` component receives the name and weather props of the `WeatherType` type. Inside the component, it renders a `div` container with a dynamic class based on the `weather.main` value.

When working on complex UIs, it is crucial to break them down into smaller, manageable components. Each component should represent a separate concept, and they can be combined together using **JSX**

(**JavaScript Extension**), similar to writing HTML code. While props are useful for passing data to components, there are situations where we need to maintain data within a component itself. This is where states come into play, allowing us to manage and update data internally.

Managing internal state in React

State in React refers to the internal data that components can hold and manage. It allows components to store and update information, enabling dynamic UI updates, interactivity, and data persistence. State is a fundamental concept in React that helps build responsive and interactive applications.

Applications feature various state types, such as a Boolean for toggle status, a loading state for network requests, or a user-input string for queries. We'll explore the useState Hook, ideal for maintaining local state within a component across re-renders. React **Hooks** are a feature introduced in React 16.8 that enables functional components to have state and lifecycle features (we'll discuss Hooks in more detail in the *Exploring common React Hooks* section later).

Let's begin by using a simple Hook for internal state management to understand how it maintains data within a component. For example, the following SearchBox component can be implemented with something like this:

```
const SearchBox = () => {
  const [query, setQuery] = useState<string>();
  const handleChange = (e: ChangeEvent<HTMLInputElement>) => {
    const value = e.target.value;
    setQuery(value);
  };

  return (
    <div className="search-box">
      <input type="text" value={query} onChange={handleChange} />
      <button>Search</button>
      <div className="search-results">{query}</div>
    </div>
  );
};
```

The code snippet showcases that SearchBox includes an input field, a search button, and a display area for search results. The useState Hook is used to create a state variable called query, initialized as an empty string. The handleChange function captures the user's input and updates the query state accordingly. Then, component renders the input field with the current value of query, a search button, and a div tag as a container displaying the search results.

Note here the useState Hook is used to manage state within the SearchBox component:

```
const [query, setQuery] = useState<string>("");
```

Let's explain this code a little more specifically:

- `useState<string>("")`: This line declares a state variable called query and initializes it with an empty string (`""`)
- `const [query, setQuery]`: This syntax uses array destructuring to assign the state variable (`query`) and its corresponding update function (`setQuery`) to variables with the same names

Now, we have the state and the setter function bound to the input box. As we enter a city name in the input box, the `search-results` area is automatically updated, along with the input value. Although there are multiple re-renders occurring as we type, the state value persists throughout the process:

Figure 2.2: Managing state with useState

The `useState` Hook is excellent for managing internal state, yet real-world projects often require handling various other state types. As applications expand, managing global-level data shared across multiple components, such as from parent to children, becomes necessary. We'll discuss different mechanisms for this kind of state management in later sections.

Now that we have gained an understanding of how props and state enable us to create dynamic components, it is important to explore how changes in data impact the rendering process in React. By understanding this process, we can take steps to optimize our code for improved efficiency and performance.

Understanding the rendering process

When the data that a React component relies on changes, whether it is through updated props or a modified state, React needs to update the UI to reflect those changes. The process is called **rendering**, and is composed of the following steps:

- **Initial render**: When a functional component is first rendered, it generates a virtual representation of the component's UI. This virtual representation describes the structure and content of the UI elements.
- **State and props changes**: When there are changes in the component's state or props, React re-evaluates the component's function body. It performs a diffing algorithm to compare the previous and new function bodies, identifying the differences between them.

> **Note**
>
> In React, a **diffing** algorithm is an internal mechanism that compares previous and new virtual **Document Object Model** (**DOM**) representations of a component and determines the minimal set of changes needed to update the actual DOM.

- **Reconciliation**: React determines which parts of the UI need to be updated based on the differences identified during the diffing process. It updates only those specific parts of the UI, keeping the rest unchanged.

- **Re-rendering**: React re-renders the component by updating the virtual representation of the UI. It generates a new virtual DOM based on the updated function body, replacing the previous virtual DOM.

- **DOM update**: Finally, React efficiently updates the real DOM to reflect the changes in the virtual DOM. It applies the necessary DOM manipulations, such as adding, removing, or updating elements, to make the UI reflect the updated state and props.

This process ensures that the UI remains in sync with the component's state and props, enabling a reactive and dynamic UI. React's efficient rendering approach minimizes unnecessary DOM manipulations and provides a performant rendering experience in functional components.

In this book, we will explore situations where writing high-performance code is crucial, ensuring that components only re-render when necessary while preserving unchanged parts. Achieving this requires utilizing Hooks effectively and employing various techniques to optimize rendering.

In an application, data management is essential, but we also encounter side effects such as network requests, DOM events, and the need for data sharing among components. To tackle these challenges, React provides a range of commonly used Hooks that serve as powerful tools for building applications. Let's explore these Hooks and see how they can greatly assist us in our development process.

Exploring common React Hooks

We briefly talked about Hooks in the *Managing internal state in React* section. In addition, Hooks allow for code reuse, improved readability, and easier testing by separating concerns and making component logic more modular.

Let's discuss a few of the most common Hooks in this section. Please be aware that in this chapter, we are focusing on the most used Hooks. As we progress through the book, we will delve into several more advanced applications of these Hooks. Regarding the last Hook, `useContext`, we will initially explore its basic usage at the end of this section to provide an introductory understanding. In later chapters, we'll employ `useContext` in more complex scenarios, allowing for a deeper and more practical grasp of its functionality.

useState

We have already seen the basic usage of `useState` Hook previously in this chapter. You can define as many states as you like inside a component, and it's quite common to do so in real-world projects. For example, a login form might include a username, a password, and a **Remember Me** flag. All these states need to be remembered before the user clicks the submit (**Login**) button:

Figure 2.3: Login form

Based on the UI, we'll need three different states for the username, password, and a Boolean flag for **Remember Me**, like so:

```
const Login = () => {
  const [username, setUsername] = useState<string>("");
  const [password, setPassword] = useState<string>("");
  const [rememberMe, setRememberMe] = useState<boolean>(false);

  return (
    <div className="login-form">
      <div className="field">
        <input
          type="text"
          value={username}
          onChange={(event) => setUsername(event.target.value)}
          placeholder="Username"
        />
      </div>

      <div className="field">
        <input
          type="password"
          value={password}
```

```
      onChange={ (event) => setPassword(event.target.value) }
      placeholder="Password"
    />
  </div>

  <div className="field">
    <label>
      <input
        type="checkbox"
        checked={rememberMe}
        onChange={ (event) => setRememberMe(event.target.checked) }
      />
      Remember Me
    </label>
  </div>

  <div className="field">
    <button>Login</button>
  </div>
 </div>
);
};
```

In the code snippet, we have to manage three different states, so it uses the useState Hook to manage state for the username, password, and rememberMe fields. The component renders input fields for username and password, a checkbox for **Remember Me**, and a **Login** button. User input updates the corresponding state variables, enabling the capture of form data.

useEffect

In React, a side effect refers to any code that is not directly related to rendering a component but has an impact outside the component's scope. Side effects often involve interacting with external resources, such as making API calls, modifying the underlying DOM (not using the normal React virtual DOM), subscribing to event listeners, or managing timers.

React provides a built-in Hook called useEffect to handle side effects within functional components. The useEffect Hook allows you to perform side effects after rendering or when specific dependencies change.

By using the useEffect Hook, you can ensure that side effects are executed at the appropriate times during the component's lifecycle. This helps maintain the consistency and integrity of the application while separating side effects from the core rendering logic.

Let's take a look at a typical use case of `useEffect`. We created an `Article` component in the *Creating components with props* section; now, let's make a list of articles. Normally, an article list could return from some API calls; in JSON format, for example. We can use the `useEffect` Hook to send the request and set state once the response is returned from an API call, like so:

```
const ArticleList = () => {
  const [articles, setArticles] = useState<ArticleType[]>([]);

  useEffect(() => {
    const fetchArticles = async () => {
      fetch("/api/articles")
        .then((res) => res.json())
        .then((data) => setArticles(data));
    };

    fetchArticles();
  }, []);

  return (
    <div>
      {articles.map((article) => (
        <Article heading={article.heading} summary={article.summary}
        />
      ))}
    </div>
  );
};
```

The code snippet demonstrates the usage of the `useEffect` Hook in a React functional component. Let's break it down:

- `useEffect(() => { ... }, []);`: This line declares the `useEffect` Hook and provides two arguments. The first argument is a callback function that contains the side effect code to be executed. The second argument is an array of dependencies that determines when the side effect should be triggered. An empty array, `[]`, indicates that the side effect should only run once during the initial render.

- `const fetchArticles = async () => { ... }`: This line declares an asynchronous function called `fetchArticles`. Inside this function, an API call is made to fetch data from the `/api/articles` endpoint.

- `fetch("/api/articles")...`: This line uses the `fetch` function to make a GET request to the specified API endpoint. The response is then processed using promises (`then`) to extract the JSON data.

- `setArticles(data)`: This line updates the component's state variable articles with the retrieved data using the `setArticles` function. This will trigger a re-render of the component with the updated data.

- `fetchArticles()`: This line invokes the `fetchArticles` function, triggering the API call and updating the article's state.

Once we have these articles, we can then use the `array.map` collection API to generate a list of articles.

It's worth mentioning that when strict mode is on, in development, React runs setup and cleanup one extra time before the actual setup. In practice, you can wrap the whole application inside the `StrictMode` built-in component from React, and your components will re-render an extra time to find bugs caused by impure rendering along with other checks.

Also, note that the second parameter of `useEffect` is critical. We used an empty array previously as we don't want the effect to trigger each time, but there are cases we would like to perform the effect whenever one of the dependencies changes.

For example, let's say we have an `ArticleDetail` component, and whenever the `id` prop of the article changes, we need to re-fetch the data and re-render:

```
const ArticleDetail = ({ id }: { id: string }) => {
  const [article, setArticle] = useState<ArticleType>();

  useEffect(() => {
    const fetchArticleDetail = async (id: string) => {
      fetch(`/api/articles/${id}`)
        .then((res) => res.json())
        .then((data) => setArticle(data));
    };

    fetchArticleDetail(id);
  }, [id]);

  return (
    <div>
      {article && (
        <Article heading={article.heading} summary={article.summary}
        />
      )}
    </div>
  );
};
```

Inside the `useEffect` Hook, the `fetchArticleDetail` function is defined to handle the API call. It fetches the article details based on the provided `id` prop, converts the response to JSON, and updates the article state using `setArticle`.

The effect is triggered when the `id` prop changes. Upon successful retrieval of the article data, the `Article` component is rendered with the `heading` and `summary` properties from the article state.

An essential feature of the `useEffect` Hook for handling side effects is the cleanup mechanism. When using `useEffect`, it's recommended to return a cleanup function that React will call upon the component's unmounting. For instance, if you set up a timer within `useEffect`, you should provide a function that clears this timer as the return value. This ensures proper resource management and prevents potential memory leaks in your application.

For example, let's say we have a component that needs to execute an effect 1 second after the initial rendering, as seen here:

```
const Timer = () => {
  useEffect(() => {
    const timerId = setTimeout(() => {
      console.log("time is up")
    }, 1000);

    return () => {
      clearTimeout(timerId)
    }
  }, [])

  return <div>Hello timer</div>
}
```

So, within the `Timer` component, the `useEffect` Hook is used to handle a side effect. As the component mounts, a `setTimeout` function is set up to log the message `time is up` after a delay of `1000` milliseconds. The `useEffect` Hook then returns a cleanup function to prevent memory leaks. This cleanup function uses `clearTimeout` to clear the timer identified by `timerId` when the component unmounts.

For the `ArticleDetail` example, the complete version with the cleanup function would be something like this:

```
useEffect(() => {
  const controller = new AbortController();
  const signal = controller.signal;

  const fetchArticleDetail = async (id: string) => {
    fetch(`/api/articles/${id}`, { signal })
```

```
      .then((res) => res.json())
      .then((data) => setArticle(data));
  };

  fetchArticleDetail(id);

  return () => {
    controller.abort();
  };
}, [id]);
```

In this code snippet, an `AbortController` component is used within a `useEffect` Hook to manage the lifecycle of a network request. When the component mounts, the `useEffect` Hook triggers, creating a new instance of `AbortController` and extracting its signal. This signal is passed to the `fetch` function, linking the request to the controller.

If the component unmounts before the request completes, the cleanup function is called, using the `abort` method of the controller to cancel the ongoing fetch request. This prevents potential issues such as updating the state of an unmounted component, ensuring better performance and avoiding memory leaks.

Let's now turn our attention to another crucial Hook that enhances performance by preventing unnecessary function creation during re-renders.

useCallback

The `useCallback` Hook in React is used to memoize and optimize the creation of callback functions. It is particularly useful when passing callbacks to child components or when using callbacks as dependencies in other Hooks. You can see it in action here:

```
const memoizedCallback = useCallback(callback, dependencies);
```

The `useCallback` Hook takes two arguments:

- `callback`: This is the function that you want to memoize. It can be an inline function or a function reference.
- `dependencies`: This is an array of dependencies that the memoized callback depends on. If any of the dependencies change, the callback will be recreated.

Let's explore a practical example. We require an editor component to modify the summary of an article. Whenever a user types a character, the summary needs to be updated, triggering a re-render. However, this re-rendering can result in the creation of a new function each time, which can impact performance. To mitigate this, we can utilize the `useCallback` Hook to optimize the rendering process and avoid unnecessary function recreations:

```
const ArticleEditor = ({ id }: { id: string }) => {
  const submitChange = useCallback(
    async (summary: string) => {
      try {
        await fetch(`/api/articles/${id}`, {
          method: "POST",
          body: JSON.stringify({ id, summary }),
          headers: {
            "Content-Type": "application/json",
          },
        });
      } catch (error) {
        // handling errors
      }
    },
    [id]
  );

  return (
    <div>
      <ArticleForm onSubmit={submitChange} />
    </div>
  );
};
```

In the `ArticleEditor` component, `useCallback` is used to memoize the `submitChange` function, which asynchronously makes a POST request to update an article, using the `fetch` API. This optimization with `useCallback` ensures that `submitChange` is only recreated when the `id` prop changes, enhancing performance by reducing unnecessary recalculations.

The component then renders `ArticleForm`, passing `submitChange` as a prop for handling form submissions:

```
const ArticleForm = ({ onSubmit }: { onSubmit: (summary: string) =>
void }) => {
  const [summary, setSummary] = useState<string>("");

  const handleSubmit = (e: FormEvent) => {
    e.preventDefault();
    onSubmit(summary);
  };

  const handleSummaryChange = useCallback(
```

```
    (event: ChangeEvent<HTMLTextAreaElement>) => {
      setSummary(event.target.value);
    },
    []
  );

  return (
    <form onSubmit={handleSubmit}>
      <h2>Edit Article</h2>
      <textarea value={summary} onChange={handleSummaryChange} />
      <button type="submit">Save</button>
    </form>
  );
};
```

`ArticleForm` uses the `useState` Hooks to track the summary state. When the form is submitted, `handleSubmit` prevents the default form action and calls `onSubmit` with the current summary. The `handleSummaryChange` function, optimized with `useCallback`, updates the summary state based on the `textarea` input. This use of `useCallback` ensures the function doesn't get recreated unnecessarily on each render, improving performance.

The React Context API

The **React Context API** is a feature that allows you to pass data directly through the component tree, without having to pass props down manually at every level. This comes in handy when your application has global data that many components share, or when you have to pass data through components that don't necessarily need the data but have to pass it down to their children.

For example, imagine that we are creating an application that includes a dark or light theme, depending on the current time (for instance, if it's daytime, we use light mode). We would need to set the theme at the root level.

So, first, we define a type `ThemeContextType` and create a context instance `ThemeContext` of the type:

```
import React from "react";

export type ThemeContextType = {
  theme: "light" | "dark";
};

export const ThemeContext = React.createContext<ThemeContextType |
undefined>(
  undefined
);
```

Then, we create a `ThemeProvider` component, which will use a React state to manage the current theme:

```
import React, { useState } from "react";
import { ThemeContext, ThemeContextType } from "./ThemeContext";

export const ThemeProvider = ({ children }) => {
  const [theme, setTheme] = useState<"light" | "dark">("light");

  const value: ThemeContextType = { theme };

  return (
    <ThemeContext.Provider value={value}>{children}</ThemeContext.
Provider>
  );
};
```

Finally, we can use the `ThemeProvider` component in our application:

```
import React from "react";
import { ThemeProvider } from "./ThemeProvider";
import App from "./App";

const Root = () => {
  return (
    <ThemeProvider>
      <App />
    </ThemeProvider>
  );
};

export default Root;
```

In any component in our application, we can now access the current theme:

```
import React, { useContext } from "react";
import { ThemeContext } from "./ThemeContext";

const ThemedComponent = () => {
  const context = useContext(ThemeContext);

  const { theme } = context;

  return <div className={theme}>Current Theme: {theme}</div>;
```

```
};

export default ThemedComponent;
```

In this setup, `ThemeContext` provides the current theme to any components in the tree that are interested in it. The theme is stored in a state variable in the `ThemeProvider` component, which is the root component of the app.

The provided code may not offer much utility since the theme cannot be modified. However, by utilizing the Context API, you can define a modifier that allows children nodes to alter the status. This mechanism proves highly beneficial for data sharing, making it a valuable tool. Let's modify the context interface a little bit:

```
type Theme = {
  theme: "light" | "dark";
  toggleTheme: () => void;
};

const ThemeContext = React.createContext<Theme>({
  theme: "light",
  toggleTheme: () => {},
});
```

We added a `toggleTheme` function in the context so that the component can modify the `theme` value when needed.

To implement the provider, we can utilize the `useState` Hook to define an internal state. By exposing the setter function, the children components can utilize it to update the value of the theme:

```
const ThemeProvider = ({ children }: { children: ReactNode }) => {
  // default theme is light
  const [theme, setTheme] = useState<"light" | "dark">("light");

  const toggleTheme = useCallback(() => {
    setTheme((prevTheme) => (prevTheme === "light" ? "dark" :
"light"));
  }, []);

  return (
    <ThemeContext.Provider value={{ theme, toggleTheme }}>
      {children}
    </ThemeContext.Provider>
  );
};
```

And then, in the calling site, it's straightforward to use the `useContext` Hook to access values in the context:

```
const Article = ({ heading, summary }: ArticleType) => {
  const { theme, toggleTheme } = useContext(ThemeContext);

  return (
    <article className={theme}>
      <h3>{heading}</h3>
      <p>{summary}</p>
      <button onClick={toggleTheme}>Toggle</button>
    </article>
  );
};
```

Then, whenever we click the **Toggle** button, it will change the theme and trigger a re-render:

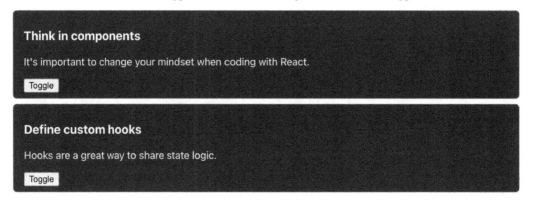

Figure 2.4: Using a theme context

In React, the Context API allows you to create and manage global state that can be accessed by components throughout your application. This capability enables you to combine multiple context providers, each representing a different slice or aspect of your application's state.

By using separate context providers, such as one for security, another for logging, and potentially others, you can organize and share related data and functionality efficiently. Each context provider encapsulates a specific concern, making it easier to manage and update related state without impacting other parts of the application:

```
import InteractionContext from "xui/interaction-context";
import SecurityContext from "xui/security-context";
import LoggingContext from "xui/logging-context";

const Application = ({ children }) => {
```

```
  const context = {}; // ... define values for context

  //... define securityContext
  //... define loggingContext

  return (
    <InteractionContext.Provider value={context}>
      <SecurityContext.Provider value={securityContext}>
        <LoggingContext.Provider value={loggingContext}>
          {children}
        </LoggingContext.Provider>
      </SecurityContext.Provider>
    </InteractionContext.Provider>
  );
};
```

This example demonstrates the usage of React's Context API to create and combine multiple context providers within an application component. `InteractionContext.Provider`, `SecurityContext.Provider`, and `LoggingContext.Provider` are used to wrap the children components and provide the respective context values.

There are several additional built-in Hooks available in React that are used less frequently. In the following chapters, we will introduce these Hooks as needed, focusing on the ones that are most relevant to the topics at hand.

Summary

In this introductory chapter, we covered essential concepts of React and laid the groundwork for your React development journey. We explored the concept of thinking in components, emphasizing the importance of breaking down applications into reusable and modular pieces. By adopting this mindset, you'll be able to create maintainable and scalable code bases.

Furthermore, we introduced you to the most commonly used Hooks in React, such as `useState` and `useEffect`, which empower you to manage state and handle side effects efficiently within functional components. These Hooks provide the flexibility and power to build dynamic and interactive UIs.

By mastering the fundamental principles of React and familiarizing yourself with the concept of thinking in components, you are now well prepared to dive deeper into the world of React development. In the upcoming chapters, we will explore more advanced topics and tackle real-world challenges, enabling you to become a proficient React developer.

Remember – React is a powerful tool that opens endless possibilities for creating modern and robust web applications. In the upcoming chapter, we will delve into the process of breaking down a design into smaller components and explore effective strategies for organizing these components. We will emphasize the importance of reusability and flexibility, ensuring that our components are adaptable to future changes.

3

Organizing Your React Application

Welcome to a chapter dedicated to unraveling the various strategies to structure a React project. Here, we'll take a step beyond code and delve into the fascinating world of application architecture – an essential aspect of software development that often doesn't receive as much attention in the frontend world as it should.

In this chapter, you will learn about different React project structuring strategies – including the feature-based structure, component-based structure, atomic design structure, and **Model-View-ViewModel** (**MVVM**) structure – and the unique advantages and potential pitfalls that each approach brings to the table. You'll also be exposed to practical examples of these structures, gain insights into when to use one over another, and explore the trade-offs that come with each decision.

But why should we care about project structure in the first place? A well-structured project can significantly enhance code maintainability, make it easier for new team members to understand the system and improve scalability, and even influence the overall success of the project. In contrast, an inefficient structure can lead to code smells and increased complexity, and it can become a source of technical debt.

By understanding these structuring strategies, you'll be better equipped to make decisions that can have a long-lasting impact on your project's health and success. You'll be able to assess your project's specific needs and constraints and use these strategies as a guiding light, enabling you to create a structure that improves code quality, fosters a productive development environment, and ultimately leads to a successful project.

In this chapter, we will cover the following topics:

- Understanding the problem of a less-structured project
- Understanding the complications of frontend applications
- Exploring common structures in React applications
- Keeping your project structure organized

Technical requirements

A GitHub repository has been created to host all the code we'll discuss in this book. For this chapter, you can find the recommended structure at `https://github.com/PacktPublishing/React-Anti-Patterns/tree/main/code/src/ch3`.

Understanding the problem of a less-structured project

The rapid growth of a project can be astonishing, leading to a sense of things spiraling out of control. Initializing a frontend project is typically straightforward, and for small-scale projects, there may be little concern regarding file structure since the number of files to manage is minimal. However, as the project expands, the need for proper file organization becomes apparent:

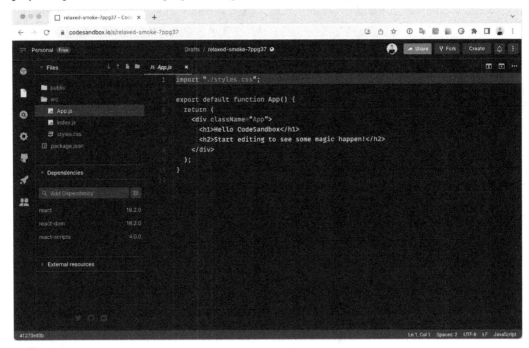

Figure 3.1: A simple project might not need a structure

The problem with having a less-structured project is that it can lead to several challenges and difficulties in managing and maintaining the code base effectively. Some of the key problems that arise from a lack of structure are as follows:

- **Code disorganization**: Without a clear structure, it becomes harder to locate specific code files or components. This can result in wasted time and effort spent searching for relevant code, especially as the project becomes larger.

- **Poor code reusability**: Without a proper structure, it becomes challenging to identify reusable components or functions. This can lead to code duplication and a lack of consistency, making it harder to maintain and update the code base in the long run.

- **Difficulty in collaboration**: When team members are working on a less-structured project, it becomes harder to understand and navigate each other's code. This can lead to communication gaps, slower development, and an increased risk of introducing bugs or conflicts.

- **Scalability issues**: As the project expands and new features are added, the lack of structure can make it challenging to integrate new components seamlessly. This can result in a tangled code base that is difficult to extend or modify, leading to decreased productivity and increased development time.

- **Maintenance complexity**: Without a clear organization, maintaining the code base becomes more complex. Making changes or fixing issues can become a time-consuming task as there may be a lack of consistency in how code is structured or named.

Before proposing a recommended project structure, let's look at the typical components of a modern frontend project. Understanding these components will provide a foundation for designing an effective project structure.

Understanding the complications of frontend applications

In a medium-sized frontend project, you may be surprised by the multitude of components required for its successful implementation. Alongside the core features, numerous other elements contribute to the project's functionality.

The folder structure of a React project provides a glimpse into the various aspects you'll need to manage within a typical React code base:

- **Source code**: This is the heart of your application and contains the JavaScript/TypeScript files that contain your application's logic, HTML files for structure, and style files for appearance. Everything that defines the operation and user interface of your application is found here.

- **Assets**: This category holds all the static files, such as images, videos, and fonts, that are utilized by your application. These files are essential in enhancing the visual experience and interaction of your application, contributing to its overall look and feel.

- **Configuration**: These files hold important parameters that control various aspects of your application. From dependency information in the `package.json` and environment-specific variables to the rules for building your project, these files are crucial for the operation and deployment of your application.

- **Tests**: This category is dedicated to ensuring the correctness and stability of your application. It holds all the unit, integration, and **end-to-end tests** that simulate user behavior, validate interactions, and check the functionality of your application, helping to catch and prevent potential bugs.

- **Documentation**: This is where all the informative documents of your application reside. From the `README` file providing an overview of the project to the API documentation and the style guide for coding, these documents help maintain consistency, understanding, and ease of use for anyone interacting with the project.

- **Build artifacts**: These are the outputs of the build process, including bundled and optimized JavaScript, CSS, and HTML files ready for deployment, and other temporary or diagnostic files that help debug build issues. They're key to distributing your application to end users.

- **Development tools and configurations**: This is the toolkit that enforces code quality, formatting, and version control and facilitates automated testing and deployment processes. They work in the background, ensuring a smooth, error-free, and efficient development process.

Collectively, these diverse components form the foundation of a typical React code base, highlighting the complexity and breadth of considerations involved in medium-sized frontend projects.

Exploring each feature folder can be an enjoyable experience as it unravels a variety of elements:

- Common components, such as modal dialogs, navigation menus, buttons, and cards

- Dedicated components tailored to specific features, such as `SpecialOffer` for special offers that only display on the menu page or `PayWithApple` for pay with ApplePay

- Style definitions using CSS-in-JS or SCSS/LESS code

- Various types of testing code, including unit tests and browser tests

- Calculation logic encapsulated within utility/helper functions

- Custom Hooks for reusable functionality

- Contexts for security, **internationalization (i18n)**, and other specific needs

- Additional configuration files such as `eslint config`, `jest config`, `webpack settings`, and more

Given the multitude of files, how can we arrange them in a manner that facilitates easy navigation and quick access for modifications? While there is no one-size-fits-all solution, consistently organizing the code base can greatly assist in this endeavor.

Consistency is paramount when it comes to naming and structuring code elements. Regardless of the approach that's chosen, it is crucial to maintain uniformity throughout the project. For example, if you decide to place style files alongside their respective components, it is essential to adhere to this convention across all components in the code base.

Similarly, if a `tests` folder is being used to house test files, ensure to maintain this convention consistently across the entire code base. For instance, other naming patterns such as `__tests__` or `specs` should be avoided to prevent confusion and maintain uniformity.

Having grasped the complexity inherent in medium to large-sized projects, and acknowledging the challenges that a disorganized code base can pose, it's time we explore some tried-and-tested approaches to structuring our code. These strategies aim to simplify the development process and make life easier for developers.

Exploring common structures in React applications

There are many different ways of organizing a large React application. In the following subsections, we will discuss the four most common structures:

- Feature-based structure

- Component-based structure

- Atomic design structure

- MVVM structure

Each structure has its own set of benefits and drawbacks, and the choice depends on the specific requirements and complexity of the project. Sometimes, we might need to mix them in some way so that they fit our project-specific needs.

To explore these different structure methods further, we'll use an online shopping application as an example since it's relatively complicated and you should have some familiarity with that domain already. The application also contains elements such as API calls, routers, and state management.

Feature-based structure

Feature-based structure means the application is organized based on features or modules. Each feature contains its own set of components, views, API calls, and state management, allowing for clear separation and encapsulation of functionality.

With a feature-based architecture in the context of online shopping, you can organize your files and folders as follows:

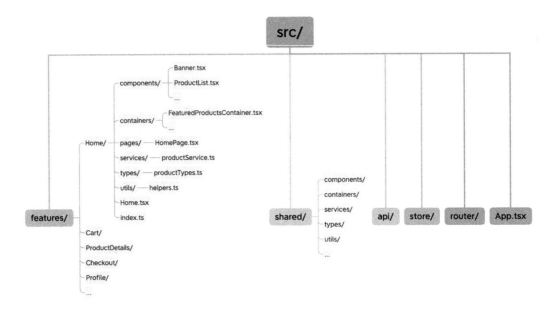

Figure 3.2: Feature-based structure

Let's take a closer look at this structure:

- The `features` directory represents different features of the application, such as Home, Cart, ProductDetails, Checkout, Profile, and more
- Each feature has a folder containing `components`, `containers`, `pages`, `services`, `types`, and `utils` related to that feature
- The `shared` directory contains reusable `components`, `containers`, `services`, `types`, and `utils` that can be shared across multiple features
- The `api` directory houses modules for making API calls
- The `store` directory contains modules for state management (for example, Redux)
- The `router` directory contains the routing configuration and related components
- The `App.tsx` file serves as the entry point of the application

This method has the following benefits:

- **Clear separation of concerns**: Each feature has a folder, making it easier to locate and modify related code
- **Modularity**: Features are self-contained, allowing for easier testing, maintenance, and reuse
- **Scalability**: New features can be added without directly impacting existing code
- **Team collaboration**: Developers can work on different features concurrently with minimal conflicts

However, it has the following drawback:

- **Potential duplication**: Features may share similar components or logic, leading to some duplication. Careful planning and refactoring can help mitigate this.

Component-based structure

Component-based structure means the application is organized around reusable components. Components are categorized based on their functionality and can be composed together to build larger views.

With a component-based architecture in the context of online shopping, you can organize your files and folders as follows:

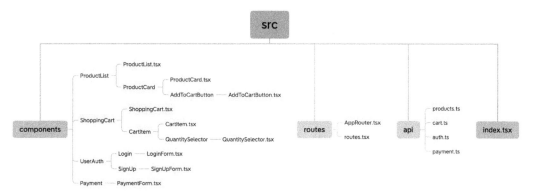

Figure 3.3: Component-based structure

Let's take a closer look at this structure:

- The `components` folder contains individual components related to various features of the online shopping application. Each component is organized into a folder, which may contain child components as necessary.

- The `routes` folder handles frontend routing in the application. It includes the main `AppRouter.tsx` file, which configures the routing logic, and the `routes.tsx` file, which defines the individual routes and their corresponding components.

- The `api` folder contains separate files for different API domains or functionalities. These files, such as `products.ts`, `cart.ts`, `auth.ts`, and `payment.ts`, handle the API calls related to their respective domains.

- The example also assumes the use of a state management library such as Redux or React Context API for managing the global application state.

This method has the following benefits:

- **Modularity**: The component-based structure promotes modularity by organizing components into separate files and folders based on their functionality. This enhances code maintainability and reusability.

- **Separation of concerns**: Each component focuses on its specific functionality, leading to clearer code and easier debugging. The separation of concerns improves code readability and maintainability.

- **Code reusability**: With components organized in a modular structure, it becomes easier to reuse components across the application or in future projects, leading to improved development efficiency.

However, it has the following drawbacks:

- **Project complexity**: As the project grows, maintaining a complex component structure can become challenging. It requires careful planning and adherence to best practices to avoid component sprawl and keep the structure manageable.

- **Learning curve**: The initial learning curve for component-based development and TypeScript may be steeper for developers who are new to these concepts. However, the benefits that are gained in terms of code organization and maintainability outweigh the initial learning.

- **Potential duplication**: Within the `components` folder, you may find smaller elements that are identical or closely resemble those in other component folders. The more you break down these components into finer parts, the greater the likelihood of identifying components that can be reused. When such reusable components emerge, it's a good practice to place them in a "shared" folder, like what is shown in a feature-based structure.

Atomic design structure

Atomic design is a methodology for designing and organizing user interfaces. It emphasizes the construction of user interfaces by breaking them down into small, reusable components called atoms, which are combined to form molecules, organisms, templates, and pages.

The key idea behind atomic design is to create a systematic approach to building UI components that encourages reusability, scalability, and maintainability. It provides a clear structure for organizing and naming components, making it easier to understand and navigate the UI code base.

Here's how the atomic design methodology categorizes UI components:

- **Atoms**: Atoms are the smallest building blocks of a UI and represent individual elements such as buttons, inputs, icons, or labels. They are typically simple and self-contained.

- **Molecules**: Molecules are combinations of atoms and represent more complex UI components. They encapsulate a group of atoms working together to form a functional unit, such as a form field or a navigation bar.

- **Organisms**: Organisms are larger components that combine molecules and/or atoms to create more significant sections of a UI. They represent distinct sections of a user interface, such as a header, sidebar, or card component.

- **Templates**: Templates provide a layout structure for arranging organisms and/or molecules. They define the overall skeleton of a page or a specific section of a UI.

- **Pages**: Pages represent complete user interface screens that are composed of templates, organisms, molecules, and atoms. They represent the final output visible to the user.

  With an atomic design architecture in the context of online shopping, you can organize your files and folders as follows:

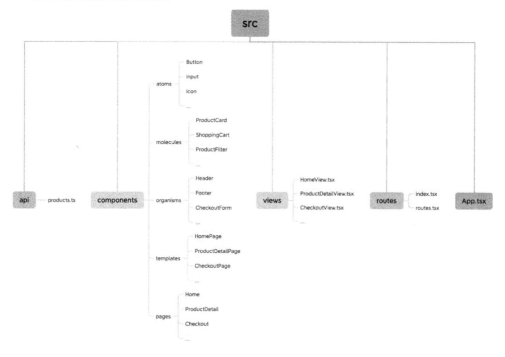

Figure 3.4: Atomic design structure

Let's take a closer look at this structure:

- The atoms, molecules, organisms, templates, and pages directories represent the different levels of component composition and abstraction

- The api directory contains the API-related files for making API calls

- The views directory contains the individual views that render the components

- The routes directory handles the routing configuration

This method has the following benefits:

- **Reusability**: Components can be easily reused across the application, promoting code efficiency
- **Consistency**: The structure encourages a consistent design language and UI pattern
- **Scalability**: The modular approach allows for easy scaling and the addition of new components
- **Maintainability**: Components are organized in a logical hierarchy, making them easier to locate and update
- **Collaboration**: The atomic design structure facilitates collaboration between designers and developers as it provides a common language for discussing UI components

However, it has the following drawbacks:

- **Learning curve**: It may require some initial learning and adaptation to understand and implement the atomic design principles effectively
- **Complexity**: As the application grows, managing a large number of components and their relationships can become challenging
- **Overengineering**: It's important to strike a balance between component reusability and overengineering as excessive abstraction can introduce unnecessary complexity

The MVVM structure

The **MVVM structure** is a software architectural pattern that's primarily used in building user interfaces:

- The *Model* represents the actual data and/or information we are dealing with. This could be a database, a file, a web service, or even a simple object.
- The *View* is what the user sees and interacts with. It's the user interface that presents the Model to the user.
- The *ViewModel* is where most of the logic resides in this pattern. It is an abstraction of the View that exposes public properties and commands, bridging the gap between the View and the Model, and processes the data from the Model into a format that is easy for the View to handle. It can perform operations on the data and decide how it should be presented to the View.

To structure a React application with the MVVM architecture in the context of online shopping, you can organize your files and folders as follows:

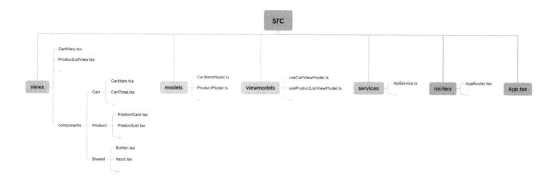

Figure 3.5: The MVVM structure

Let's take a closer look at this structure:

- The `components` directory contains reusable UI components, organized by their respective features

- The `models` directory includes the data models or entities representing the application's domain objects, such as `CartItemModel` and `ProductModel`

- The `viewmodels` directory holds the Hooks responsible for managing the state, logic, and interactions of the views

- The `services` directory contains modules for handling API calls and other external services

- The `views` directory includes the view components that display the UI based on the `ViewModel` state

- The `routers` directory houses the routing configuration and components

- The `App.tsx` file serves as the entry point of the application

This method has the following benefits:

- **Separation of concerns**: The ViewModel separates the business logic from the UI components, promoting cleaner and more maintainable code

- **Testability**: The ViewModel can be easily unit tested without the need for the actual UI components

- **Reusability**: Components, models, and services can be reused across different features and views

- **Scalability**: New features and views can be added while reusing existing ViewModel and service modules

However, it has the following drawbacks:

- **Complexity**: Implementing the MVVM pattern may introduce additional layers of abstraction and complexity to the application, especially for smaller projects
- **Learning curve**: Developers need to understand the concepts and principles of MVVM to effectively structure and manage the application

Now that we have explored these four popular structures, let's delve into the continuous evolution of our application's structure. This ongoing process ensures that the structure remains beneficial for developers in terms of easy navigation, seamless addition of new features, and the ability to maintain scalability over time.

Keeping your project structure organized

The feature-based structure is always a good starting point. As the project expands and patterns of duplication start to emerge, an additional layer can be introduced to eliminate redundancy.

For instance, let's use the online shopping application again. It contains various pages:

- Home page
- Log in/sign up
- Store address search
- Product list
- Shopping cart
- Order details
- Payment
- Profile
- Coupon

In the initial stages, organizing pages based on their features is a common approach. We can create a folder for each feature and put all the related components, styles, and tests inside that folder.

Implementing the initial structure

The initial folder structure in the `src` directory is quite straightforward and follows a feature-based approach, with each page having its own folder:

```
├── Address
│      ├── AddressList
│      └── Store
├── Home
```

```
├── Login
├── Order
├── Payment
├── Product
├── Profile
│      └── Coupon
└── SignUp
```

However, as the project evolves, you may encounter duplication of components or functionalities across different pages. To address this, it becomes necessary to introduce an additional layer of abstraction.

For example, if both the `Login` and `Order` pages require a `Button` component, it would be impractical to have separate implementations of the button on each page. Instead, you can extract the `Button` component into a separate layer, such as a components or shared folder. This way, `Button` can be reused across multiple pages without duplication.

Adding an extra layer to remove duplicates

By adding this extra layer, you promote reusability and maintainability in your code base. It helps in eliminating redundancy, streamlining development efforts, and ensuring consistency throughout the application. As the project expands, this modular approach allows for easy management and scalability, making it easier to add new features or make changes without impacting the entire code base.

So, you can create a `components` folder for all the reusable components and a `pages` folder for all the feature pages, like so:

```
├── components
│    ├── Accordion
│    ├── GenericCard
│    ├── Modal
│    ├── Offer
│    │    └── SpecialOffer
│    └── StackView
└── pages
     ├── Address
     │    ├── AddressList
     │    └── Store
     ├── Home
     ├── Login
     ├── Order
     ├── Payment
     ├── Product
     ├── Profile
     │    └── Coupon
     └── SignUp
```

As the project expands, it becomes necessary to create a separate components folder to house reusable components that are shared across different pages. In this structure, each component is organized within its respective folder, promoting modularity and code reuse. Additionally, you can introduce nested folders to represent component hierarchies, such as the `Offer` folder, which contains a specific component called `SpecialOffer`.

Alongside the `components` folder, you may need folders for other essential elements. The `pages` folder contains feature-specific pages, while the `hooks` folder houses React Hooks that provide reusable logic and functionality. The `context` folder is used for managing the global state and provides different contexts that can be shared throughout the application.

It's important to note that not all components need to be moved to the `components` folder. Only components that exhibit duplication across different pages should be lifted to the shared folder, ensuring that you maintain a balance between modularity and unnecessary complexity.

This file structure allows for better organization, code reuse, and scalability as the project grows. It promotes maintainability by reducing redundancy and ensuring consistency across the application. Additionally, having a separate folder for Hooks and contexts helps centralize related code and makes it easier to manage and maintain global state and reusable logic.

Naming files

In an individual component, there are different approaches to naming files, and each approach has its advantages and considerations. Let's explore two approaches.

Naming files with index.tsx and explicit component names

In this approach, each file within the component folder has an explicit name that corresponds to the component it represents:

```
components/Button
├── Button.test.tsx
├── Button.tsx
├── index.tsx
└── style.css
```

The `index.tsx` file serves as the default export file, allowing you to import the component from the folder directly. `Button.tsx` is the JSX for the component, and `Button.test.tsx` is the corresponding test file, while `style.css` defines CSS styles.

This approach promotes clear and self-descriptive filenames, making it easier to understand the purpose and content of each file. However, it can result in a long list of index files when browsing or searching for components in an editor or file explorer.

Naming files with kebab case

In this approach, the files within the `components` folder are named using **kebab case**, a naming convention where words are lowercase and separated by hyphens. If there is only one word, simply use lowercase – this follows a consistent convention that's used in the JavaScript community:

```
components
├── button.test.tsx
├── button.tsx
├── index.tsx
└── style.css
```

The filename of the component is explicitly named using kebab case (for example, `button.tsx`) to match the component's name.

This approach maintains consistency with the convention of kebab case filenames and promotes a unified naming structure throughout the project. However, it may require specifying the filename explicitly when importing the component.

Both approaches have their merits, and the choice depends on personal preference and the project's requirements or team conventions. It is crucial to establish and maintain consistency within the project to enhance collaboration and understanding among team members.

Either way, you can use ESlint and FolderLint to ensure your team has the same naming standard for files and folders. For example, the following screenshot shows that filenames should be in the kebab case and suggests changing `Button.tsx` into `button.tsx`:

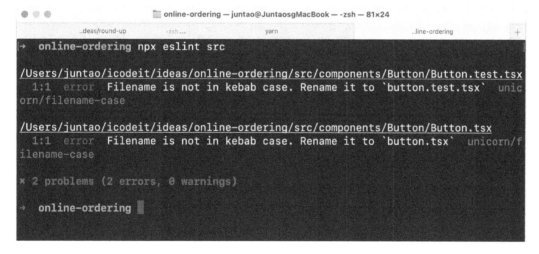

Figure 3.6: ESlint checks

Exploring a more customized structure

As your application grows and different types of abstractions are added, it becomes necessary to organize the project structure accordingly. Relying solely on any previously discussed structure may not be ideal for your specific scenario. It's often necessary to customize the structure so that it aligns well with your project's needs. Remember, the primary goal of establishing a project structure is to simplify and streamline the development process for developers.

Starting with the feature-based structure, we need to adjust our current folder structure to the following folder structure to reflect this evolution:

- `api`: This folder represents the module or directory for managing API-related code, including functions for making network requests, handling responses, and interacting with the backend services.

- `components`: This folder contains reusable UI components that can be used across different pages or features of the application. It includes components such as `Accordion`, `Button`, `GenericCard`, `Modal`, `Offer`, and `StackView`. These components can be organized into subfolders based on their functionality or purpose.

- `context`: This folder represents the module or directory for managing React context, which allows for global state management and data sharing across components.

- `hooks`: This folder contains custom React Hooks that encapsulate reusable logic and behavior. These Hooks can be shared across different parts of the application.

- `mocks`: This folder holds mock data or mock implementations for testing purposes. It includes subfolders for `graphql` and `rest`, which represent mocks for GraphQL and REST APIs, respectively.

- `pages`: This folder represents the different pages or features of the application. Each page or feature has a folder. The folders that are included are `Address`, `Home`, `Login`, `Order`, `Payment`, `Product`, `Profile`, `SignUp`, as well as their respective subfolders. The subfolders may contain additional components, Hooks, or context related to that specific page or feature.

By structuring the project in this way, you can achieve a modular and organized code base that facilitates code reuse, separation of concerns, and scalability. Each directory represents a specific aspect of the application, making it easier to locate and manage code related to that particular functionality.

You can see this in the following figure, where we are returning to our shopping example:

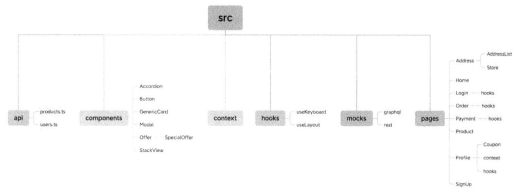

Figure 3.7: A mixed structure for an online shopping application

While this structure provides a solid foundation, it's important to adapt it based on the specific needs and scale of your project. Regularly reviewing and refactoring the structure can help maintain its effectiveness and accommodate future changes.

As the application becomes larger, it may be beneficial to extract the components folder into a shared library that can be used across multiple projects or as an internal design system. This approach promotes code reuse, consistency, and maintainability. The shared library can be hosted on an internal registry or published to *npmjs Registry* (https://www.npmjs.com/) for easy distribution and consumption.

Also, as your application evolves and new features are introduced, the existing structure may no longer fully meet your requirements. In such cases, it can be beneficial to incorporate architectural patterns such as MVVM, which follows a layered approach. This allows for better separation of concerns and facilitates the management of complex features and state in a more organized manner. We'll have an in-depth discussion about using layered architecture in *Chapter 11*.

Summary

In this chapter, we explored the challenges that arise when managing a large React application and the importance of establishing a solid project structure. We discussed various styles of structuring a React application, including feature-based, component-based, MVVM, and atomic design. Each approach offers its benefits and considerations, allowing developers to choose the most suitable structure for their specific project requirements.

Additionally, we proposed a continuously evolving approach to shaping the folder structure as the project grows. Starting with a simple initial structure, we emphasized the need to adapt and introduce new layers and abstractions to reduce duplication and maintain code organization. By continuously refining the structure and adhering to consistent conventions, developers can navigate, add new features, and maintain scalability effectively.

Throughout this chapter, we highlighted the importance of keeping the project structure flexible and evolving to meet the changing needs of the application. By staying proactive in shaping the folder structure, developers can mitigate the challenges of managing a large React application and ensure maintainability and scalability in the long run.

In the forthcoming chapter, we will delve into prevalent design patterns and strategies for component implementation. These techniques will allow us to craft code that is amenable to feature additions, intuitive to comprehend, and requires less maintenance effort.

4

Designing Your React Components

Welcome to this pivotal chapter on mastering React component design. In this chapter, we'll embark on an enriching journey to recognize and eradicate common anti-patterns in designing React components, including issues such as large monolithic components, prop drilling, and other prevalent pitfalls that often perplex developers and hamper the maintainability and scalability of React applications.

First, we'll introduce the single responsibility principle. In the realm of React, this guides us to ensure that each component has one specific purpose. Adhering to this principle makes components easier to understand, test, and maintain, all while making your code more readable and manageable.

Next, we'll explore the don't repeat yourself principle. One of the core tenets of effective programming, this encourages developers to minimize repetition and promote reuse. In the context of React, this principle can be the key to unlocking a more streamlined, efficient, and maintainable code base.

Finally, we'll delve into the component composition principle. Composition allows us to build complex UIs by combining simpler, reusable components. In React, composition is favored over inheritance, leading to more flexible and easier-to-manage components.

Throughout this chapter, we'll take a deep dive into each of these principles, providing real-world examples and practical applications. By doing so, we aim to guide you in crafting more efficient components, bolstering your understanding of React's potential, and enhancing your problem-solving skills in this powerful library.

So, in this chapter, we will cover the following topics:

- Exploring the single responsibility principle
- Learning about the don't repeat yourself principle
- Using composition
- Combining component design principles

Technical requirements

A GitHub repository has been created to host all the code we discuss in the book. For this chapter, you can find the recommended structure under https://github.com/PacktPublishing/React-Anti-Patterns/tree/main/code/src/ch4.

Exploring the single responsibility principle

The **single responsibility principle** (**SRP**) is one of the fundamental concepts in software engineering, asserting that a function, class, or, in the context of React, a component, should have only one reason to change. In other words, each component should ideally handle a single task or functionality. Following this principle can make your code more readable, maintainable, and easier to test and debug.

Let's illustrate this with an example. Suppose you initially have a `BlogPost` component that fetches blog post data, displays the post, and handles the user liking the post, all in one component:

```
import React, { useState, useEffect } from "react";

import fetchPostById from "./fetchPostById";

interface PostType {
  id: string;
  title: string;
  summary: string;
}

const BlogPost = ({ id }: { id: string }) => {
  const [post, setPost] = useState<PostType>(EmptyBlogPost);
  const [isLiked, setIsLiked] = useState(false);

  useEffect(() => {
    fetchPostById(id).then((post) => setPost(post));
  }, [id]);

  const handleClick = () => {
    setIsLiked(!isLiked);
  };

  return (
    <div>
      <h2>{post.title}</h2>
      <p>{post.summary}</p>
      <button onClick={handleClick}>
        {isLiked ? "Unlike" : "Like"}
      </button>
```

```
        </div>
    );
};
```

```
export default BlogPost;
```

The code defines a functional component called `BlogPost` that takes an `id` prop of the `string` type. Inside the component, there are two state variables defined using the `useState` Hook: `post` and `isLiked`. The `post` state represents the blog post data, initialized with a default value of an empty blog post. The `isLiked` state represents whether the post is liked or not, initialized as `false`.

Following this, we need to manage the side effect (sending network requests) in the `useEffect` Hook. It is used to fetch the blog post data from the server based on the provided `id` prop. It triggers the `fetch` operation whenever the `id` prop changes. Once the data is fetched, the `post` state is updated with the retrieved post using the `setPost` function.

Inside the `useEffect` Hook call, for the network request, there is a function called `fetchPostById`. The function is simply a `fetch` call to a remote API endpoint. We can assume the function is implemented with something like the following code snippet:

```
const fetchPostById = (id: string) => {
  return new Promise((resolve, reject) => {
    setTimeout(() => resolve({}), 2000);
  })
};
```

The component renders the title and summary of the blog post from the `post` state. It also renders a button that toggles the `isLiked` state when clicked, displaying **Like** or **Unlike** based on the current value of `isLiked`.

While this code works, it violates the SRP. It's doing three separate things: fetching data, displaying the blog post, and handling the like functionality. Instead, let's refactor it into smaller, single-responsibility components:

```
const useFetchPost = (id: string): PostType => {
  const [post, setPost] = useState<PostType>(EmptyBlogPost);

  useEffect(() => {
    fetchPostById(id).then((post) => setPost(post));
  }, [id]);

  return post;
};
```

```
const LikeButton: React.FC = () => {
```

```
    const [isLiked, setIsLiked] = useState(false);

    const handleClick = () => {
      setIsLiked(!isLiked);
    };

    return <button onClick={handleClick}>
        {isLiked ? "Unlike" : "Like"}
    </button>;
};

const BlogPost = ({ id }: { id: string }) => {
  const post = useFetchPost(id);

  return (
    <div>
      <h2>{post.title}</h2>
      <p>{post.summary}</p>
      <LikeButton />
    </div>
  );
};
```

Here, we've refactored BlogPost into smaller, single-responsibility components:

- useFetchPost is a custom Hook responsible for fetching the blog post data

- LikeButton is a component responsible for handling the like functionality

- BlogPost is now just responsible for rendering the blog post content and LikeButton

Each part has a single responsibility and could be tested and maintained independently, leading to a more manageable code base.

> **Note**
>
> In a real-world application, clicking a **Like** button may send an API call to update the database; for example, it could be another fetch request that is sent to an endpoint such as https://post.service/post/<id> to change the isLiked status.

So, in the first section, we explored the SRP. This principle encourages each component to take charge of a single piece of functionality, making our code more maintainable and understandable. Here, we applied this principle to break down large, monolithic components into smaller, more manageable pieces.

As we advance further into our design journey, our next section leads us to a principle that intertwines closely with the philosophy of SRP – the don't repeat yourself principle.

Don't repeat yourself

The **don't repeat yourself** (**DRY**) principle is a fundamental concept in software development that aims to reduce repetition within the code. Following this principle leads to better maintainability, readability, and testability, and can prevent bugs that occur due to the duplication of logic.

Let's say that you have a shopping website, and you want to display a list of products and the user's cart side by side, something like this:

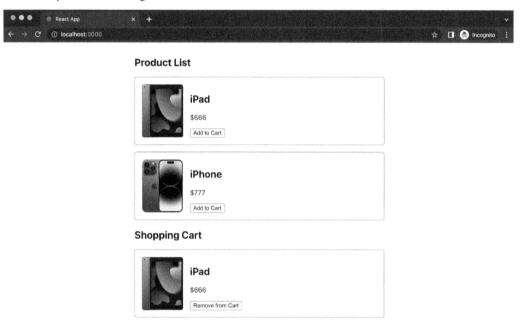

Figure 4.1: The product list page

The `ProductList` component will display the product's image, name, and price, with an **Add to Cart** button, while the `Cart` component will display a list of cart items with a **Remove from Cart** button.

A naive implementation of `ProductList` might look like this:

```
type Product = {
  id: string;
  name: string;
  image: string;
  price: number;
};

const ProductList = ({
  products,
```

```
    addToCart,
}: {
  products: Product[];
  addToCart: (id: string) => void;
}) => (
  <div>
    <h2>Product List</h2>
    {products.map((product) => (
      <div key={product.id} className="product">
        <img src={product.image} alt={product.name} />
        <div>
          <h2>{product.name}</h2>
          <p>${product.price}</p>
          <button onClick={() => addToCart(product.id)}>Add to Cart
          </button>
        </div>
      </div>
    ))}
  </div>
);

export default ProductList;
```

This functional component named `ProductList` accepts two props: `products` (an array of product objects) and `addToCart` (a function used to add a product to a shopping cart).

Each product object is of the `Product` type, which has the `id`, `name`, `image`, and `price` properties.

The component maps over the `products` array and renders a `div` for each product, including an image, product name, price, and an **Add to Cart** button. When the **Add to Cart** button is clicked, the `addToCart` function is invoked with the corresponding product's `id` prop as an argument.

The `Cart` component has a similar structure, as you can imagine; it requires a list of items and renders a button with the text **Remove from Cart**, and a callback function for the user to invoke:

```
const Cart = ({
  cartItems,
  removeFromCart,
}: {
  cartItems: Product[];
  removeFromCart: (id: string) => void;
}) => (
  <div>
    <h2>Shopping Cart</h2>
    {cartItems.map((item) => (
```

```
      <div key={item.id} className="product">
        <img src={item.image} alt={item.name} />
        <div>
          <h2>{item.name}</h2>
          <p>${item.price}</p>
          <button onClick={() => removeFromCart(item.id)}>
            Remove from Cart
          </button>
        </div>
      </div>
    ))}
  </div>
);
```

The `Cart` component iterates over the `cartItems` array and, for each item, it renders a `div` with the item's image, name, price, and a **Remove from Cart** button. When this button is clicked, it invokes the `removeFromCart` function with the respective item's `id` prop as an argument, signifying that this item should be removed from the cart.

To reduce the duplication and make each component only do one thing, we can extract a `LineItem` component:

```
import { Product } from "./types";

const LineItem = ({
  product,
  performAction,
  label,
}: {
  product: Product;
  performAction: (id: string) => void;
  label: string;
}) => {
  const { id, image, name, price } = product;

  return (
    <div key={id} className="product">
      <img src={image} alt={name} />
      <div>
        <h2>{name}</h2>
        <p>${price}</p>
        <button onClick={() => performAction(id)}>{label}</button>
      </div>
    </div>
```

```
    );
  };
```

```
  export default LineItem;
```

We defined a functional component called `LineItem` that renders a product's details and a button. It accepts properties for `product`, `performAction`, and `label`, and uses destructuring to extract the necessary values. The component returns JSX code to display the product's information and trigger the `performAction` function when the button is clicked.

For the `ProductList` and `Cart` components, you can simply pass in different props to the `LineItem` component to reduce the duplication we had before:

```
  const ProductList = ({
    products,
    addToCart,
  }: {
    products: Product[];
    addToCart: (id: string) => void;
  }) => (
    <div>
      <h2>Product List</h2>
      {products.map((product) => (
        <LineItem
          key={product.id}
          product={product}
          performAction={addToCart}
          label="Add to Cart"
        />
      ))}
    </div>
  );
```

The new `ProductList` component receives `products` and `addToCart` as props. It renders a list of products, with each product having an **Add to Cart** button.

Similarly, for the `Cart` component, we'll have a similar structure that reuses the `LineItem` component for rendering the product details (`image`, `name`, and `price`):

```
  const Cart = ({
    cartItems,
    removeFromCart,
  }: {
    cartItems: Product[];
    removeFromCart: (id: string) => void;
```

```
    }) => (
      <div>
        <h2>Shopping Cart</h2>
        {cartItems.map((item) => (
          <LineItem
            key={item.id}
            product={item}
            performAction={removeFromCart}
            label="Remove from Cart"
          />
        ))}
      </div>
    );
```

This is a more maintainable and reusable approach by following the DRY principle. There is less chance of introducing bugs because changes only need to be made in one place, and if we must add new features of `LineItem`, we only need to touch a single component.

In this section, we dove into the DRY principle. It guided us to eliminate redundancy in our code, reducing the likelihood of inconsistencies and bugs. By avoiding code duplication, we've simplified maintenance as changes in functionality need to be addressed in a single place. As we refined our understanding of DRY, we prepared ourselves to enhance our component structure using a key concept in React – composition.

Using composition

In React, **composition** is a natural pattern of the component model. For instance, JSX's markup language syntax enables us to pair a `div` with an h2 tag seamlessly, without the need to incorporate anything new.

The custom component is nothing more special than the built-in ones like a `div`; you can use your `Cart` component with a `div` just as you can use a `p` tag with it. This pattern enables more straightforward reuse of components, which can contribute to cleaner and more maintainable code.

Let's consider an example. Suppose we're building a `UserDashboard` component that displays user information. The profile includes an avatar, a name, and a list of the user's friends and the latest posts. Here's how it might look:

```
type User = {
  name: string;
  avatar: string;
  friends: string[];
};

type Post = {
```

```
    author: string;
    summary: string;
};


type UserDashboardProps = {
  user: User;
  posts: Post[];
};

function UserDashboard({ user, posts }: UserDashboardProps) {
  return (
    <div>
      <h1>{user.name}</h1>
      <img src={user.avatar} alt="profile" />
      <h2>Friends</h2>
      <ul>
        {user.friends.map((friend) => (
          <li key={friend}>{friend}</li>
        ))}
      </ul>
      <h2>Latest Posts</h2>
      {posts.map((post) => (
        <div key={post.author}>
          <h3>{post.author}</h3>
          <p>{post.summary}</p>
        </div>
      ))}
    </div>
  );
}

export default UserDashboard;
```

In this simplified example, `UserDashboard` is responsible for rendering the user's profile, a list of friends, and the latest posts, which violates the SRP. We can break it down into smaller components, each responsible for one thing.

First, we can extract the profile-related JSX into a `UserProfile` component that displays the user's profile, which includes an h1 tag (the user's name) and an `avatar` image:

```
const UserProfile = ({ user }: { user: User }) => {
  return (
    <>
      <h1>{user.name}</h1>
```

```
        <img src={user.avatar} alt="profile" />
      </>
    );
};
```

Next, we create a `FriendList` component that displays a list of the user's friends; it includes an h2 tag and a `friends` list:

```
const FriendList = ({ friends }: { friends: string[] }) => {
    return (
        <>
            <h2>Friends</h2>
            <ul>
                {friends.map((friend) => (
                    <li key={friend}>{friend}</li>
                ))}
            </ul>
        </>
    );
};
```

Finally, we create a `PostList` component that displays a feed of posts, which includes an h2 tag and a list of `posts`:

```
const PostList = ({ posts }: { posts: Post[] }) => {
    return (
        <>
            <h2>Latest Posts</h2>
            {posts.map((post) => (
                <div key={post.author}>
                    <h3>{post.author}</h3>
                    <p>{post.summary}</p>
                </div>
            ))}
        </>
    );
};
```

Now, our `UserDashboard` component becomes simpler and delegates its responsibilities to these smaller components:

```
function UserDashboard({ user, posts }: UserDashboardProps) {
    return (
        <div>
            <UserProfile user={user} />
```

```
      <FriendList friends={user.friends} />
      <PostList posts={posts} />
    </div>
  );
}
```

The refactored version of the `UserDashboard` component is superior due to several reasons:

- **Separation of Concerns**: By separating different parts of the component (user profile, friend list, and post list) into their own components (`UserProfile`, `FriendList`, and `PostList`), you ensure that each component is responsible for one task. This improves the maintainability of the code.

- **Readability**: The new version of `UserDashboard` is easier to read and understand. It becomes immediately clear what this component is rendering: a user profile, a list of friends, and a list of posts. There's no need to read through details about how each of these parts is rendered.

- **Reusability**: The `UserProfile`, `FriendList`, and `PostList` components can now be reused in other parts of the application if needed, thereby promoting code reuse and reducing redundancy.

- **Testability**: Smaller, single-responsibility components are easier to test, as they tend to have less complex interactions and dependencies. We'll cover the testing and testability in *Chapter 5*.

This is a simple example, but it illustrates the basic idea of composition in React. Composition can become more complex as you deal with components that have their own state or logic, but the core principle remains the same: building larger components from smaller, reusable parts.

This section brought us to the power of composition in React. With composition, we could efficiently structure and combine our components, creating complex user interfaces from simpler, single-responsibility components. We observed how composition allowed us to fully leverage the principles of SRP and DRY, leading to the creation of sophisticated UIs that remain easy to understand, test, and maintain.

Combining component design principles

We've separately analyzed the principles of single responsibility, don't repeat yourself, and composition. However, in practical coding scenarios, things can get intricate, necessitating the simultaneous application of multiple principles to enhance the readability and maintainability of the code.

Let's consider an example of a `Page` component, which might have many responsibilities such as managing the state and behavior of a header, sidebar, and main content area. Also, there are a bunch of props for configuring each of these sections. It's typical to encounter such code when individuals simply replicate the existing code base without much consideration or critical thinking; so the prop list grows as new features are added.

Here is a simplified example:

```
import React from "react";

type PageProps = {
  headerTitle: string;
  headerSubtitle: string;
  sidebarLinks: string[];
  isLoading: boolean;
  mainContent: React.ReactNode;
  onHeaderClick: () => void;
  onSidebarLinkClick: (link: string) => void;
};

function Page({
  headerTitle,
  headerSubtitle,
  sidebarLinks,
  mainContent,
  isLoading,
  onHeaderClick,
  onSidebarLinkClick,
}: PageProps) {
  return (
    <div>
      <header onClick={onHeaderClick}>
        <h1>{headerTitle}</h1>
        <h2>{headerSubtitle}</h2>
      </header>
      <aside>
        <ul>
          {sidebarLinks.map((link) => (
            <li key={link} onClick={() => onSidebarLinkClick(link)}>
              {link}
            </li>
          ))}
        </ul>
      </aside>
      {!isLoading && <main>{mainContent}</main>}
    </div>
  );
}
```

We defined a `Page` component; the component uses the preceding props to render a page with a clickable header, a sidebar containing clickable links, and a main content section. The component expects an object of the `PageProps` type as its properties.

Let's take a closer look inside `PageProps`:

- `headerTitle`: This string will be displayed as the main title in the page's header
- `headerSubtitle`: This string will be displayed as the subtitle in the page's header
- `sidebarLinks`: This is an array of strings, where each string represents a link that will be displayed in the page's sidebar
- `isLoading`: This is a flag to determine whether the main content is ready or not
- `mainContent`: This can be any valid React node (a component, an element, null, etc.) that represents the main content of the page
- `onHeaderClick`: This function will be executed when the header section of the page is clicked
- `onSidebarLinkClick`: This function will be executed when any sidebar link is clicked. The function will receive the clicked link as an argument

The `Page` component has multiple responsibilities, and it has a long list of props that could make it hard to work with. A long prop list – when a component has over five props – typically signals a need for component breakdown. This is because remembering the purpose of each prop can be challenging, and it also increases the likelihood of passing the wrong prop or misordering them.

We can group the props based on how they are used. The `headerTitle`, `headerSubtitle`, and `onHeaderClick` props can be split out into a group, while `isLoading` and `mainContent` belong to another group.

Extracting a small part of the large component is always a good starting point. Note that there might be many ways to do the extracting; if the information looks related to each other, we can group them and create a new component for that group of data. For example, we can extract a `Header` component first:

```
type HeaderProps = {
  headerTitle: string;
  headerSubtitle: string;
  onHeaderClick: () => void;
};

const Header = ({
  headerTitle,
  headerSubtitle,
  onHeaderClick,
}: HeaderProps) => {
  return (
```

```
    <header onClick={onHeaderClick}>
      <h1>{headerTitle}</h1>
      <h2>{headerSubtitle}</h2>
    </header>
  );
};
```

This `Header` component in React takes three props – `headerTitle`, `headerSubtitle`, and `onHeaderClick` – and renders a header with the provided title and subtitle. The `onHeaderClick` prop is then called when the header is clicked.

Now, because `title`, `subtitle`, and the `onClick` callback are already in the `Header` component, we don't need the `header` prefix in the prop names. Let's rename these props:

```
type HeaderProps = {
  title: string;
  subtitle: string;
  onClick: () => void;
};

const Header = ({
  title,
  subtitle,
  onClick,
}: HeaderProps) => {
  return (
    <header onClick={onClick}>
      <h1>{title}</h1>
      <h2>{subtitle}</h2>
    </header>
  );
};
```

It's now much clearer regarding what `Header` does – it accepts `title`, `subtitle`, and `onClick` and doesn't need to know anything beyond that. This extraction also increases the reusability of `Header`, meaning we might reuse the component in a different place.

Now, we can extract a `Sidebar` component with the same approach:

```
type SidebarProps = {
  links: string[];
  onLinkClick: (link: string) => void;
};

const Sidebar = ({ links, onLinkClick }: SidebarProps) => {
```

```
    return (
      <aside>
        <ul>
          {links.map((link) => (
            <li key={link} onClick={() => onLinkClick(link)}>
              {link}
            </li>
          ))}
        </ul>
      </aside>
    );
  };
```

The `Sidebar` component accepts an array of `links` and an `onLinkClick` function as props and generates a list of clickable items from the `links` array. The `onLinkClick` function is triggered when a link is clicked, passing the clicked link as an argument.

After we extracted `Header` and `Sidebar`, the only thing left in `Page` is the part related to the main content. We can apply the same approach for the main content, extracting a `Main` component with the simple JSX fragment, as in the following code:

```
type MainProps = {
  isLoading: boolean;
  content: React.ReactNode;
};

const Main = ({ isLoading, content }: MainProps) => {
  return <>{!isLoading && <main>{content}</main>}</>;
};
```

As we extracted most of the content out of the `Page` component, we can now use these simple components without changing the public interface of `Page`:

```
function Page({
  headerTitle,
  headerSubtitle,
  sidebarLinks,
  mainContent,
  isLoading,
  onHeaderClick,
  onSidebarLinkClick,
}: PageProps) {
  return (
    <div>
      <Header
```

```
        title={headerTitle}
        subtitle={headerSubtitle}
        onClick={onHeaderClick}
      />
      <Sidebar links={sidebarLinks} onLinkClick={onSidebarLinkClick}
        />
      <Main isLoading={isLoading} content={mainContent} />
    </div>
  );
}
```

The Page component arranges the Header, Sidebar, and Main components and takes in several props. It then passes these props to the respective child components – Header gets the title, subtitle, and a click handler; Sidebar receives a list of links and a click handler; and the Main component gets the main content and a loading state.

The refactored Page looks much nicer, but it's not perfect. Let's consider a common issue with the current code. What happens if we need to pass in new props to Sidebar or Main?

To accept the new props passed into Sidebar or Main, we need to extend the prop list, which already has seven props. For people who use the Page component, as more props are added, they will have to remember even more props, which wouldn't be a good experience (not to mention the additional testing efforts because of these props).

Instead of accepting these detailed descriptions to customize Header or Sidebar, we can pass in an instance of Header and then just plug it into the correct slot (to replace the Header component):

```
type PageProps = {
  header: React.ReactNode;
  sidebarLinks: string[];
  isLoading: boolean;
  mainContent: React.ReactNode;
  onSidebarLinkClick: (link: string) => void;
};

function Page({
  header,
  sidebarLinks,
  mainContent,
  isLoading,
  onSidebarLinkClick,
}: PageProps) {
  return (
    <div>
      {header}
```

```
      <Sidebar links={sidebarLinks}
        onLinkClick={onSidebarLinkClick} />
      <Main isLoading={isLoading} content={mainContent} />
    </div>
  );
}
```

Now, the Page component accepts a header prop (along with a list of sidebar links, a loading state, main content, and a link click handler as props) and renders the Header component directly. That means we can pass in any header instance from outside of Page.

Similarly, we can do the same for Sidebar and Main:

```
type PageProps = {
  header: React.ReactNode;
  sidebar: React.ReactNode;
  main: React.ReactNode;
};

function Page({ header, sidebar, main }: PageProps) {
  return (
    <div>
      {header}
      {sidebar}
      {main}
    </div>
  );
}
```

The Page component accepts three props – header, sidebar, and main – with each expected to be a **ReactNode**, a type that includes practically anything that can be rendered in React (strings, elements, arrays, etc.). The Page component simply renders these three props in a div in the order they are provided, effectively forming a simple page layout with a header, a sidebar, and a main section.

You can then use Page in the most flexible way – you can pass in a fully customized Header, Sidebar, and Main as parameters into the Page component:

```
const MyPage = () => {
  return (
    <Page
      header={
        <Header
          title="My application"
          subtitle="Product page"
          onClick={() => console.log("toggle header")}
```

```
          />
        }
      sidebar={
        <Sidebar
          links={["Home", "About", "Contact"]}
          onLinkClick={() => console.log("toggle sidebar")}
        />
      }
      main={<Main isLoading={false}
            content={<div>The main</div>} />}
    />
  );
};
```

This MyPage component renders a Page component, passing in Header, Sidebar, and Main components as props, while click events on the Header and Sidebar components will log certain messages to the console.

Note that here you can pass anything into Page to define header, sidebar, or main. Here's an example:

```
const MySimplePage = () => {
  return (
    <Page
      header={
        <h1>A simple header</h1>
      }
      sidebar={
        <aside>
          <ul>
            <li>Home</li>
            <li>About</li>
          </ul>
        </aside>
      }
      main={<div>The main content</div>}
    />
  );
};
```

The MyPage component wraps a Page component. The Page component receives three props: header, sidebar, and main, each containing JSX elements that specify what's to be rendered in each respective section of the page. The header prop has a heading, the sidebar prop includes a list with **Home** and **About** items, and the main section contains the main content of the page.

The original `Page` component was heavily burdened with a multitude of responsibilities, leading to a long list of props. This design presented a **prop drilling** problem, where a large amount of data had to be passed down through multiple layers of components. This setup was both complex and hard to maintain.

With that, let's review our process of how we applied different principles. The refactoring process started by breaking down the monolithic `Page` component into smaller, more manageable components – `Header`, `Sidebar`, and `Main` – using the SRP. These sub-components were designed to handle their respective responsibilities, thus simplifying their individual prop requirements.

Once these components were extracted, we modified the `Page` component to accept these sub-components (`Header`, `Sidebar`, and `Main`) as props using composition. This approach significantly reduced the prop drilling issue, as each sub-component now receives props directly at the point of usage.

This refactoring exercise streamlined the `Page` component, resulting in a cleaner, more manageable code base. It utilized the principles of component composition and single responsibility to solve the prop drilling problem effectively.

Summary

This chapter covered several key principles in designing and developing components in React: the SRP, DRY, and the use of component composition. Each of these principles provides different strategies for achieving clean, maintainable, and scalable code bases.

By understanding and applying these principles, we can create a solid foundation for our React applications. These strategies lead to more organized, scalable, and robust code bases, ultimately making our work as developers more effective and enjoyable.

In the next chapter, we'll start to look into an exciting topic in React applications – testing – and see how good structured tests can protect us from making mistakes while helping us to improve the code quality.

Part 2: Embracing Testing Techniques

In this part, you will delve into the significance of testing in frontend development, exploring various testing methodologies and refactoring techniques that will ensure the robustness and maintainability of your React applications.

This part contains the following chapters:

- *Chapter 5, Testing in React*
- *Chapter 6, Exploring Common Refactoring Techniques*
- *Chapter 7, Introducing Test-Driven Development with React*

5
Testing in React

Welcome to this immersive chapter on testing in React. In this chapter, we will learn the importance of software testing, understand the different types of testing – including unit, integration, and **end-to-end** (**E2E**) testing – and delve into the use of popular testing tools such as Cypress, Jest, and the React Testing Library. In addition, we will demystify concepts such as stubbing and mocking, ensuring you are well-equipped to handle complex testing scenarios.

Our overarching goal is to foster a solid understanding of testing strategies and their implementation in React. We aim to enhance your ability to write tests that make your application resilient to bugs and regressions and ensure the seamless addition of new features.

By the end of this chapter, you'll have a comprehensive understanding of React testing and be ready to implement efficient testing practices in your projects. So, let's get started and step into the exciting world of React testing!

In this chapter, we will cover the following topics:

- Understanding why we need tests
- Learning about different types of tests
- Testing individual units with Jest
- Learning about integration tests
- Learning about E2E tests using Cypress

Technical requirements

A GitHub repository has been created to host all the code we'll discuss in this book. For this chapter, you can find the recommended structure at `https://github.com/PacktPublishing/React-Anti-Patterns/tree/main/code/src/ch5`.

Understanding why we need tests

Testing is not just an optional best practice; it's a critical part of building reliable and maintainable software. Without tests, you're essentially navigating the complex seas of software development without a compass. Let's understand the multiple benefits that testing brings:

- **Ensuring code correctness**: Tests serve as a seal of validation that your code performs exactly the way it's supposed to. A well-written test verifies that your functions return the expected output for a given input, your components render correctly, and your application behaves as anticipated.

- **Preventing regression**: As applications grow and evolve, new code can sometimes unintentionally break existing functionality. This is known as a **regression**. Automated tests act as a safety net, catching these regressions before they reach production.

- **Facilitating refactoring and maintenance**: Fear often surrounds the process of refactoring or updating legacy code. Tests alleviate this fear. They provide a comfort zone, assuring that if you accidentally break something during the update or refactoring process, your tests will catch it.

- **Boosting confidence in code quality**: Tests elevate the confidence level of your team. When a suite of well-written tests backs your code, you have a quantifiable measure of your code's quality. This assurance is especially beneficial when you're adding new features or making changes to the system.

- **Documentation**: Tests also serve as a form of documentation. They provide a clear understanding of what a function or component is supposed to do, helping new developers on the team understand the project's functionality.

In the subsequent sections, we'll delve deeper into the various types of testing you'll commonly use in React applications and learn how to use testing tools effectively. Buckle up for an engaging ride into the realm of software testing.

Learning about different types of tests

Testing, in the realm of software development, isn't a one-size-fits-all approach. Rather, it is categorized into different types, each serving a distinct purpose and offering unique insights into the functionality and reliability of the application. It is important to understand these categories to ensure the overall health and robustness of your application. Typically, you will have unit tests, integration tests, and E2E tests in one code base.

We will define each type here briefly and discuss each type in detail in the following sections:

- **Unit tests**: These tests focus on testing individual components or functions in isolation to ensure they work as expected

- **Integration tests**: These tests examine the interactions between different modules or services to verify they work together cohesively

- **E2E tests**: These tests test the entire application flow from start to finish, mimicking real-world user behavior to validate that the system works as a whole

How you structure your tests in a project also matters. For example, you should have a lot of unit tests that run fast and can provide detailed feedback, and you should have only a few E2E tests to ensure all the parts work together. This approach aligns with the principles of the test pyramid.

Originally conceived by Mike Cohn, the **test pyramid** recommends having a larger number of unit tests compared to integration or E2E tests. The reasoning is simple – unit tests are quicker, simpler, and more cost-effective to maintain:

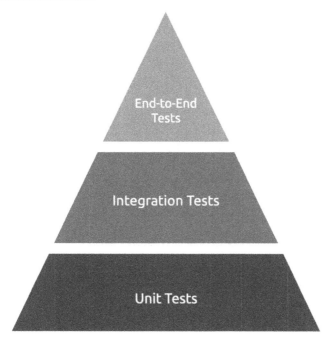

Figure 5.1: The traditional test pyramid

However, in the modern frontend world, this model is evolving. More value is being placed on integration and E2E tests due to the increasing complexity and interactivity of frontend applications. Tools such as Cypress and Puppeteer facilitate writing E2E tests that emulate user behavior on the browser, while libraries such as the React Testing Library encourage more integration tests by making it easier to test component interactions.

New types of tests are also introduced in frontend applications. The visual regression tests is one of them. **Visual regression testing** is a method of testing in which the visual aspects of a web application are captured and compared to previous states or versions. This type of testing is particularly useful in catching unintended visual bugs and changes in a user interface that may be introduced during development.

Visual regression tests work by taking screenshots (or snapshots) of web pages or components at different stages, and then comparing these screenshots pixel by pixel to identify any visual differences. When a difference is detected, it is flagged for review. The review can then determine if the change is expected (due to a new feature or design update) or if it's an unintended regression that needs to be fixed.

In frontend testing, **static checks** involve analyzing code without executing it to identify errors and ensure coding standards. This includes checking for syntax errors, enforcing coding style through linting, verifying correct data types with type checking, analyzing code complexity, examining dependencies, and identifying security vulnerabilities.

The exact shape of your test pyramid might vary depending on your application's needs, but the critical takeaway is to have a balanced testing strategy that provides quick and useful feedback at different levels of your application:

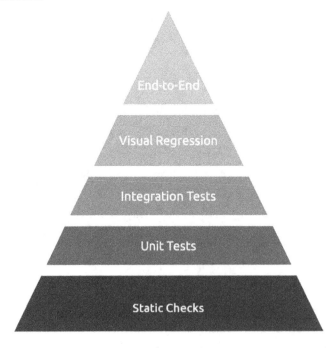

Figure 5.2: The enhanced test pyramid

The next sections in this chapter will give you hands-on experience in writing these types of tests for a React application, ensuring that you are well-equipped to bring these concepts into your projects. Let's forge ahead!

Testing individual units with Jest

Unit tests are the smallest and most foundational part of the testing pyramid, verifying the behavior of individual units of code in isolation, such as functions, methods, or components. These tests are quick to write and execute, offering immediate feedback to developers.

We'll use Jest to write unit tests and integration tests in this book. Jest is a comprehensive JavaScript testing framework built by Facebook, with a strong focus on simplicity. It's feature-rich and supports asynchronous testing, mocking, and snapshot testing, making it a great choice for React applications.

Writing your first test

Let's write a simple test. Say you have an add function in a file called math.ts:

```
export function add(a: number, b: number) {
  return a + b;
}
```

To test this function, you must create a math.test.ts file in the same directory:

```
import { add } from './math';

test('add adds numbers correctly', () => {
  expect(add(1, 2)).toBe(3);
});
```

You've now written your first test! The test function takes two arguments: a string description of the test and a callback function that implements the test. expect is a Jest function that takes the actual value, and toBe is a matcher function that compares the actual value with the expected value.

Another way of writing a test is to use the it function. In Jest, test and it are actually the same function and can be used interchangeably; the names just come from different testing conventions:

- test: This is a common name for a test function in many testing frameworks and languages. If you come from a background of using other testing libraries, you might find test to be more intuitive or familiar.

- it: This comes from **behavior-driven development** (BDD) style frameworks such as Jasmine or Mocha.

The idea of using it is to make the tests read more like sentences. For example, it ("adds 1 + 2 to equal 3", () => expect(1 + 2).toBe(3)) reads like "it adds 1 + 2 to equal 3."

> **Note**
>
> BDD is a software development approach that emphasizes collaboration between developers, QA, and non-technical participants in a software project. It highlights the need to start with a clear understanding of desired behavior before development starts, thereby aligning development with business needs.
>
> BDD encourages expressing software behaviors in plain, descriptive language that can be read and understood by all stakeholders. It leverages executable specifications, often written in a language such as Gherkin, that guide development and serve as acceptance criteria.
>
> BDD aims to reduce misunderstandings by encouraging collaboration, making the behavior of a system explicit and understandable by all, and ensuring that the software developed truly meets the needs of the business.

It's a matter of team preference and what aligns best with your team's testing philosophy – some teams prefer the sentence-like structure that it provides as it often makes it clearer what a test is trying to verify, especially to non-developers, while others might find `test` to be more straightforward and less verbose. We're going to write tests that follow the BDD style in this book.

Grouping tests

Grouping related tests in one block significantly improves the readability of your test files. By clearly delineating different areas of functionality, a block allows anyone reading the tests to understand the context of the test suite at a glance. This enhanced understanding is crucial for comprehension of what functionality is being verified. In a large code base, with numerous tests, this organization can greatly decrease the cognitive load required to understand how different parts of the application are tested.

In Jest, we can use the `describe` function to group related tests into one unit. For instance, consider a function, `add`, that includes multiple cases: the addition of negative numbers, the combination of one negative and one positive number, decimal sums, or even computations involving imaginary numbers. It would be prudent to gather all these distinct cases under one `describe` block, like so:

```
import { add } from './math';

describe('math functions', () => {
  it('adds positive numbers correctly', () => {
    expect(add(1, 2)).toBe(3);
  });

  it('adds negative numbers correctly', () => {
    expect(add(-1, -2)).toBe(-3);
  });

  // More tests...
});
```

The describe function is used to group related tests – in this case, tests for some math functions. Within this group, there are two it functions, each representing a single test. The first test checks if the add function correctly adds two positive numbers, and the second test checks if the add function correctly adds two negative numbers.

With Jest, you can nest describe blocks to organize your tests more systematically. For example, suppose we're expanding our suite to include subtraction, multiplication, and division in our calculator functionality. We can structure our test suite in the following manner:

```
describe('calculator', () => {
  describe('addition', () => {
    it('adds positive numbers correctly', () => {
        expect(add(1, 2)).toBe(3);
    });

    it('adds negative numbers correctly', () => {
        expect(add(-1, -2)).toBe(-3);
    });

    // More tests...
  })

  describe('subtraction', () => {
    it('subtracts positive numbers', () => {});
  })

  // Other describe blocks for multiplication and division
});
```

In this code snippet, we have a top-level describe block labeled calculator. Within this block, we have nested describe blocks for each mathematical operation. For instance, in the addition block, we have individual it tests for different scenarios of adding numbers. Similarly, we start a new describe block for subtraction. This nested structure makes our test suite more organized, readable, and easier to navigate, particularly when dealing with a large number of tests or complex scenarios.

Testing React components

As we mentioned previously, Jest is a great tool for testing different types of applications, and it supports React applications out of the box. Although it's possible to use Jest alone, it would be a bit more cumbersome and verbose than using a dedicated library such as the **React Testing Library**.

The React Testing Library is a lightweight yet powerful library for testing React components. It's built on top of the popular JavaScript testing framework, Jest, and adds specific utilities for working with React components. The philosophy of the React Testing Library is to encourage writing tests that closely resemble how your software is used. It encourages you to interact with your app just like how users would, meaning you test the functionality and not the implementation details. This approach leads to more robust and maintainable tests that will give you confidence that your app will work in production.

In the code provided in this book, the project has already been set up for you with the React Testing Library. Simply clone the code mentioned in the *Technical requirements* section into your local directory and you are good to go.

All right – let's start with a simple React component to see how we can test it with the React Testing Library. The Section component is a presentational component that accepts two props, heading and content, and renders the props in an article tag:

```
type SectionProps = {
  heading: string;
  content: string;
};

const Section = ({ heading, content }: SectionProps) => {
  return (
    <article>
      <h1>{heading}</h1>
      <p>{content}</p>
    </article>
  );
};

export { Section };
```

To test the component, we can create a new file next to Section.tsx, which we will call Section.test.tsx. This is where our test code will live. Then, we'll use the React Testing Library to check the Section component:

```
import React from "react";
import { render, screen } from "@testing-library/react";

import { Section } from "../component/Section";

describe("Section", () => {
  it("renders a section with heading and content", () => {
    render(<Section heading="Basic" content="Hello world" />);

    expect(screen.getByText("Basic")).toBeInTheDocument();
    expect(screen.getByText("Hello world")).toBeInTheDocument();
  });
});
```

This test code makes use of `@testing-library/react` to verify that the `Section` component behaves as expected – the text **Basic** and **Hello world** should be present in the HTML document. The render function provided by `@testing-library/react` is used to render the `Section` component with specific props: a heading of **Basic** and content of **Hello world**.

Following the rendering, the `screen.getByText` function is used to query the DOM (which represents the rendered output of the `Section` component) for elements containing specific text.

Next, `expect` and `toBeInTheDocument` are then used to make assertions about the state of these elements. Specifically, the test is asserting that there is an element with the **Basic** text and an element with the **Hello world** text present in the DOM, which would indicate that the `Section` component has correctly rendered its heading and content props.

This straightforward unit test for a React component serves as a useful starting point. However, in complex real-world projects, we often encounter scenarios where multiple components need to interact harmoniously. For instance, consider a checkout page that integrates an address collection component, a payment component, and a price calculation logic component.

To confidently ensure the seamless interaction of these distinct components, we must employ a more comprehensive testing strategy: integration tests.

Learning about integration tests

Integration tests are positioned above unit tests in the pyramid, validating the interactions between multiple units of code. These could be component interactions or interactions between the client side and server side. Integration tests aim to identify issues that may arise when different parts of the system are combined.

One such scenario involves testing the interaction between two separate components to verify that they function correctly together – this is integration testing at a UI component level. Additionally, if you're looking to ensure smooth collaboration between your frontend code and backend services, the tests you write for this purpose would also be classified as integration tests, which verify that different layers of your application are working correctly together.

Let's have a look at an example of an integration test for a React component. In *Figure 5.3*, there is a **Terms and Conditions** section, which includes a long text about the legal information, and a checkbox for the user to consent. There is also a **Next** button, which is disabled by default. However, once the user selects **Accept the Terms and Conditions**, the button will be enabled, and the user can proceed:

Terms and Conditions

Welcome to our platform. We value your trust, and strive to maintain a secure and respectful environment for all users. By accessing our platform, you agree to adhere to our terms and conditions. This includes respecting all copyright laws, refraining from harassing behavior, and ensuring all content posted by you does not violate any local, national, or international laws. The information and services provided on this platform are offered on an 'as is' basis and we are not responsible for any damage or loss you may incur as a result of your use of the platform. Please review these terms regularly, as they may be updated from time to time.

☑ I accept the terms and conditions

Next

Figure 5.3: The Terms and Conditions component

This integration test can be described using the following code snippet – we are not testing the **Checkbox** and **Next** buttons separately, but verifying the interaction between them:

```
describe('Terms and Conditions', () => {
  it("renders learn react link", () => {
    render(<TermsAndConditions />);
    const button = screen.getByText('Next');
    expect(button).toBeDisabled();

    const checkbox = screen.getByRole('checkbox');

    act(() => {
      userEvent.click(checkbox);
    })

    expect(button).toBeEnabled();
  });
})
```

The `describe` function is used to group all tests associated with the `TermsAndConditions` component, forming a so-called test suite. Within this suite, we have a single test case denoted by the it function. The description of this test is **renders learn react link**, which appears to be a misnomer considering the operations carried out in this test. A more suitable description might be **Enables the next button upon accepting terms and conditions**.

Initially, the `render` function is invoked to display the `TermsAndConditions` component. This function produces a series of output, or render results, that can be queried in various ways to assess whether the component behaves as expected.

We then try to find a button by its text, **Next**, using the `screen.getByText` function – which returns the element found on the page. At this point, we expect this button to be disabled, so we confirm this expectation by calling `expect(button).toBeDisabled()`.

Next, we look for the checkbox using the `screen.getByRole` function. This function allows us to find the checkbox based on its role, which is `checkbox`.

The user interaction of ticking the checkbox is simulated using the `userEvent.click` function, which is wrapped in React's `act` function. The `act` function ensures that all updates related to these actions are processed and applied before moving forward; this way, our assertions will examine the component in its updated state.

Finally, we verify that the button is enabled after the checkbox has been clicked. This is done using `expect(button).toBeEnabled()`. If this statement holds true, we know that our component behaves as intended – that is, disabling the **Next** button until the user accepts the terms and conditions.

Now, let's look at how the code is written. The `TermsAndConditions` component under test is composed of a few components – `heading`, `LegalContent`, and `UserConsent`. Plus, `UserConsent` itself is composed of `CheckBox` and `Button`:

```
const TheLegalContent = () => {
  return (
    <p>
      {/*...*/}
    </p>
  );
};
type CheckBoxProps = {
  label: string;
  isChecked: boolean;
  onCheck: (event: any) => void
}

const CheckBox = ({label, isChecked, onCheck}: CheckBoxProps) => {
  return (
    <label>
      <input
        type="checkbox"
        checked={isChecked}
        onChange={onCheck}
      />
      {label}
    </label>
  )
```

```
}

type ButtonProps = {
  type: 'standard' | 'primary' | 'secondary';
  label: string;
  disabled?: boolean;
}

const Button = ({label, disabled = true}: ButtonProps) => {
  return (
    <div style={{margin: '0.5rem 0'}}>
      <button disabled={disabled}>{label}</button>
    </div>
  )
}

const UserConsent = () => {
  const [isChecked, setIsChecked] = useState(false);

  const handleCheckboxChange = (event: React.
   ChangeEvent<HTMLInputElement>) => {
    setIsChecked(event.target.checked);
  };

  return (
    <>
      <CheckBox isChecked={isChecked} onCheck={handleCheckboxChange}
       label="I accept the terms and conditions" />
      <Button type="primary" label="Next" disabled={!isChecked} />
    </>
  );
};

const TermsAndConditions = () => {
  return (
    <div>
      <h2>Terms and Conditions</h2>
      <TheLegalContent />
      <UserConsent />
    </div>
  );
};

export { TermsAndConditions };
```

The sole component that gets exported in this code is `TermsAndConditions`, which is the primary subject of our testing strategy. In our tests, we employ `userEvent.click` to initiate a click event within the realm of a `jsdom` environment.

Essentially, our focus is not on testing the isolated React components (such as `CheckBox` and `Button`; they should have their own unit tests), but rather on the DOM elements and their interactions. It's important to clarify that we're not invoking a full-fledged browser here, but rather a headless `jsdom` variant that exists in memory. Yet, despite the simulated environment of these integration tests, they still provide us with the confidence that the click event and button enablement are functioning as expected.

> **Note**
>
> **jsdom** is a JavaScript-based headless browser that can be used to create a realistic testing environment that simulates a web browser's environment. It is an implementation of web standards such as HTML, DOM, CSS, and others, entirely in JavaScript.
>
> When we run JavaScript that manipulates the DOM in a browser, the browser provides the DOM. However, when we are running tests using a testing framework such as Jest in a Node.js environment, there isn't a DOM by default. This is where `jsdom` comes into play. `jsdom` provides a virtual DOM, thereby allowing our tests to run as though they were in a browser-like environment, even when they're running in Node.js.
>
> Why do we need `jsdom`? In modern frontend development, particularly with frameworks such as React, Angular, and Vue, our JavaScript code often interacts directly with the DOM. For our tests to be useful, they need to be able to simulate this interaction. `jsdom` allows us to do this without needing to open a browser window.

In integration tests, we concentrate on the interactions between various modules. However, even if these interactions function as expected, there's still a possibility that the broader system may break. User journeys often involve multiple steps, so it's essential to have a process that seamlessly connects these steps to ensure the software continues to work reliably.

Learning about E2E tests using Cypress

E2E tests are at the top of the test pyramid. E2E tests simulate real user flows and interactions, testing the system as a whole. These tests help ensure that all parts of the application work together as expected, from the user interface to the backend systems.

We're going to use Cypress as the E2E test framework in this book. **Cypress** is a powerful tool for E2E testing of modern web applications. Its unique approach sets it apart from many other testing tools – instead of using Selenium, a common engine for many testing systems, Cypress operates directly on the actual browser, resulting in more reliable tests and a superior debugging experience.

Installing Cypress

You can either install Cypress into an existing project (like what we're doing in this book) or install it in another folder other than your project. Cypress has been added as a project dependency in the code base in GitHub (provided in the *Technical requirements* section), so you only need to run npm install in the project root (refer to the official documentation for more information: https://docs.cypress.io/guides/getting-started/installing-cypress).

Once you have installed the package, simply run npx cypress open to launch the configuration wizard:

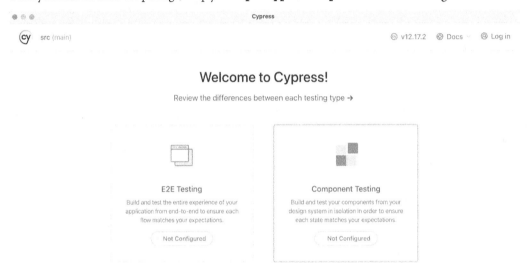

Figure 5.4: The Cypress wizard – choosing a test type

Follow the wizard to configure **E2E Testing**, and choose **Chrome** as the browser for running all the tests. After that, choose **Create new spec**:

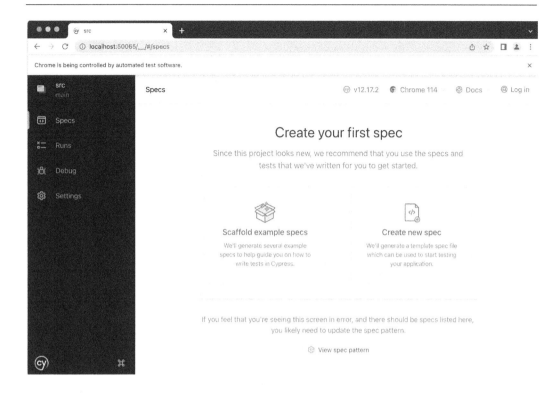

Figure 5.5: The Cypress wizard – creating a spec from a template

Cypress will create a folder with all the necessary files for us:

```
cypress
├── downloads
├── e2e
│   └── quote-of-the-day.spec.cy.js
├── fixtures
│   └── example.json
└── support
    ├── commands.js
    └── e2e.js
```

Let's break his structure down:

- At the top level, we have the `cypress` directory, which is the root directory for all the Cypress-related files.

- The `downloads` directory is usually where files downloaded during Cypress tests would be stored; we're not going to use it here as we don't have anything to save at this stage.

- The e2e directory is where E2E test files are located. In this case, it contains `quote-of-the-day.spec.cy.js` (generated from the Cypress wizard), a Cypress test file for testing the quote-of-the-day feature of an application.

- The `fixtures` directory is a place to put external static data that your tests will use. We can put some static files that can be used in our tests (for example, if our tests need some JSON data for mocking the network's response).

- The `support` directory houses Cypress commands and support files, which we will not touch either.

Once we have the folder structure set up, we can proceed and write our first test.

Running our first E2E test

Let's modify the `quote-of-the-day.spec.cy.js` file to make it access a remote website. Cypress will actively watch the files under the `cypress/e2e/` folder, and whenever the content changes, it will rerun the test.

Make sure you have launched cypress in a terminal window (either Terminal for MacOS/Linux or Windows Terminal) with `npx cypress open`:

```
describe('quote of the day', () => {
  it('display the heading', () => {
    cy.visit('https://icodeit-juntao.github.io/quote-of-the-day/');
  })
});
```

In this code snippet, `describe` is used to declare a test suite – in this case, for the quote of the day feature. Within this suite, there's a single test case defined by it, labeled `display the heading`. The purpose of this test case is to visit a web page – in this instance, `https://icodeit-juntao.github.io/quote-of-the-day/` – and this web page returns a random quote each time the user refreshes the page.

However, it's important to note that this test case doesn't perform any actual tests or assertions yet. It merely navigates to the page. To make this a meaningful test, you would typically add assertions to check the state of specific elements on the page, such as the heading or a quote displayed:

```
it('display the heading', () => {
  cy.visit('https://icodeit-juntao.github.io/quote-of-the-day/');
  cy.contains("Quote of the day");
})
```

This code snippet is a meaningful test now. After visiting `https://icodeit-juntao.github.io/quote-of-the-day/`, this test now contains an additional check with the `cy.contains()` method. The `cy.contains()` method is used to search for and get a DOM element that contains the specified text – in this case, **Quote of the day**. This method will get the first element it finds that contains the text, and it will fail the test if no such element is found.

If the test can pass, we're confident that the URL is accessible to the public, and the page doesn't throw any exceptions:

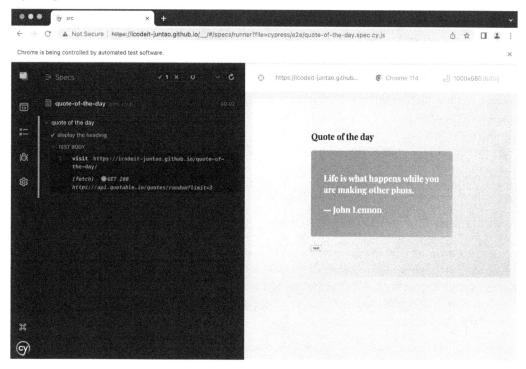

Figure 5.6: Running E2E tests inside Cypress Test Runner

Note that in *Figure 5.6*, on the right-hand side of the screen, you can see what is displayed on the real browser, while on the left-hand side, you can see the test cases and steps. You can even use the mouse to hover on a step to see the page snapshot at that point.

In addition, we can add another test case to verify that a quote container is present on the page; that is the most important part of the quote of the day application – to make sure a quote shows up:

```
it('display a quote', () => {
  cy.visit('https://icodeit-juntao.github.io/quote-of-the-day/');
  cy.get('[data-testid="quote-container"]').should('have.length', 1);
})
```

In this test, the `cy.get()` method is used to retrieve a DOM element by its `data-testid` attribute. This attribute is typically used for testing, allowing you to select elements without the need to worry about their CSS selectors or contents, which might change over time.

The element that's being selected in this test has a `data-testid` attribute of `quote-container`. Once the element is retrieved, the `should()` method is invoked to assert something about the state of that element. In this case, it checks that the length of the element (that is, the number of matching elements) is `1`.

So, in this test, after navigating to the web page, it looks for an element with the `data-testid` attribute of `quote-container`, and checks that exactly one such element exists. If it does, the test will pass; if not (either because there are no matching elements or more than one), the test will fail.

That is awesome, but there is a problem here: what if the page isn't blank and the heading is rendered correctly, but the actual content of a quote doesn't show up for some reason? Alternatively, what if the quotes are visible but we're uncertain about the expected quotes when we're writing the tests? Consider, for instance, the `https://icodeit-juntao.github.io/quote-of-the-day/` website, which generates random quotes each time it's accessed. Different users may encounter different quotes at various times. To address these variables, we need a structured method for testing applications with such unpredictable behavior.

Intercepting the network request

In some cases, we don't want to send actual network requests for the UI to work, while in other cases, it's not practical to rely on the response directly. We want to verify whether the quote is rendered correctly by checking the content, but as the quoted content is generated randomly, we cannot predict it before we make the network request. This means we need a mechanism to pin down the response, but we would also like to send the request.

One way to achieve that is to intercept the network request that's sent to the endpoint and return some fixed data. In Cypress, we can do that through the `cy.intercept` API.

Firstly, we can define a data array in the `quote-of-the-day.spec.cy.js` file. It's a normal JavaScript array that contains the data we expect to return from the server side:

```
const quotes = [
  {
    content:
      "Any fool can write code that a computer can understand. Good
       programmers write code that humans can understand.",
    author: "Martin Fowler",
  },
  {
    content: "Truth can only be found in one place: the code.",
    author: "Robert C. Martin",
```

```
    },
    {
      content:
        "Optimism is an occupational hazard of programming: feedback is
          the treatment.",
      author: "Kent Beck",
    },
  ];
```

In the testing code, we aim to capture any network requests that are sent to URLs beginning with
`https://api.quotable.io/quotes/random`. Whenever the request is sent from React,
Cypress will cancel the request and return the `quotes` array instead; this means the test doesn't
depend on whether the remote service is working or not. That way, our test is more stable. We can
see the code here:

```
it("display the quote content", () => {
  cy.intercept("GET", "https://api.quotable.io/quotes/random*", {
    statusCode: 200,
    body: quotes,
  });

  cy.visit("https://icodeit-juntao.github.io/quote-of-the-day/");

  cy.contains(
    "Any fool can write code that a computer can understand. Good
      programmers write code that humans can understand."
  );

  cy.contains(
    "Martin Fowler"
  );
});
```

The `cy.intercept` function is being used to stub the HTTP GET request to the quote API. When
such a request is detected, rather than letting the request go through to the actual API, Cypress will
respond with a predefined HTTP response. This response has a status code of 200, indicating success,
and the body of the response is set to be our predefined quotes data. This technique allows us to
control the data being returned, making our test more deterministic and isolated from any potential
instability or variation in the actual API.

The test then navigates to the quote web page. After the page is loaded, it verifies if the page contains
the expected quote text and the quote author. If these two checks pass, the test case succeeds.

Something is interesting here that we need to highlight. An E2E test, by definition, tests the whole software stack from the frontend through to the backend, including all the intermediate layers, such as databases and network infrastructure. E2E testing aims to simulate real-world scenarios and confirm that the entire application is functioning correctly.

However, when we use the `cy.intercept` function to stub HTTP requests, we are indeed modifying this behavior. We are no longer testing the complete E2E flow because we are controlling and replacing the actual backend response with a mock response. This technique transforms the test from an E2E test into something more akin to an integration test for the frontend as we are testing the integration of different components of the frontend while mocking the backend responses.

This is not necessarily a bad thing, however. Often, in testing, especially in complex systems, it is beneficial to isolate different parts of the system to gain more control over what we are testing and to ensure we can test different scenarios more reliably and deterministically.

With that, we've covered the basics of Cypress for E2E testing and you're now equipped to write robust E2E tests for your web applications.

Summary

In this chapter, we embarked on an exploration of the world of testing in a React application. We understood that the necessity of testing goes beyond mere validation of code correctness; it paves the path toward maintainability, improves readability, and drives the evolution of our application, ultimately ensuring we build software that meets expectations consistently.

Testing is a vital practice in software development – one that ensures our application not only works correctly but is also resilient to future changes. The React ecosystem, with tools such as Jest, the React Testing Library, and Cypress, provides us with a powerful arsenal to implement comprehensive testing strategies, thus bolstering the robustness and reliability of our applications.

In the next chapter, we'll look into the common refactoring techniques and see how tests can help us during the refactoring process.

6

Exploring Common Refactoring Techniques

Welcome to the fascinating world of refactoring! In this chapter, we're going to explore the basics of this fundamental practice, essential to every developer in maintaining and improving a code base. We aim to introduce you to the most common refactoring techniques, providing a solid foundation for understanding and employing these valuable tools. Remember, our objective is not to provide an exhaustive guide, but rather to familiarize you with the essentials that you'll use time and time again in your programming journey.

Refactoring doesn't discriminate among languages or frameworks – it's a universal concept applicable anywhere you write code. The techniques we'll discuss include renaming variables, changing function declarations, extracting functions, moving fields, and more. These techniques might appear simple at first glance, but they are incredibly powerful tools for crafting clean, understandable, and maintainable code.

Also remember that refactoring is not a one-time task, but rather an ongoing process of small, iterative changes that gradually enhance the structure and quality of your code. It is these frequent, incremental improvements that keep a code base healthy, robust, and easier to work with. By introducing you to the basics, we hope to equip you with the essential tools and techniques that will be a stepping stone toward more advanced refactoring methods.

While we'll delve into more complex refactoring techniques in later chapters, the practices you'll learn here will serve as a valuable starting point. By the end of this chapter, you'll have a toolkit of common refactoring practices and a newfound understanding of their importance in enhancing code quality. Ultimately, the refactoring skills you begin to develop here will empower you to write cleaner, more efficient code, and set you on the path to becoming a more proficient developer. Let's dive in!

In this chapter, we will cover the following topics:

- Understanding refactoring
- Adding tests before refactoring
- Using Rename Variable
- Using Extract Variable
- Using Replace Loop with Pipeline
- Using Extract Function
- Using Introduce Parameter Object
- Using Decompose Conditional
- Using Move Function

Technical requirements

A GitHub repository has been created to host all the code we discuss in the book. For this chapter, you can find the recommended structure at `https://github.com/PacktPublishing/React-Anti-Patterns/tree/main/code/src/ch6`.

Before we dive into the refactorings, let's align with some tooling that would help us to make changes easily. When it comes to refactoring tools, there are many **integrated development environments (IDEs)** and source code editors available in the frontend world – WebStorm and Visual Studio Code (VS Code) are the most popular ones that offer an impressive range of features, including robust refactoring capabilities.

WebStorm, developed by JetBrains, is a powerful and feature-rich IDE specifically designed for JavaScript and its related technologies such as TypeScript, HTML, and CSS. One of its most notable features is its advanced automated refactoring, but it also offers an extensive list of refactoring options such as rename, extract, inline, move, and copy, which can be applied to variables, classes, functions, and other elements. It also has a smart duplication detection feature, helping you to locate and resolve repetitive blocks of code.

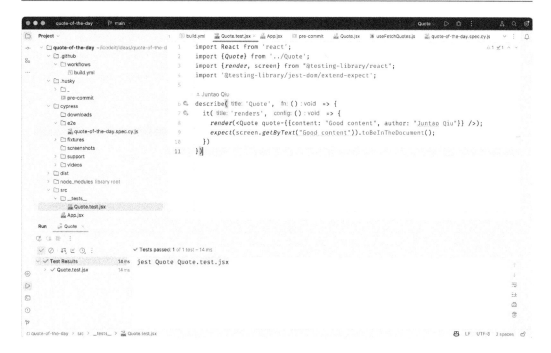

Figure 6.1: The WebStorm IDE

WebStorm's IntelliSense, auto-complete, and code navigation are quite robust, giving you a lot of help when writing and exploring the code. However, WebStorm is a commercial product, and while it does offer a trial period, you will need to purchase a license for continued use.

Visual Studio Code (**VS Code**), on the other hand, is a free, open source IDE developed by Microsoft. It's lightweight compared to WebStorm and is known for its speed and flexibility. VS Code also supports a wide range of languages beyond JavaScript, thanks to its extension marketplace. Refactoring capabilities in VS Code are strong as well, with support for common operations such as renaming, extracting functions or variables, and changing function signatures. VS Code's refactoring capabilities can be further enhanced by installing extensions, and its customizability is one of its key strengths.

Figure 6.2: VS Code

While VS Code may not have as many automated refactoring features as WebStorm out of the box, it can be tailored to match and sometimes exceed WebStorm's capabilities through these extensions.

Choosing between the two often boils down to personal preference and the specific needs of your project. If you value a highly automated, feature-rich environment and don't mind paying for it, WebStorm might be your best bet. However, if you prioritize speed, flexibility, and customization and are comfortable setting up your environment through extensions, VS Code could be the better choice.

I prefer WebStorm as my IDE at work – part of the reason is I am already very familiar with the keymaps, and I love the built-in auto-refactoring capability. However, I still use VS Code for casual projects.

Understanding refactoring

Refactoring is a disciplined, systematic process of improving the design of an existing code base without changing its external behavior. It's a fundamental aspect of everyday coding, a practice integral to the iterative and incremental nature of software development. The concept is universally applicable, and not bound to any specific programming language, framework, or paradigm. Whether you're writing in JavaScript, Python, or any other language, and whether you're using React, Angular, or a homegrown framework, refactoring is crucial to maintaining a healthy code base.

The term "refactoring" was first introduced by William Opdyke and Ralph Johnson in a 1990 paper titled *Refactoring: An Aid in Designing Application Frameworks and Evolving Object-Oriented Systems*; however, the concept and practice of refactoring have roots in earlier practices in software engineering. The art of refactoring gained significant prominence with Martin Fowler's book *Refactoring: Improving the Design of Existing Code*, published in 1999. In this book, Fowler describes refactoring as "a controlled technique for improving the design of an existing code base," emphasizing its role in mitigating the buildup of technical debt, which makes the code easier to understand, maintain, and extend.

Refactoring isn't about making one grand, sweeping change to perfect the code base. Instead, it's about making small, incremental improvements consistently over time. Each individual change might not dramatically alter the quality of the code, but collectively, over time, these small changes can significantly enhance the structure, readability, and maintainability of the code base.

Although refactoring doesn't add new functionality, it directly influences the team's ability to deliver new features more quickly, with fewer bugs, and to respond more flexibly to changing requirements. By continuously refactoring, we keep our code clean and easy to work with and set the stage for long-term, sustainable development.

In conclusion, refactoring is a critical tool in a developer's toolkit, irrespective of the technology stack or the size and scope of the project. It's a long-term investment in the code base and the team, and ultimately, it's an investment in the quality of the software that is delivered.

The common mistakes of refactoring

The biggest mistake people make in refactoring is that they restructure code rather than refactoring it. The terms "refactoring" and "restructuring" are often used interchangeably, but they have distinct meanings in software development.

Refactoring is a disciplined technique for improving the design of an existing code base, making it cleaner and easier to understand and work with. It involves changing the internal structure of the software without modifying its external behavior. This is generally done in small steps, and each refactoring step is expected to maintain the software's functionality. It doesn't add new features; instead, it makes the code more readable, maintainable, and prepared for future changes.

For example, in a React application, refactoring could involve breaking down a large component into smaller, more manageable components, or replacing complex conditional logic with a strategy pattern.

Restructuring, on the other hand, can be seen as a broader and more drastic process. It often involves large-scale changes that not only impact the internal structure of the software but can also affect its external behavior. Restructuring can encompass changes to the software's architecture, data models, interfaces, and more. It is often driven by the need to introduce major changes or additions to the software's features or capabilities, to improve performance, or to address significant technical debt.

In the context of a React application, restructuring might involve changing the state management solution (such as moving from Redux to the React Context API), updating the routing mechanism, or transitioning from a monolithic architecture to a microfrontend architecture.

While both refactoring and restructuring aim to improve the quality of the code base, refactoring is typically smaller in scope, involves no change in functionality, and is part of the regular development process. In contrast, restructuring is generally larger in scope, can change functionality, and is often part of a larger project or initiative to address more significant challenges or changes in requirements.

As well as a misunderstanding between refactoring and restructuring, another mistake people tend to make is that they don't test as often – sometimes this is because they don't have many tests, while at other times they think it's safe to make these "small" changes without testing. Let's look at testing in the next section.

Adding tests before refactoring

Because we don't want to make any observable behavior changes during refactoring, we need to inspect the code to make sure we have enough tests to cover the current behavior. It's easy to mess up without the right tests in place, and that's not only risky but also less efficient, as we need to check the changed code manually and repeatedly.

Let's say we have some TypeScript code from an online shopping application – the code works fine, but there aren't any tests associated with it. To improve the code so that it's easier to understand and extend, we need to refactor it:

```typescript
interface Item {
  id: string;
  price: number;
  quantity: number;
}

class ShoppingCart {
  cartItems: Item[] = [];

  addItemToCart(id: string, price: number, quantity: number) {
    this.cartItems.push({ id, price, quantity });
  }

  calculateTotal() {
    let total = 0;
    for (let i = 0; i < this.cartItems.length; i++) {
      let item = this.cartItems[i];
      let subTotal = item.price * item.quantity;
      if (item.quantity > 10) {
```

```
      subTotal *= 0.9;
    }
    total += subTotal;
  }
  return total;
}
}


export { ShoppingCart };
```

So, this code defines a shopping cart model. Firstly, it defines an `Item` interface, which represents an item to be added to the cart. An `Item` component consists of an ID, a price, and a quantity. Then, it defines a `ShoppingCart` class with a `cartItems` property, which is an array of `Item` objects, initially empty.

The `ShoppingCart` class has two methods:

- The `addItemToCart` method accepts an ID, price, and quantity, and then creates an item using these parameters. This item is then added to the `cartItems` array.

- The `calculateTotal` method calculates the total price of the items in the cart. For each item, it multiplies the item's price by its quantity to get a subtotal. If the quantity of the item is more than 10, a 10% discount is applied to the subtotal. The subtotal of each item is then added together to get the total. The total is then returned by the method.

There are two important calculations here: compute the total price (price by quantity) and apply the discount when eligible. We normally should pay more attention to the logic regarding these calculations.

For example, we need to verify both sides of an `if-else` statement. As we have `if-else` inside the `for` loop, we will at least need to add two test cases before making changes. Let's add the following Jest tests to describe both calculations – with and without a discount:

```
import { ShoppingCart } from "../ShoppingCart";

describe("ShoppingCart", () => {
  it("calculates item prices", () => {
    const shoppingCart = new ShoppingCart();
    shoppingCart.addItemToCart("apple", 2.0, 2);
    shoppingCart.addItemToCart("orange", 3.5, 1);

    const price = shoppingCart.calculateTotal();
    expect(price).toEqual(7.5);
  });

  it('applies discount when applicable', () => {
```

```
      const shoppingCart = new ShoppingCart();
      shoppingCart.addItemToCart("apple", 2.0, 11);

      const price = shoppingCart.calculateTotal();
      expect(price).toEqual(19.8);
    })
  });
```

The first test, `calculates item prices`, is verifying that the `calculateTotal` method works as expected when no discounts are applied. Here, a `ShoppingCart` object is instantiated, and two items (`apple` and `orange`) are added to the cart. The total price of these items is calculated and expected to be 7.5, as there are two apples at $2 each and one orange at $3.5.

The second test, `applies discount when applicable`, is checking that the `calculateTotal` method correctly applies a 10% discount when the quantity of an item is more than 10. In this case, a `ShoppingCart` object is instantiated, and one type of item (`apple`) is added to the cart with quantity 11. The total price of this item should be $19.8 after applying the 10% discount on the subtotal of $22 (11 apples at $2 each). The calculated total price is then checked against this expected value.

Once we have test cases to cover the important logic, we can safely make changes. During refactoring, we'll need to run these tests regularly.

Refactorings are small steps that can improve the code. Let's have a look at our very first and maybe the simplest refactoring technique: **Rename Variable**.

Using Rename Variable

Let's start with a simple refactoring technique called Rename Variable. Rename Variable is a very straightforward yet effective method to improve the readability and maintainability of the code. It involves changing the name of a variable to better reflect its purpose and the data it holds, or to follow a certain naming convention or standard.

Sometimes, during the initial phases of coding, developers might choose names for variables that make sense at that time, but as the code evolves, the purpose of the variable might change or become clearer. The variable name, however, often remains the same. This can cause confusion and make the code harder to understand and maintain. Renaming variables to describe their purposes more accurately can reduce the cognitive load for future readers of the code, including the future self of the current coder.

Let's return to our `ShoppingCart` example. The variable name `cartItems` inside the `ShoppingCart` class is a little redundant; however, we can rename it to simply `items` to be more concise and clean:

```
class ShoppingCart {
  items: Item[] = [];

  addItemToCart(id: string, price: number, quantity: number) {
```

```
    this.items.push({ id, price, quantity });
  }

  calculateTotal() {
    let total = 0;
    for (let i = 0; i < this.items.length; i++) {
      let item = this.items[i];
      let subTotal = item.price * item.quantity;
      if (item.quantity > 10) {
        subTotal *= 0.9;
      }
      total += subTotal;
    }
    return total;
  }
}
```

After the change, make sure to run the tests again to see whether we accidentally made any mistakes.

It's important to establish a habit of running tests regularly after making some changes, and whenever the tests fail, we need to stop and examine what is wrong. Once all the tests are back to passing, we can then proceed.

Using Extract Variable

Extract Variable is a common refactoring technique that is used to improve the readability and maintainability of code. The process involves taking a section of code that calculates a value, replacing it with a new variable, and assigning the result of the original expression to this new variable. There is a similar refactoring called **Extract Constant** that can be used to extract a value that doesn't change at runtime.

This refactoring technique is particularly useful when you have a complex expression or a duplicated calculation; by extracting parts of the expression to variables with meaningful names, the code becomes more understandable and easier to manage.

In the `ShoppingCart` example, the `0.9` discount rate deserves its own name; we can extract a variable and reference it at the point where the function is called. As the value of the variable isn't going to change at runtime, we can call it **Extract Constant** in this case:

```
const DISCOUNT_RATE = 0.9;

class ShoppingCart {
  //...
  calculateTotal() {
    let total = 0;
```

```
    for (let i = 0; i < this.items.length; i++) {
      let item = this.items[i];
      let subTotal = item.price * item.quantity;
      if (item.quantity > 10) {
        subTotal *= DISCOUNT_RATE;
      }
      total += subTotal;
    }
    return total;
  }
  //...
}
```

For the sake of clarity, portions of the code that aren't relevant to this particular change have been left out of the discussion; however, the important thing to note is that in this instance, we've created a constant named `DISCOUNT_RATE` and used it in place of the previous hard-coded value of `0.9` where it's utilized in the code. At times, we may wish to assign a name to an expression other than a hard-coded value, so we can create a variable to stand in for the expression and then refer to that variable.

It's a tiny step, but it improves the code slightly. If we need to change the discount rate in the future, the constant name is much easier to search and understand than the hard-coded value of `0.9`.

Now we can investigate another refactoring technique to make the `for` loop a bit simpler.

Using Replace Loop with Pipeline

The **Replace Loop with Pipeline** refactoring technique, as the name implies, is about replacing a loop structure with a pipeline of transformations, commonly achieved by using higher-order functions or methods such as `map`, `filter`, and `reduce` in functional programming languages such as JavaScript.

In the case of JavaScript, the Array prototype has methods such as `map`, `filter`, and `reduce` that can be chained together to form a pipeline. Each of these methods receives a function as an argument and applies this function to each element in the array, effectively transforming the array in some manner.

However, keep in mind that while replacing loops with pipelines can make the code cleaner and more readable, it might not always be the most efficient option, especially when dealing with very large datasets. So, as with all refactorings, you need to balance readability and maintainability with performance requirements in cases when you need to iterate through a large dataset multiple times.

The `for` loop in the previous section can be replaced by the `reduce` function (and we don't have to explicitly define an index variable or save the boilerplate code):

```
class ShoppingCart {
  //...
  calculateTotal() {
```

```
    return this.items.reduce((total, item) => {
      let subTotal = item.price * item.quantity;
      return total + (item.quantity > 10 ? subTotal * DISCOUNT_RATE :
        subTotal);
    }, 0);
  }
  //...
}
```

The `calculateTotal()` method is using the `reduce()` function to calculate the total price of the items in the shopping cart. The `reduce()` function is a higher-order function that applies a function against an accumulator and each element in the array (from left to right) to reduce it to a single output value.

The total starts at 0 and then for each item in the shopping cart, it adds the `subTotal` variable of that item to the total. The `subTotal` variable is calculated by multiplying the price and quantity of each item.

Next, we need to re-run all the tests to check whether everything goes well. As our tests are still passing, let's see how we can make the code even better by extracting lines into a smaller function.

Using Extract Function

Extract Function is a refactoring technique that helps to improve code readability and maintainability by breaking down a large or complex function into smaller, more manageable parts.

Let's say you come across a function that's performing multiple tasks. Maybe it's doing some data validation, then some computations, and finally logging the result or updating some state. The function is long and complex, making it hard to understand at a glance what it's doing. Extract Function refactoring is all about identifying those distinct pieces of functionality, pulling them out into their own separate functions, and then calling those new functions from the original one.

One key benefit is that it makes the code more self-documenting. If you extract a part of your function to a new function and give it a meaningful name, it can often make the code much easier to understand since the function name can describe what the code is doing. It also improves the reusability of the code, since these smaller functions can be reused elsewhere if needed.

The logic of how to calculate the `subTotal` variable can be extracted from `calculateTotal` as a separate unit:

```
function applyDiscountIfEligible(item: Item, subTotal: number) {
  return item.quantity > 10 ? subTotal * DISCOUNT_RATE : subTotal;
}

class ShoppingCart {
```

```
//...

calculateTotal() {
  return this.items.reduce((total, item) => {
    let subTotal = item.price * item.quantity;
    return total + applyDiscountIfEligible(item, subTotal);
  }, 0);
}
}
```

In this code snippet, we see the result of an Extract Function refactoring. The logic to apply a discount if the item quantity is greater than 10 has been extracted into its own function named `applyDiscountIfEligible`.

In the `ShoppingCart` class, the `calculateTotal` method calculates the total price of the items in the cart using the `reduce` function. For each item, it computes the subtotal as the product of the item's price and quantity, then adds this subtotal (after applying any eligible discount) to the total.

The `applyDiscountIfEligible` function takes an item and its quantity as arguments. If the quantity of the item is more than 10, it applies a discount rate (represented by `DISCOUNT_RATE`) to the argument `subTotal`; otherwise, it simply returns the argument `subTotal` as it is.

This refactoring makes the `calculateTotal` method more concise and easier to read, by abstracting away the details of how discounts are applied into a separate, appropriately named function.

Let's look at another refactoring method that could make the passed-in parameter easy to modify.

Using Introduce Parameter Object

Introduce Parameter Object is a refactoring technique used when a function has a large number of parameters, or when multiple functions share the same parameters. In this technique, you group related parameters into a single object and pass that object to the function instead.

A large number of parameters in a function can be confusing and difficult to manage. Grouping related parameters together into an object can increase code readability and make it easier to understand what the function does. It also makes the function call simpler and cleaner. Furthermore, if the same group of parameters is used in multiple function calls, this technique reduces the chances of passing parameters in the wrong order.

For example, consider a `calculateTotalPrice(quantity, price, discount)` function. We could refactor this using the Introduce Parameter Object technique to become calculateTotalPrice({ quantity, price, discount }). Now, the quantity, price, and discount parameters are grouped together into an object (with type Item), like so:

```
class ShoppingCart {
  items: Item[] = [];

  addItemToCart({id, price, quantity}: Item) {
    this.items.push({ id, price, quantity });
  }

  //...
}
```

On top of these benefits, Introduce Parameter Object refactoring can often reveal or inspire domain concepts that were previously hidden and implicit in your code. The parameter object might become a class of its own, with its own behavior and data manipulation methods. This can lead to more object-oriented and encapsulated code.

Next, let's explore another refactoring technique designed to streamline your if-else statements and enhance code readability.

Using Decompose Conditional

Decompose Conditional is a refactoring technique where the logic within a conditional statement (if-else or switch) is extracted into separate functions. This technique helps to improve the readability of the code, making it more understandable.

The condition, if clause, and else clause (if it exists) all get their own function. These functions are then named according to what they do or what they are checking for. This refactoring is beneficial because it replaces code that might need comments to understand with well-named functions, making the code self-explanatory.

For example, the logic in the applyDiscountIfEligible function can actually be simplified by this refactoring; we can extract a small function called isDiscountEligible to replace the item.quantity > 10 check, like in the following:

```
function isDiscountEligible(item: Item) {
  return item.quantity > 10;
}

function applyDiscountIfEligible(item: Item, subTotal: number) {
  return isDiscountEligible(item) ? subTotal * DISCOUNT_RATE :
subTotal;
}
```

In this code snippet, the extraction of logic into a separate function might appear superfluous because it adds an additional function call. However, it enhances readability and reusability:

```
function isDiscountEligible(item: Item) {
  return item.quantity > 10;
}

function applyDiscountIfEligible(item: Item, subTotal: number) {
  return isDiscountEligible(item) ? subTotal * DISCOUNT_RATE :
    subTotal;
}
```

In this code snippet, we've separated the logic that determines whether an item is eligible for a discount into a standalone `isDiscountEligible` function. This extraction makes our `applyDiscountIfEligible` function cleaner and its intention more evident. Additionally, it allows for the `isDiscountEligible` logic to be updated independently if needed in the future, improving maintainability.

After extracting these smaller functions, they don't have to reside in the current file. We can relocate them to a separate module and import them as needed; this not only shortens the length of the current module but also improves its readability. Let's look at that next.

Using Move Function

Move Function is a refactoring method that involves changing the location of a function to a more suitable or appropriate place. This could be within the same class, to a different class, or even to a separate module. The objective of this method is to enhance the readability, maintainability, and structure of the code by ensuring that functions are placed where they logically fit best.

This kind of refactoring becomes necessary when the responsibilities of your classes evolve over time. You might find that a function makes more sense in a different class, or perhaps you have a group of functions within a class that work together and would be better suited in their own class or module.

Move Function refactoring can help reduce the complexity of the class by moving functions to the places where their functionality is most relevant or required. This promotes the principle of cohesion where related code is kept together. It also aids in achieving loose coupling by minimizing unnecessary dependencies between different parts of the code.

In our `ShoppingCart` component, we can move the type definition into a new file called `types.ts`. We can also move `DISCOUNT_RATE`, `isDiscountEligible`, and `applyDiscountIfEligible` into a separate file called `utils.ts`:

```
import { Item } from "./types";

const DISCOUNT_RATE = 0.9;

function isDiscountEligible(item: Item) {
  return item.quantity > 10;
}

export function applyDiscountIfEligible(item: Item, subTotal: number)
{
  return isDiscountEligible(item) ? subTotal * DISCOUNT_RATE :
    subTotal;
}
```

Note that in the code, only `applyDiscountIfEligible` is a public function and can be accessed outside of the file. This refactoring also improves the encapsulation of the code.

After Move Function is used, the `ShoppingCart` component is simplified significantly and only has the necessary parts:

```
import { Item } from "./types";
import { applyDiscountIfEligible } from "./utils";

class ShoppingCart {
  items: Item[] = [];

  addItemToCart({ id, price, quantity }: Item) {
    this.items.push({ id, price, quantity });
  }

  calculateTotal() {
    return this.items.reduce((total, item) => {
      let subTotal = item.price * item.quantity;
      return total + applyDiscountIfEligible(item, subTotal);
    }, 0);
  }
}

export { ShoppingCart };
```

As with all refactoring, care should be taken when moving functions to ensure that the overall behavior of the system is not altered. Tests should be in place to verify that the functionality remains the same after refactoring.

Summary

This chapter focused on a variety of code refactoring techniques that are essential to maintaining and improving the structure, readability, and maintainability of your code base.

The refactoring techniques introduced include Rename Variable, which enhances code clarity by using more descriptive variable names, Extract Variable, which simplifies complex expressions by breaking them into smaller, more manageable parts, and Replace Loop with Pipeline, which transforms traditional `for`/`while` loops into more concise, declarative higher-order functions such as `map`, `filter`, and `reduce`.

As well as this, Extract Function encourages code modularity and reusability by breaking down large functions into smaller ones, each with a single, well-defined responsibility, while Introduce Parameter Object groups related parameters into a single object, thereby reducing the complexity of function signatures. Plus, Decompose Conditional breaks down complex conditional logic into separate functions, enhancing readability, and Move Function ensures that functions are placed in the most logical and appropriate location in your code base, promoting high cohesion and loose coupling.

Throughout all these techniques, we emphasized the importance of maintaining the same overall system behavior and relying on tests to ensure that functionality remains consistent despite refactoring. These methods, when properly applied, can lead to a more understandable, easier to maintain, and more robust code base.

In the next chapter, we will explore an exceptional approach to enhancing the quality of our code – the method known as test-driven development.

7

Introducing Test-Driven Development with React

Welcome to a chapter that could potentially revolutionize your approach to React development – **test-driven development** (or **TDD** for short). If you've been building React applications, you know how complex and intricate they can get. With various states to manage, components to juggle, and user interactions to facilitate, ensuring the reliability of your code base can be challenging. That's where TDD comes in.

In the ever-changing landscape of software development, where features are continuously added or modified, TDD serves as a lighthouse that guides you safely through the rough seas of bugs and regressions. By writing tests before your actual code, you not only confirm that your code does what it's supposed to, but you also create a safety net that makes future changes less risky.

This chapter aims to deepen your understanding of TDD and how to implement it effectively in React applications. We'll introduce the core principles of TDD, explore various styles, including unit test-driven development, **acceptance test-driven development** (**ATDD**), and **behavior-driven development** (**BDD**), and even examine the nuanced differences between the Chicago and London styles of TDD.

But we won't stop at theory – to make these concepts come alive, we'll walk you through a practical example of creating a pizza store menu page. From setting up the initial structure to managing complex features, we'll guide you through each step with the TDD approach. By the end of this chapter, you'll have a firm grasp of TDD's capabilities, and you'll be well equipped to start writing more reliable, robust React applications.

So, get ready to dive into a world where tests lead the way and code follows, creating a harmonious balance that results in better, more reliable software.

In this chapter, we will cover the following topics:

- Understanding TDD
- Introducing tasking
- Introducing the online pizza store application
- Breaking down the application requirements
- Implementing the application headline
- Implementing the menu list
- Creating the shopping cart
- Adding items to the shopping cart
- Refactoring the shopping cart

Technical requirements

A GitHub repository has been created to host all the code we'll discuss in this book. For this chapter, you can find the recommended structure at `https://github.com/PacktPublishing/ React-Anti-Patterns/tree/main/code/src/ch7`.

Understanding TDD

TDD isn't exactly a new kid on the block. Originating from **Extreme Programming** (**XP**), a software development methodology that encourages frequent releases in short cycles, TDD has roots going back to the late 1990s. It was Kent Beck, one of the original signatories of the Agile Manifesto, who popularized this practice as a core part of XP. The practice has since grown beyond the realm of XP and is now commonly utilized in various methodologies and frameworks, React included.

At the heart of TDD is a very simple, yet profoundly effective cycle known as the **Red-Green-Refactor loop**:

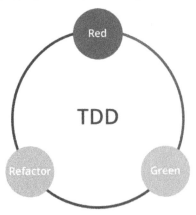

Figure 7.1: The Red-Green-Refactor loop

As you can see, there are essentially three steps when practicing TDD:

- **Red**: At this stage, you write a test that defines a function or improvements of a function. This test should initially fail because the function isn't implemented yet. In most test frameworks (for example, Jest), there will be some red text to indicate the failure.

- **Green**: At this stage, you write the minimum amount of code necessary to pass the test. The key here is to write as little code as possible to make the test pass and make the text turn green – no more than that.

- **Refactor**: Finally, you need to clean up the code while keeping it functional. The refactor phase is about making the code efficient, readable, and understandable without changing its behavior. The tests that are written should still pass after the refactoring.

When developers first encounter TDD, it often feels counter-intuitive, as the practice of writing tests before the actual code contradicts traditional development instincts. However, once you get past the initial discomfort, the advantages of TDD become hard to ignore:

- **Focused problem-solving**: By writing a test for a specific functionality first, you focus your attention solely on solving one problem at a time, making the development process less overwhelming.

- **Predictable next steps**: When you follow a test-driven approach, you always know what to do next: make the test pass. This reduces the cognitive load, making it easier to focus on the task at hand.

- **Simple, maintainable design**: The process naturally encourages the simplest code necessary to pass tests, resulting in a design that is as minimal as possible, and thereby easier to understand and maintain.

- **Facilitates mental flow**: The loop provides a structured approach to coding that helps maintain a "mental flow," helping you stay focused on tasks by reducing the constant context-switching that interrupts a productive coding session.

- **Automatic test coverage**: TDD ensures that your application has robust test coverage by default. You're not adding tests as an afterthought; they're integral to the development process, ensuring a more stable codebase.

TDD is a practice deeply rooted in the principles of Agile and XP but has found relevance far beyond those methodologies. With its structured Red-Green-Refactor loop, TDD provides a solid framework for writing high-quality code. Although it may appear counter-intuitive initially, adopting TDD can result in more focused problem-solving, predictable development, simpler design, enhanced productivity, and robust test coverage.

Different styles of TDD

The core principles of TDD have been adapted and extended into various styles, each offering different perspectives on how best to approach testing and development. Let's explore some of these styles to understand how they can be applied to React development.

The original form of TDD, simply referred to as TDD, mainly focuses on unit tests. In this style, you write tests for the smallest pieces of your code – often individual methods or functions. The aim is to ensure that each part of your code base works as expected in isolation. While this is powerful for testing logic and algorithms, it may not fully capture how various parts interact, especially in a complex UI framework such as React.

ATDD extends TDD by beginning the development process with user acceptance tests. This means that before writing any code, you define what "done" looks like from a user's perspective, often in collaboration with stakeholders. These acceptance tests are then used as the foundation for developing features. ATDD is particularly useful for ensuring that you're building what the user needs and wants:

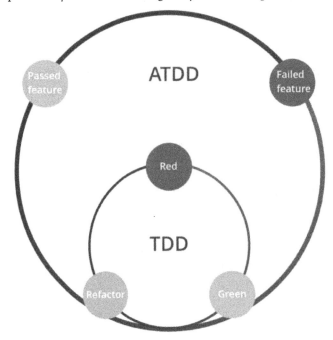

Figure 7.2: The ATDD loop

Note that when you write an acceptance test, it can usually be broken down into smaller unit tests. For example, a user logging into the system can be an acceptance test, but there will be forgotten passwords, incorrect passwords or usernames, remember me functions, and more to cover in the lower-level unit tests.

BDD is a further refinement of TDD and ATDD, focusing on the behavior of an application for a given input. Rather than writing tests that check if a particular method returns an expected value, BDD tests check if a system behaves as expected when subjected to certain conditions. BDD often uses more descriptive language to define tests, making it easier for non-technical stakeholders to understand what is being tested.

BDD often makes use of tools such as **Cucumber** to define behavior specifications in a human-readable format. In a Cucumber test, you specify behavior using a plaintext language called **Gherkin**. Here's a simple example of a BDD test case using Cucumber for a pizza ordering feature (we will continue working on this pizza example later in this chapter):

```
Feature: Pizza Ordering

  Scenario: Customer orders a single pizza
    Given I'm on the PizzaShop website
    When I select the "Order Pizza" button
    And I choose a "Margherita" pizza
    And I add it to the cart
    Then the cart should contain 1 "Margherita" pizza

  Scenario: Customer removes a pizza from the cart
    Given I'm on the PizzaShop website
    And the cart contains 1 "Margherita" pizza
    When I remove the "Margherita" pizza from the cart
    Then the cart should be empty
```

This Gherkin file defines the expected behavior of the pizza ordering functionality. Each line is called a step and can be interpreted as a statement in the test. The scenarios describe the test's behavior in terms of the steps to be performed and the expected outcomes.

Gherkin syntax is more than just readable documentation – it's executable. Tools such as Cucumber can parse the Gherkin files and execute tests based on them – for example, **Given I'm on the PizzaShop website** is transformed into `cypress.visit("http://pizzashop.com")`. This ensures that the software behaves exactly as described in the feature files, making it a source of truth that evolves along with the application.

BDD feature files (Gherkin) serve as a form of living documentation that gets updated as the application changes. This makes them incredibly valuable for new team members, or even for seasoned developers, to understand the expected behavior of the application quickly.

Focusing on user value

Regardless of the style you choose, when working with React, it's crucial to focus on the user's perspective. React components are pieces of UI that users interact with, so your tests should reflect that interaction. The user doesn't care about how your state is managed or how efficient your life cycle methods are; they care about whether clicking a button shows a dropdown, or whether a form submission produces the expected result.

Kent C. Dodds, the creator of the React Testing Library, said "*The more your tests resemble the way your software is used, the more confidence they can give you.*" This principle is universally applicable, irrespective of the framework or library you're using. The focus should always be on the user's experience.

This user-centric approach aligns well with BDD and ATDD, where the focus is on the result of an interaction, not the minutiae of the implementation. By adhering to these principles, you can ensure your React components not only work well but also deliver the user experience you aim to achieve.

Now that we've understood what TDD is and how its various styles can aid in delivering value to our customers, the next question to tackle is: how do we go about implementing it?

Introducing tasking

Tasking is an essential step in the TDD process that involves breaking down a feature or user story into small, manageable tasks, which then serve as the basis for your test cases. The goal of tasking is to create a clear roadmap for what you're going to code, how you'll test it, and in what order you'll proceed.

Breaking the big requirement into smaller chunks has a lot of benefits:

- **It clarifies scope**: Breaking down a feature into tasks helps establish a better understanding of what needs to be done and how to approach it
- **It simplifies the problem**: By dissecting a complex problem into smaller tasks, you make it easier to tackle
- **It prioritizes work**: Once the tasks have been laid out, they can be prioritized to deliver the most value first or to build logically upon one another
- **It focuses effort**: Tasking ensures that each test you write serves a clear, immediate purpose, making your TDD cycle more efficient
- **It facilitates collaboration**: Team members can pick up individual tasks, safe in the knowledge that they are all contributing to a cohesive whole

Now, you might be wondering, if it is so good and helpful, how can we do tasking? It's not anything fancy – you might have already done it without noticing. You just follow these steps:

1. **Review the user story or requirement**: Understand the user story or feature you are supposed to implement.
2. **Identify logical components**: Break the story down into its logical components, which often correspond to domain concepts, business rules, or individual steps in a user workflow.

3. **Create a task list**: Write down a list of tasks. These tasks should be small enough that you can write a few test cases and the corresponding implementation code in a short amount of time (say, 15 to 30 minutes).

4. **Sequence the tasks**: Determine the most logical order for completing these tasks, often starting with the "happy path" – the default scenario where everything goes as expected, without encountering any errors – and then moving on to edge cases and error handling.

5. **Map the tasks to tests**: For each task, identify the tests that will verify that part of the functionality. You don't need to write the tests at this stage; you're simply identifying what they'll be.

Tasking might be a part of your daily workflow without you even realizing it. It's a systematic approach to problem-solving that involves breaking down a requirement into manageable, sequential tasks. These tasks should ideally be completable within a few minutes to an hour.

The process of TDD is akin to the art of painting. You begin with a sketch or draft, outlining basic shapes and lines with a pencil, much like framing the initial structure of your code. In the beginning, the vision might be vague, a mere idea or concept in your mind. But as you draw – or write tests and code – the image begins to take shape. More elements are added, details emerge, and adjustments are made, allowing for continuous refinement. With each layer or iteration, clarity emerges, yet the exact final appearance remains a mystery until the very last stages. Just as an artist crafts a masterpiece through gradual development, TDD shapes a robust and elegant piece of software.

All right, we have covered a lot of theory so far. Let's look into a concrete example to fully understand how to do tasking and use tasks as a guideline for applying the Red-Green-Refactor loop.

Introducing the online pizza store application

In this section, we'll be diving into the TDD process through a deliciously practical example: *The Code Oven*, an online pizza store. Named to celebrate the fusion of coding and culinary arts, The Code Oven aims to serve both your appetite and your intellectual curiosity. This digital storefront will offer us a comprehensive sandbox where we can apply all the TDD principles and techniques we discuss.

Here's what you can expect to see in The Code Oven:

*   **Pizza menu**: At the heart of The Code Oven is an appetizing menu of eight delectable pizzas. Each pizza is presented with its name and cost, designed to whet your appetite and inform your choice.

*   **An Add button**: Beside each mouth-watering option is an **Add** button. This enables users to start the ordering process by adding their chosen pizzas to a virtual shopping cart.

*   **Shopping cart**: A designated section on the screen shows users their current shopping cart, complete with the names and prices of each selected pizza.

- **Modify cart**: Should you get second thoughts or just want more pizza, The Code Oven allows you to modify your cart by adding or removing items dynamically.

- **Order total**: There's no need for manual calculations – The Code Oven's cart automatically computes and displays the total price of your chosen items.

- **A Place my order button**: A prominent **Place my order** button serves as the final step, which would, in a real-world application, process the order for delivery or pick-up:

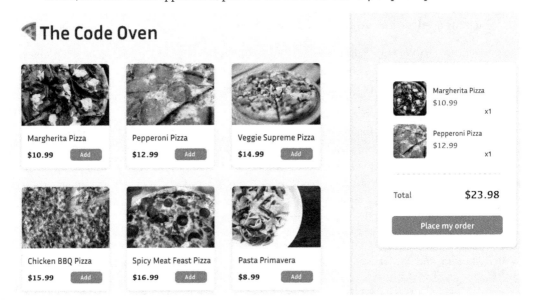

Figure 7.3: The Code Oven

As we build out The Code Oven, we'll be applying TDD at every stage to ensure that our virtual pizzeria is not just functional but robust and easily maintainable. Get ready to roll up your sleeves, both for coding and for some virtual pizza-making!

Breaking down the application requirements

There isn't a universal right way to break down the requirements of the application you are making; however, there are typically two different styles – the bottom-up style and the top-down style.

In the **bottom-up** style of TDD, developers start by writing tests and implementing functionality for the smallest and most fundamental components of the system. This approach emphasizes the construction of individual units or classes, thoroughly testing them before integrating them into higher-level components. It provides strong validation for the underlying parts of the system and helps in creating a robust foundation.

However, this style might lead to challenges in integrating the components if the bigger picture and interactions between the units are not carefully considered.

Back to the online pizza store, we can break the whole page down into the following tasks:

- Implement a single `PizzaItem` component with a pizza name
- Add a price to `PizzaItem`
- Add a button to `PizzaItem`
- Implement a `PizzaList` component (render three items in a row, for example)
- Implement a simple `ShoppingCart` component with a button
- Support the ability to add/remove items to the `ShoppingCart` component
- Add a calculation for the total number of pizzas
- Implement the whole application with these individual standalone components

As you can see, each task focuses on an individual component at a time. The components start simple, with only the minimal function; then, we incrementally add more features to them, including test cases to cover the functionality required, as well as other reasonable edge cases.

So, we start from a single `PizzaItem` component (which only has a name in it) and then give it a price, and then a button. After the individual items are built, we start to implement `PizzaList`, and then `ShoppingCart`. Then, once `PizzaList` and `ShoppingCart` are done, we integrate them and test a few overall functions from the user's perspective.

For example, as demonstrated in the following screenshot, we might start with a `PizzaItem` component, implementing the component gradually without worrying about anything else in the application. Once we have a full implementation of `PizzaItem` (with an image, name, price and **Add** button), we can move on to the next component, `ShoppingCart`:

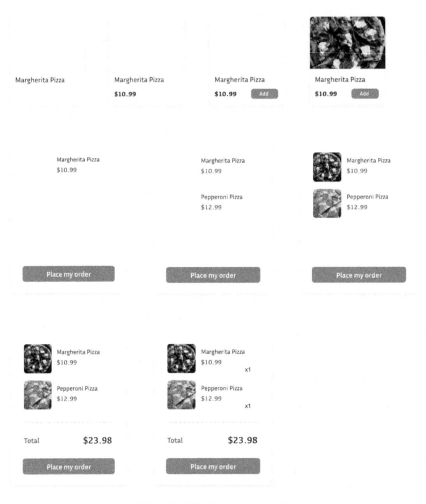

Figure 7.4: The bottom-up style

The **top-down** style of TDD takes the opposite approach, beginning with the high-level architecture and overall functionality of the system. Developers first write tests and implement features for the main components and then gradually work their way down to the more detailed and specific functionalities.

This style helps ensure that the system's primary objectives and workflow are established early on, providing a clear roadmap for the development process. It can foster better integration and alignment with the overall goals but may sometimes require the use of temporary "stubs" or "mocks" to simulate lower-level components before they are developed. For instance, we could break the feature down into the following list:

- Implement the page title
- Implement a menu list containing the pizza names
- Implement a `ShoppingCart` component with only a button (disabled by default)

- Add an item to `ShoppingCart` when the button is clicked, after which the `ShoppingCart` button is enabled

- Add a price to the `ShoppingCart` component

- Add a total number of selected items to `ShoppingCart`

- Remove an item from `ShoppingCart`, with the total number changing accordingly

For the top-down approach, we don't have a clear picture of the individual units but the working application as a whole – so we see the application from outside without knowing the implementation details.

For example, there isn't a `PizzaItem` component at the beginning, and the smaller components are gradually extracted from the bigger component when we find that the component is too big. This means we will always have functional software running (even if we don't have the small well-designed components up-front), allowing us to stop at any time without breaking the functionality.

A possible breakdown with the top-down approach is shown in the following diagram. We start with an empty list, then a list with pizza names, and then a shopping cart that allows users to add items and proceed to the next step:

Figure 7.5: The top-down style

(The textual detail in the previous figure is minimized and is not directly relevant to your understanding of it. If you would like to see the textual detail, please refer to the free downloadable eBook.)

Both styles have contributed to the rich variety of methodologies in modern software development, and neither is definitively "right" or "wrong." Instead, they offer different perspectives and tools that developers can choose from based on their particular needs and preferences.

In the following parts of this chapter, we are going to use the top-down style as it forces us to think from the user's perspective. We'll explore the bottom-up approach in more detail in the following chapters when we introduce other design patterns.

Implementing the application headline

Let's start with the implementation of the pizza store application. If you have cloned the repository mentioned in the *Technical requirements* section, simply go to the `react-anti-patterns-code/src/ch7` folder.

As we're applying TDD, the first thing to do here is to write a test that fails. In the previous section, we mentioned what we want to test: implement the page title.

So, let's create a file called `App.test.tsx` with the following code:

```
import React from 'react';
import {render, screen} from '@testing-library/react';

describe('Code Oven Application', () => {
  it('renders application heading', () => {
    render(<PizzaShopApp />);
    const heading = screen.getByText('The Code Oven');
    expect(heading).toBeInTheDocument();
  });
});
```

We're writing a test for the yet-to-be-created `PizzaShopApp` React component. Using the React Testing Library, we will render this component and verify whether it includes a heading labeled **The Code Oven**. The `expect(heading).toBeInTheDocument();` assertion confirms that the heading is successfully rendered.

Now, let's run the test with the following command in your terminal window:

```
npm run test src/ch7
```

An error will appear in the terminal saying `ReferenceError: PizzaShopApp is not defined`, like so:

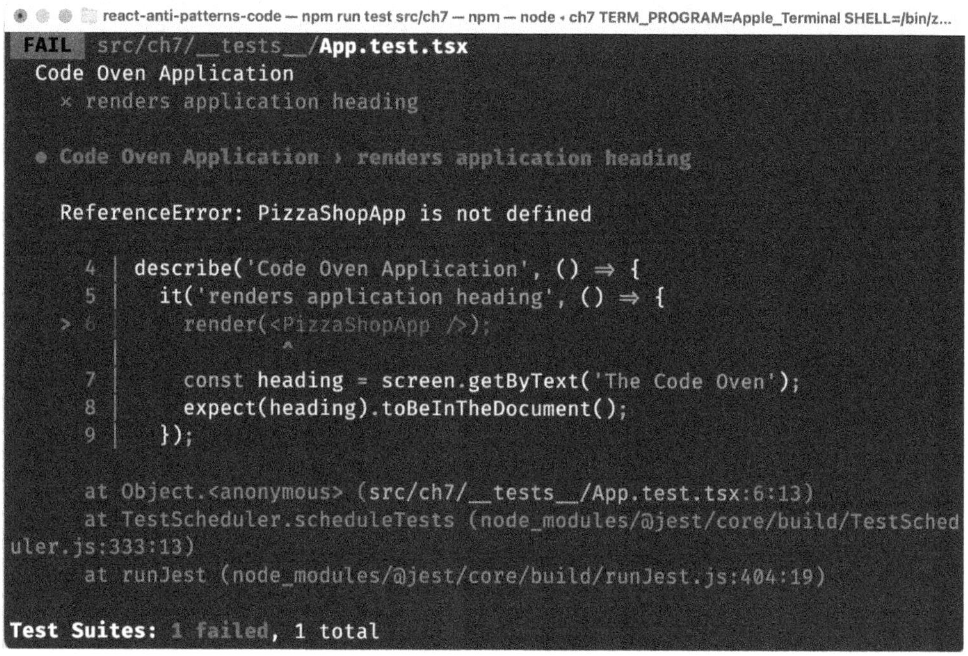

Figure 7.6: The failed test

We're in the red stage of the Red-Green-Refactor loop now, so we need to make the code pass using the simplest code possible. A static component that returns **The Code Oven** would be simple enough to make the test pass. This means we can simply define a function component, `PizzaShopApp`, in the test file that returns just the string:

```
import React from 'react';
import {render, screen} from '@testing-library/react';

function PizzaShopApp() {
  return <>The Code Oven</>;
}

describe("Code Oven Application", () => {
  it("renders application heading", () => {
    render(<PizzaShopApp />);
    const heading = screen.getByText("The Code Oven");
    expect(heading).toBeInTheDocument();
  });
});
```

When we re-run the test, it passes since `PizzaShopApp` does exactly the thing the test expects – it shows **The Code Oven**. Now, we're at the green stage of the Red-Green-Refactor loop. Next, we can look into opportunities for improvement.

We don't want to write all our code inside the test file – instead, we can use the **Move Function** refactoring method we learned about in the previous chapter and move `PizzaShopApp` into a separate file called `App.tsx`. Now, the implementation lives in its own file, allowing us to change the test and the component separately:

```
import React from "react";

export function PizzaShopApp() {
    return <>The Code Oven</>;
}
```

Awesome! With that, we have done a complete Red-Green-Refactor loop. We can now remove that task from our task list and move on to the next one.

> **Note**
>
> The code doesn't have to be perfect at the beginning as we know TDD is an iterative process; we always have a chance to make the code better as we have good tests protecting us.

Implementing the menu list

Even a basic menu list featuring just the names of pizzas can be valuable for customers who are looking to browse and decide what to eat. While The Code Oven may not be set up for online ordering yet, it serves as a useful starting point.

Looking at the second task on our list, we can write our second test like so:

```
it("renders menu list", () => {
    render(<PizzaShopApp />);
    const menuList = screen.getByRole('list');
    const menuItems = within(menuList).getAllByRole('listitem');

    expect(menuItems.length).toEqual(8);
});
```

This test starts by rendering the component. Then, it identifies the HTML element tagged with the `list` role from the rendered component. Using the `within` function, it narrows down the search to only that list and locates all items within it tagged with `listitem`. Finally, it asserts that the number of such items should be equal to 8 (the number of items the pizza shop has to offer). Essentially, we want eight list items to show up on the page.

Now, the test has failed. To make the test pass easily, we can hard-code eight empty list items on the page:

```
import React from "react";

export function PizzaShopApp() {
  return <>
    <h1>The Code Oven</h1>
    <ol>
      <li></li>
      <li></li>
      <li></li>
      <li></li>
      <li></li>
      <li></li>
      <li></li>
      <li></li>
    </ol>
  </>;
}
```

It doesn't look too good, but it makes the test pass all the same. This is important to remember – during TDD, we always want to make the test pass first and then look for opportunities to improve afterward. The advantage of this mindset forces us to think about delivery and production readiness; we should be able to stop coding at any point and release the app to production – even if the code isn't perfect yet.

Now, re-run the test to see if it passes; if so, we can start refactoring it. To reduce the long hard-coded <li> (the list item tag in HTML), we can use an array with eight elements and use map to generate the <li> dynamically inside an ordered list (<ol>):

```
import React from "react";

export function PizzaShopApp() {
  return <>
    <h1>The Code Oven</h1>
    <ol>
      {new Array(8).fill(0).map(x => <li></li>)}
    </ol>
  </>;
}
```

Inside this list, an array with eight elements (all initialized to 0) is mapped over, generating eight empty list items (<li>). This matches the test criteria of having a menu list with eight items and the tests pass with the new structure.

With that, we've done another Red-Green-Refactor loop. Now, we can verify that the pizza names are displayed correctly. Let's add a few more lines to the second test case:

```
it("renders menu list", () => {
  render(<PizzaShopApp />);
  const menuList = screen.getByRole('list');
  const menuItems = within(menuList).getAllByRole('listitem');

  expect(menuItems.length).toEqual(8);

  expect(within(menuItems[0]).getByText('Margherita Pizza')).
    toBeInTheDocument();
  expect(within(menuItems[1]).getByText('Pepperoni Pizza')).
    toBeInTheDocument();
  expect(within(menuItems[2]).getByText('Veggie Supreme Pizza')).
    toBeInTheDocument();
  //...
});
```

To make all the newly added lines pass, we'll need to define a list of pizza names in `PizzaShopApp`, and then use the map function in the `pizzas` array to map through these names into list items:

```
const pizzas = [
  "Margherita Pizza",
  "Pepperoni Pizza",
  "Veggie Supreme Pizza",
  "Chicken BBQ Pizza",
  "Spicy Meat Feast Pizza",
  "Pasta Primavera",
  "Caesar Salad",
  "Chocolate Lava Cake"
];

export function PizzaShopApp() {
  return <>
    <h1>The Code Oven</h1>
    <ol>
      {pizzas.map((x) => <li>{x}</li>)}
    </ol>
  </>;
}
```

The tests are now successfully passing. While the code may be overly simplified, the passing tests give us the confidence to make further changes without having to worry about any accidental feature breaks.

It's great to have a menu list, but the purpose of The Code Oven is to help users order online. So, let's look into how we can create a shopping cart.

Creating the shopping cart

To develop a `ShoppingCart` component, we will start with a simple test that expects an empty container to show on the page. Inside the container, there should be a button for the user to place their order.

To do this, we will start with a test that simply checks that the container and button are present:

```
it('renders a shopping cart', () => {
  render(<PizzaShopApp />);

  const shoppingCartContainer = screen.getByTestId('shopping-cart');
  const placeOrderButton = within(shoppingCartContainer).
  getByRole('button');

  expect(placeOrderButton).toBeInTheDocument();
})
```

The Jest test renders the `PizzaShopApp` component and then locates a shopping cart container by its `data-testid`. Within this container, it looks for a button element by its role. The test concludes by using the `toBeInTheDocument()` matcher to verify that this button is present in the rendered output.

To make this test pass, we can add an empty `div` as a container with `data-testid`, and put an empty button inside it:

```
export function PizzaShopApp() {
  return <>
    <h1>The Code Oven</h1>
    <ol>
      {pizzas.map((x) => <li>{x}</li>)}
    </ol>

    <div data-testid="shopping-cart">
      <button></button>
    </div>
  </>;
}
```

As the tests pass, we can add more details to the test, checking if the button is disabled by default.

> **Note**
>
> Observe how we oscillate between the test code and the actual implementation, especially in the beginning. As you become more accustomed to the Red-Green-Refactor cycle, you'll be able to write increasingly complex tests and adjust your code to pass them. The key objective initially is to establish this rapid feedback loop.

We should now add a few more details to the test, to check the button text and the disabled status by default – we want to make sure users cannot interact with the button:

```
it('renders a shopping cart', () => {
  render(<PizzaShopApp />);

  const shoppingCartContainer = screen.getByTestId('shopping-cart');
  const placeOrderButton = within(shoppingCartContainer).
   getByRole('button');

  expect(placeOrderButton).toBeInTheDocument();
  expect(placeOrderButton).toHaveTextContent('Place My Order');
  expect(placeOrderButton).toBeDisabled();
})
```

With the new assertions added, the test failed again, waiting for us to add more details to the implementation. It's straightforward to make the test pass by adding the text and `disabled` status:

```
export function PizzaShopApp() {
  return <>
    <h1>The Code Oven</h1>
    <ol>
      {pizzas.map((x) => <li>{x}</li>)}
    </ol>

    <div data-testid="shopping-cart">
      <button disabled>Place My Order</button>
    </div>
  </>;
}
```

The tests are all passing again, so that's another task to tick off (note how maintaining a task list can help us focus and gradually shape our application code).

Next, we will look at the next task – adding items from the menu to the shopping cart.

Adding items to the shopping cart

Once we have the basic structure of the `ShoppingCart` component, we need to add a few more assertions to verify it works. We will start by adding one item to the cart, which can be done with the following code:

```
it('adds menu item to shopping cart', () => {
  render(<PizzaShopApp />);

  const menuList = screen.getByRole('list');
  const menuItems = within(menuList).getAllByRole('listitem');

  const addButton = within(menuItems[0]).getByRole('button');
  userEvent.click(addButton);

  const shoppingCartContainer = screen.getByTestId('shopping-cart');
  const placeOrderButton = within(shoppingCartContainer).
    getByRole('button');

  expect(within(shoppingCartContainer).getByText('Margherita Pizza')).
    toBeInTheDocument();
  expect(placeOrderButton).toBeEnabled();
})
```

This test renders the `PizzaShopApp` component, fetches the menu list, and grabs all the list items within it. Then, it simulates a user clicking the **Add** button of the first menu item. Next, it locates the shopping cart container and checks two things:

- The added item, **Margherita Pizza**, appears in the cart
- The **Place My Order** button is enabled

Let's add the button to a menu item first, and then add a state to manage the user selection and enable the **Place My Order** button according to the selection:

```
export function PizzaShopApp() {
  const [cartItems, setCartItems] = useState<string[]>([]);

  const addItem = (item: string) => {
    setCartItems([...cartItems, item]);
  }

  return <>
    <h1>The Code Oven</h1>
    <ol>
```

```
      {pizzas.map((x) => <li>
        {x}
        <button onClick={() => addItem(x)}>Add</button>
      </li>)}
    </ol>

    <div data-testid="shopping-cart">
      <ol>
        {cartItems.map(x => <li>{x}</li>)}
      </ol>
      <button disabled=>Place My Order</button>
    </div>
  </>;
}
```

The `PizzaShopApp` function component uses React's `useState` Hook to manage an array of `cartItems`. It defines a function, `addItem`, to add items to this cart. The component renders a list of pizzas, each with an **Add** button. Clicking the **Add** button invokes the `addItem` function, adding the corresponding pizza to the `cartItems` array.

The shopping cart displays the items in `cartItems` in a list. The **Place My Order** button's disabled state is controlled by the length of the `cartItems` array. Specifically, the button is disabled when the cart is empty – (`cartItems.length === 0`).

The implementation looks great, but if we run the tests, something weird happens. The test failed in the terminal with the following error message: `TestingLibraryElementError: Found multiple elements with the role "list"`. This is because we have two lists (one in the menu and the other in the shopping cart) on the screen now, and the React Testing Library is confused about which one should look for the **Add** button, and which one should look for the added items. We can fix that by adding a more specific `data-testid` to the menu list and modifying the test accordingly.

Firstly, let's change our `PizzaShopApp` component and move the first `<ol>` (the ordered list tag) into a `div` element attributed with `data-testid="menu-list"`:

```
<div data-testid="menu-list">
  <ol>
    {pizzas.map((x) => <li>
      {x}
      <button onClick={() => addItem(x)}>Add</button>
    </li>)}
  </ol>
</div>
```

Then, we must modify the test so that it looks as follows (note that we explicitly ask the React Testing Library to search inside menu-list for all list items):

```
it('adds menu item to shopping cart', () => {
  render(<PizzaShopApp />);

  const menuItems = within(screen.getByTestId('menu-list')).
   getAllByRole('listitem');

  const addButton = within(menuItems[0]).getByRole('button');
  userEvent.click(addButton);

  const shoppingCartContainer = screen.getByTestId('shopping-cart');
  const placeOrderButton = within(shoppingCartContainer).
   getByRole('button');

  expect(within(shoppingCartContainer).getByText('Margherita Pizza')).
   toBeInTheDocument();
  expect(placeOrderButton).toBeEnabled();
})
```

When we re-run the test, it fails again with this message: TestingLibraryElementError: Unable to find an element with the text: Margherita Pizza. This could be because the text is broken up by multiple elements. In this case, you can provide a function for your text matcher to make your matcher more flexible.

The expected **Margherita Pizza** doesn't show up in the shopping cart. This is because we use an event to trigger React to re-render by modifying the cartItems state. But when React detects the state change and re-renders, the test isn't waiting for that to happen. In other words, it's too early for the test to see the updated cartItems. We need to give React a bit of time to digest the change and re-render. We can mark the test case as async and wait for userEvent.click to make the state change:

```
it('adds menu item to shopping cart',  async () => {
  render(<PizzaShopApp />);

  const menuItems = within(screen.getByTestId('menu-list')).
 getAllByRole('listitem');

  const addButton = within(menuItems[0]).getByRole('button');
  await userEvent.click(addButton);

  const shoppingCartContainer = screen.getByTestId('shopping-cart');
  const placeOrderButton = within(shoppingCartContainer)
   .getByRole('button');

  expect(within(shoppingCartContainer).getByText('Margherita Pizza')).
```

```
      toBeInTheDocument();
    expect(placeOrderButton).toBeEnabled();
  })
```

In this code snippet, the use of `async` and `await` ensures that the asynchronous operations are completed before they move on to the next step in the test. The test function itself is marked as async, making it return a Promise, which Jest will wait for before considering the test complete.

The `await userEvent.click(addButton);` line is particularly important here. `userEvent.click` simulates a real user clicking a button and might trigger state updates or effects in your React component. Using `await` ensures that all associated updates and effects are fully completed before moving on to the subsequent lines of the test.

By ensuring that `userEvent.click` has been fully processed, the test will then safely proceed to query and assert against the updated DOM or state. This is crucial for preventing false negatives, where the test might fail not because the code is incorrect, but because the test is checking the DOM before all updates have occurred.

Since all the tests are passing again, it's time to look into other opportunities for improvement.

Refactoring the code

The code we have now isn't too hard to understand, but it has some room for improvement. Let's quickly look at what we have got so far:

```
export function PizzaShopApp() {
  const [cartItems, setCartItems] = useState<string[]>([]);

  const addItem = (item: string) => {
    setCartItems([...cartItems, item]);
  }

  return <>
    <h1>The Code Oven</h1>
    <div data-testid="menu-list">
      <ol>
        {pizzas.map((x) => <li>
          {x}
          <button onClick={() => addItem(x)}>Add</button>
        </li>)}
      </ol>
    </div>

    <div data-testid="shopping-cart">
```

```
      <ol>
        {cartItems.map(x => <li>{x}</li>)}
      </ol>
      <button disabled={cartItems.length === 0}>Place My Order
        </button>
    </div>
  </>;
}
```

Now, let's make some changes. Firstly, we could use the **Rename Variable** refactoring to change x to item, to make it a bit more meaningful. Also, there is a warning in the terminal now, saying `Warning: Each child in a list should have a unique "key" prop` – as React expects a unique key for each item it renders, we need to have a key for each `<li>` element. For now, we can use the item (the pizza name) as the key to fix this issue:

```
export function PizzaShopApp() {
  const [cartItems, setCartItems] = useState<string[]>([]);

  const addItem = (item: string) => {
    setCartItems([...cartItems, item]);
  }

  return <>
    <h1>The Code Oven</h1>
    <div data-testid="menu-list">
      <ol>
        {pizzas.map((item) => <li key={item}>
          {item}
          <button onClick={() => addItem(item)}>Add</button>
        </li>)}
      </ol>
    </div>

    <div data-testid="shopping-cart">
      <ol>
        {cartItems.map(item => <li key={item}>{item}</li>)}
      </ol>
      <button disabled={cartItems.length === 0}>Place My Order
        </button>
    </div>
  </>;
}
```

As another change, the menu item list looks pretty self-contained and doesn't depend on anything out of the context it lives in, so we can extract a new component here to encapsulate that logic:

```
const MenuList = (({
  onAddMenuItem,
}: {
  onAddMenuItem: (item: string) => void;
}) => {
  return (
    <div data-testid="menu-list">
      <ol>
        {pizzas.map((item) => (
          <li key={item}>
            {item}
            <button onClick={() => onAddMenuItem(item)}>Add</button>
          </li>
        ))}
      </ol>
    </div>
  );
};
```

The `MenuList` component takes a single prop, `onAddMenuItem`, which is a function that accepts a string argument representing a menu item. The component renders a list of pizzas, which presumably is an array of strings. For each pizza, it creates a list item and an **Add** button. When this button is clicked, the `onAddMenuItem` function is called with the corresponding pizza name as an argument. The component uses the `data-testid="menu-list"` attribute to make it easier to query this section during testing. Overall, this is a presentational component that's designed to display a list of pizzas and handle the addition of menu items through the provided callback.

Similarly, we can extract a new component for the shopping cart, like so:

```
const ShoppingCart = ({ cartItems }: { cartItems: string[] }) => {
  return (
    <div data-testid="shopping-cart">
      <ol>
        {cartItems.map((item) => (
          <li key={item}>{item}</li>
        ))}
      </ol>
      <button disabled={cartItems.length === 0}>Place My Order
      </button>
```

```
        </div>
    );
};
```

The `ShoppingCart` component takes an array of `cartItems` as its prop. This array holds the names of the items that have been added to the shopping cart. The component renders an ordered list (`<ol>`) where each list item (`<li>`) corresponds to an item in the cart. It uses the `data-testid="shopping-cart"` attribute to make it easier to identify this component in tests. Additionally, a **Place My Order** button is rendered at the bottom of the list. The button is disabled if the `cartItems` array is empty, meaning there are no items in the cart. Overall, this component is designed to display the items in the shopping cart and provide an option to place an order.

After these extractions, we can use these components in the main component, `PizzaShopApp`:

```
export function PizzaShopApp() {
  const [cartItems, setCartItems] = useState<string[]>([]);

  const addItem = (item: string) => {
    setCartItems([...cartItems, item]);
  };

  return (
    <>
      <h1>The Code Oven</h1>
      <MenuList onAddMenuItem={addItem} />
      <ShoppingCart cartItems={cartItems} />
    </>
  );
}
```

During these relatively big changes, our tests always stay in the green state – meaning no functions are broken. We haven't implemented all the tasks we have broken down, but I believe you have got the idea of the Red-Green-Refactor loop. You can use the remaining tasks as exercises, making sure you always write the test first, with only the minimal code, and looking for improvements after the test passes.

You may initially find this coding approach challenging as it requires you to resist the temptation to immediately delve into implementation. Instead, take incremental steps and savor the journey. You'll soon discover the strength that lies in taking small steps, as well as how maintaining a steady rhythm can enhance your focus and productivity.

Summary

In this chapter on TDD, we've explored various forms of TDD, emphasizing the importance of breaking down complex problems into manageable tasks through tasking. We delved into two key approaches – top-down and bottom-up, each with its distinct merits and use cases. To illustrate these concepts, we used a practical example of building a pizza shop application.

This hands-on example helped solidify the theories and methodologies we discussed, providing a comprehensive understanding of how TDD can be employed effectively in different scenarios.

In the upcoming chapter, we'll delve deeper into the intricate world of data management in React applications. Specifically, we'll explore various design patterns that are commonly adopted for efficient data access and manipulation.

Part 3: Unveiling Business Logic and Design Patterns

This part looks at business logic and design patterns, which are essential in tackling common challenges in state management and adhering to principles, such as the single responsibility principle, in order to maintain a clean and efficient code base.

This part contains the following chapters:

- *Chapter 8, Exploring Data Management in React*
- *Chapter 9, Applying Design Principles in React*
- *Chapter 10, Diving Deep into Composition Patterns*

8
Exploring Data Management in React

In modern frontend development, the way we handle state and data access can make or break an application. Whether you're a solo developer or part of a large team, understanding best practices and common pitfalls is critical. This chapter aims to elevate your proficiency in state management and data handling within React applications, focusing on scalable and maintainable approaches.

State management is challenging, particularly in React, and there are many issues that developers tend to face in their day-to-day work. One of the challenges is where you can locate the business logic in your code base. When business logic infiltrates UI components, it compromises their reusability. Many domain objects, along with computational logic, are scattered in UI components either deliberately or unintentionally, which can lead to tangled logic that's hard to follow, debug, and test. It can also lead to performance issues, which negatively affect the user experience.

Another issue is prop drilling, where passing props from a parent component to deeply nested children becomes both cumbersome and susceptible to errors. This often leads to code duplication as the same snippets find their way into multiple files, making any future updates a complicated task.

Lastly, sharing state in a React application presents its own set of challenges. Various mechanisms exist for this, but choosing the most efficient way to share stateful logic across components can be quite perplexing. We'll dive deep to explore the issues of sharing state and see how React's Context API can help.

In this chapter, we will cover the following topics:

- Understanding business logic leaks
- Introducing the anti-corruption layer
- Exploring the prop drilling issue
- Using the Context API to resolve prop drilling

Technical requirements

A GitHub repository has been created to host all the code we'll discuss in this book. For this chapter, you can find the recommended structure at `https://github.com/PacktPublishing/ React-Anti-Patterns/tree/main/code/src/ch8`.

Understanding business logic leaks

Business logic refers to the rules, calculations, and processes that are essential to the operation of a business application. When this business logic "leaks" into components or areas of the application where it doesn't belong, this is known as a **business logic leak**.

This issue frequently crops up in various projects, partly because there's no widely agreed-upon approach for handling business logic in React. The framework's flexibility allows you to implement this logic directly in components, Hooks, or helper functions; as a result, developers often end up embedding the logic directly into components, where it's immediately needed – hence the leakage.

This leakage can cause many problems. Business logic leaks can result in tightly coupled components that become difficult to test, maintain, or reuse. When business logic is scattered across different parts of the application, it leads to code duplication and inconsistency, making the application more prone to errors and harder to debug. Additionally, this scattering complicates any future modifications to the business rules as changes will likely have to be made in multiple places, increasing the risk of introducing new issues.

There are various indicators that business logic is leaking into your code, but the most prevalent sign is the incorporation of data transformation directly within views or UI components. In this section, we'll delve into this issue in depth; in the following section, we'll explore solutions to mitigate this problem.

Data transformation is a function that takes one shape (or format) of data (usually from another module or a remote service) and maps the data to the shape that fits another usage. The following is a typical example you would see in many React applications, showing a `UserProfile` function:

```
function UserProfile({ id }: { id: string }) {
  const [user, setUser] = useState<User | null>(null);

  useEffect(() => {
```

```
  async function fetchUser() {
    const response = await fetch(`/api/users/${id}`);
    const data = await response.json();

    setUser({
      id: data.user_identification,
      name: data.user_full_name,
      isPremium: data.is_premium_user,
      subscription: data.subscription_details.level,
      expire: data.subscription_details.expiry,
    });
  }

  fetchUser();
}, [id]);

if (!user) {
  return <div>Loading...</div>;
}

return (
  <div data-testid="user-profile">
    <h1>{user.name}</h1>
  </div>
);
}
```

The `UserProfile` function component fetches user data from a backend API. The `useEffect` Hook ensures that data fetching happens whenever the ID changes. The fetched data is then stored in a local state variable, `user`, and the component displays the user's name once the data is available. If the data is still loading, a **Loading...** message is displayed.

In the `useEffect` block, the fetched data transforms being stored in the `user` state variable. Specifically, the keys from the fetched JSON response are mapped to new names that are more suitable for the frontend application – for example, `data.user_identification` becomes `id` and `data.user_full_name` becomes `name`. This transformation allows for easier handling and readability within the React component.

As you might imagine, this type of transformation can happen in many places in an application, and it isn't limited to the inside of a React component; sometimes, this transformation can be present in Hooks and other places, as demonstrated in the following figure:

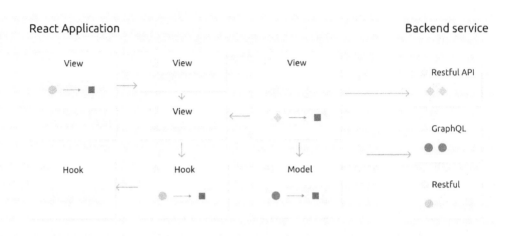

Figure 8.1: Using data transformation in views

The backend service can serve data in various formats that are supported by different technologies – some utilize RESTful APIs, while others employ GraphQL. From the perspective of the frontend code, the specifics of these formats are abstracted away. For instance, one component may be responsible for transforming XML data (indicated by an orange diamond shape) into an internal type, X (depicted as a blue square). Meanwhile, another component may interact with a GraphQL endpoint, processing the received data (represented by a red circle) into the same internal type, X.

This discrepancy necessitates data transformations across multiple areas in the code. When such transformations are duplicated, there's a higher risk of overlooking changes, especially if the backend alters the structure of their data.

All these varied transformations can be centralized into a single location where data reshaping occurs, along with empty field checks, field renaming, and the elimination of unnecessary fields. This segues nicely into our next topic: the **anti-corruption layer** (**ACL**).

Introducing the ACL

In software development, an ACL acts like a translator or a mediator between different subsystems that may not speak the same "language," so to speak. Imagine that you have two systems, each with its own set of rules, structures, and complexities. If these systems interact directly, there's a risk that they could influence each other in unintended ways, leading to what is called *corruption* in the domain logic.

In the context of frontend development, especially in complex applications, an ACL becomes crucial for managing the interactions between the frontend and various backends or APIs. Frontend developers often have to deal with multiple services that may have inconsistent or convoluted data formats. Implementing an ACL in the frontend allows you to create a unified interface to interact with these services.

For example, if your frontend application has to communicate with multiple RESTful APIs, GraphQL services, and even WebSocket servers, each may have its own set of rules, data structures, and complexities. A frontend ACL would take on the role of translating these disparate forms of data into a format that your frontend application understands. This means that your UI components don't have to worry about the intricate details of each service's data format, making the components easier to develop, test, and maintain.

The ACL can also be a strategic place to handle caching, error transformations, and other cross-cutting concerns. By centralizing these functionalities, you avoid scattering similar logic all over your frontend code base, thus adhering to the **Don't Repeat Yourself (DRY)** principle:

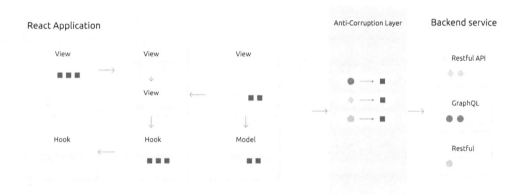

Figure 8.2: Introduced ACL for data transforming

As illustrated in *Figure 8.2*, all data transformations are now centralized, eliminating the need for such operations in the views. You might be curious about how to put this into practice in your code.

Introducing a typical usage

To get started, let's build on the example from the previous section and introduce a basic function as the starting point for our ACL. We should identify the external data format and what we consume, then define functions as the transformers before putting them in a common place.

First, let's define a type for the user data format we receive from the remote server. By using TypeScript, we gain the advantage of compile-time checks, thereby ensuring that any inconsistencies in the data format are flagged before the application runs:

```
type RemoteUser = {
  user_identification: string;
  user_full_name: string;
  is_premium_user: boolean;
  subscription_details: {
    level: string;
```

```
    expiry: string;
  }
}
```

We will also define the local `User` type – it includes all fields (`id`, `name`, and so on) that we use in the `UserProfile` component:

```
type UserSubscription = "Basic" | "Standard" | "Premium" |
"Enterprise";

type User = {
  id: string;
  name: string;
  isPremium: boolean;
  subscription: UserSubscription;
  expire: string;
};
```

The `type` definition specifies the structure of a user object that will be used in React components. Note that the `subscription` property uses a custom type, `UserSubscription`, which can take one of four string values: **Basic**, **Standard**, **Premium**, or **Enterprise**. Also, `expire` is a string that indicates when the user's subscription will expire.

With this setup, we can define a new function called `transformUser` in a file called `transformer.ts`. The file simply returns the mapped object with the `User` type we just defined:

```
import {RemoteUser, User, UserSubscription} from "./types";

export const transformUser = (remoteUser: RemoteUser): User => {
  return {
    id: remoteUser.user_identification,
    name: remoteUser.user_full_name,
    isPremium: remoteUser.is_premium_user,
    subscription: remoteUser.subscription_details.level as
     UserSubscription,
    expire: remoteUser.subscription_details.expiry,
  };
};
```

With this new extracted function in `transformer.ts`, our component can be simplified like so:

```
async function fetchUserData<T>(id: string) {
  const response = await fetch(`/api/users/${id}`);
  const rawData = await response.json();

  return transformUser(rawData) as T;
```

```
  }


  function UserProfile({ id }: { id: string }) {
    const [user, setUser] = useState<User | null>(null);

    useEffect(() => {
      async function fetchUser() {
        const response = await fetchUserData<User>(id);
        setUser(response);
      }

      fetchUser();
    }, [id]);

    if (!user) {
      return <div>Loading...</div>;
    }

    return (
      <div data-tested="user-profile">
        <h1>{user.name}</h1>
      </div>
    );
  }
```

The `UserProfile` component relies on the `fetchUserData` helper function to retrieve and process user data from an API. This design insulates `UserProfile` from any knowledge of the remote data structure. If there are future changes to the `RemoteUser` type, `UserProfile` remains unaffected as all the adjustments will be confined to `transformer.ts`.

It's advantageous to have a distinct function dedicated to managing remote data and molding it to suit the requirements of higher-level views. However, complications arise when the backend fails to deliver the necessary data. In such scenarios, additional logic is necessitated in this layer to establish fallback or default values.

Using the fallback or default value

Another frequently observed issue related to data transformation is the excessive use of defensive programming in React views. While defensive programming is generally good practice and useful in various contexts, overloading React components with too many null checks and fallbacks can clutter the code and make it difficult to comprehend.

> **Note**
>
> **Defensive programming** is a practice that involves writing code in a way that anticipates possible errors, failures, or exceptions, and handles them gracefully. The goal is to make your application more resilient and maintainable by minimizing the impact of unexpected scenarios.

For instance, in the `UserProfile` example, you might encounter situations where certain values from the remote service are empty. Instead of displaying `null` or `undefined` to end users, you would need to implement fallback values.

Let's review the `transformUser` function we extracted previously:

```
export const transformUser = (remoteUser: RemoteUser): User => {
  return {
    id: remoteUser.user_identification,
    name: remoteUser.user_full_name,
    isPremium: remoteUser.is_premium_user,
    subscription: remoteUser.subscription_details.level as
     UserSubscription,
    expire: remoteUser.subscription_details.expiry,
  };
};
```

What if `subscription_details` doesn't exist, or what happens when `expiry` isn't a valid date format from the backend? These mismatches can cause runtime exceptions, so we should fall back to some default value when the remote data isn't in the right format.

We could put the fallback logic into components, right before we render them. Without the ACL, we might end up with some logic in `UserProfile`, like this:

```
function UserProfile({ user }: { user: User }) {
  const fullName = user && user.name ? user.name : "Loading"…";
  const subscriptionLevel =
    user && user.subscription ? user.subscription": "Basic";
  const subscriptionExpiry = user && user.expire ? user.expire":
   "Never";

  return (
    <div>
      <h1>{fullName}</h1>
      <p>Subscription Level: {subscriptionLevel}</p>
      <p>Subscription Expiry: {subscriptionExpiry}</p>
    </div>
  );
}
```

The UserProfile function component takes a user object as a prop. It displays the user's full name, subscription level, and subscription expiry date. If any of these values are missing or falsy, it provides default fallback text such as **Loading…**, **Basic**, or **Never**.

As such, logic begins to infiltrate the UserProfile component, increasing the component's length and therefore complexity.

This kind of logic can be better managed by moving it into a function such as transformUser, where it can be thoroughly tested:

```
export const transformUser = (remoteUser: RemoteUser): User => {
  return {
    id: remoteUser.user_identification ?? 'N/A',
    name: remoteUser.user_full_name ?? 'Unknown User',
    isPremium: remoteUser.is_premium_user ?? false,
    subscription: (remoteUser.subscription_details?.level ?? 'Basic')
      as UserSubscription,
    expire: remoteUser.subscription_details?.expiry ?? 'Never',
  };
};
```

The transformUser function maps fields from the remote user data structure to the application's expected user data structure, providing default values for each field in case they are missing or null. For example, if remoteUser.user_identification is null, it will use **N/A** as the default ID.

Note that here, we use **optional chaining** (?), which allows you to access deeply nested properties without checking each level of nesting. If subscription_details or level is null or undefined, the result, subscription, will also be undefined and no errors will be thrown. We also used **nullish coalescing** (??) for falling back – it takes the value on its left if that value isn't null or undefined; otherwise, it takes the value on its right.

All this transforming and fallback logic is now encapsulated in a common place – the ACL. Any further changes to the remote or local data shape can easily happen in this layer, and we don't have to look up the entire code base for different usages.

Excellent – the ACL pattern effectively isolates business logic from your views. However, there are additional challenges in managing data within a React application, such as sharing data between components and avoiding prop drilling. In the following section, we'll explore how to tackle these issues using the Context API.

Exploring the prop drilling issue

Prop drilling is an issue that arises when you have to pass data through multiple levels of components that don't need the data, just so it can reach a component deeper in the hierarchy that does need it. This often makes the code harder to follow, understand, and maintain.

Consider a standard scenario in React where we have a universal searchable list component. This component takes in a list and displays each item, whether it's a list of books, menus, tickets, or anything else you can think of. In addition to displaying the list, the component also includes a search box, allowing users to easily filter through a lengthy list:

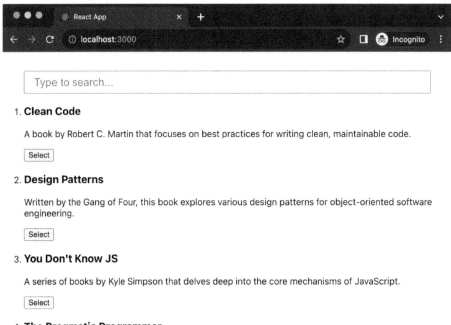

Figure 8.3: The searchable list component

At first glance, the implementation seems straightforward and not overly complicated:

```
import React, { ChangeEvent, useState } from "react";

export type Item = {
  id: string;
  name: string;
  description: string;
};

const SearchableList = ({ items }: { items: Item[] }) => {
  const [filteredItems, setFilteredItems] = useState<Item[]>(items);

  const handleChange = (e: ChangeEvent<HTMLInputElement>) => {
    setFilteredItems(
```

```
      items.filter((item) => item.name.includes(e.target.value))
    );
  };

  return (
    <div>
      <input type="text" onChange={handleChange} />
      <ul>
        {filteredItems.map((item, index) => (
          <li key={index}>{item.name}</li>
        ))}
      </ul>
    </div>
  );
};

export default SearchableList;
```

The code defines a `SearchableList` component in React that filters and displays a list of items based on user input. It starts with a full list of items and updates the filtered list whenever the text in the input box changes.

Over time, as the component evolves and is used in more diverse scenarios, the code base becomes increasingly complex, resulting in additional layout changes and more lines of code. As illustrated in *Figure 8.4*, on the right-hand side, we can break the searchable list input into three sub-components called `SearchInput`, `List`, and `ListItem`:

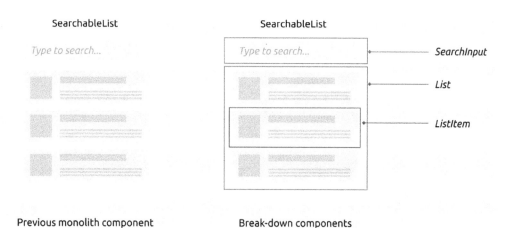

Figure 8.4: Breaking a searchable list into smaller components

On the right-hand side, `SearchInput` accepts the user's input (in the top red rectangle). It is a sibling of the `List` component (inside the green rectangle), which contains multiple `ListItem` (in the purple rectangle) – each `ListItem` represents an item (one might have a title, description, or buttons in it).

Let's look at each of these extracted components in detail:

```
const ListItem = ({ item }: { item: Item }) => {
  return (
    <li>
      <h2>{item.name}</h2>
      <p>{item.description}</p>
    </li>
  );
};
```

`ListItem` displays the name and description of an item. For any further details that are needed, we only need to modify this file directly.

Then, each `ListItem` is wrapped inside a container component, `List`, like so:

```
const List = ({ items }: { items: Item[] }) => {
  return (
    <section data-testid="searchable-list">
      <ul>
        {items.map((item) => (
          <ListItem item={item} />
        ))}
      </ul>
      <footer>Total items: {items.length}</footer>
    </section>
  );
};
```

This `List` acts as the container for all the items. It also includes a footer to show some summary information of the items.

Finally, we have the `SearchInput` component, which is responsible for collecting user input and triggering searches as the user is typing:

```
const SearchInput = ({ onSearch }: { onSearch: (keyword: string) =>
void }) => {
  const handleChange = (e: ChangeEvent<HTMLInputElement>) => {
    onSearch(e.target.value);
  };

  return <input type="text" onChange={handleChange} />;
```

```
};

const SearchableList = ({ items }: { items: Item[] }) => {
  const [filteredItems, setFilteredItems] = useState<Item[]>(items);

  const onSearch = (keyword: string) => {
    setFilteredItems(items.filter((item) => item.name.
     includes(keyword)));
  };

  return (
    <div>
      <SearchInput onSearch={onSearch} />
      <List items={filteredItems} />
    </div>
  );
};
```

Note that this code breakdown is only an internal structural change – we made the change only to make each part easy to read and understand. People who use `SearchableList` aren't aware of such changes at all – the props of `SearchableList` haven't been changed so far.

However, the consumer has requested a new feature: they wish to track user interactions for analytics, specifically to gauge the popularity of items and the utilization of the search function. To meet this requirement, two new props are being introduced: an `onItemClicked` callback to capture when an item is clicked, and an `onSearch` callback to monitor when a search is performed.

So, we need to modify our code to meet these requirements, starting from the new type used in `SearchableList`:

```
type SearchableListProps = {
  items: Item[];
  onSearch: (keyword: string) => void;
  onItemClicked: (item: Item) => void;
};

const SearchableList = ({
  items,
  onSearch,
  onItemClicked,
}: SearchableListProps) => {
  //...
}
```

To pass `onSearch` and `onItemClicked`, we'll make some changes to `ListItem`. We need to change the props list (adding `onItemClicked`) and then call the function when the list is clicked:

```
const ListItem = ({
  item,
  onItemClicked,
}: {
  item: Item;
  onItemClicked: (item: Item) => void;
}) => {
  return (
    <li onClick={() => onItemClicked(item)}>
      <h2>{item.name}</h2>
      <p>{item.description}</p>
    </li>
  );
};
```

However, as `ListItem` is not exposed directly to the outside world, the props are passed from its parent component, `List`. So, we also need to update the `List` component's props list to add `onItemClicked`:

```
const List = ({
  items,
  onItemClicked,
}: {
  items: Item[];
  onItemClicked: (item: Item) => void;
}) => {
  return (
    <section data-testid="searchable-list">
      <ul>
        {items.map((item) => (
          <ListItem item={item} onItemClicked={onItemClicked} />
        ))}
      </ul>
      <footer>Total items: {items.length}</footer>
    </section>
  );
};
```

The `List` component has to accept `onItemClicked` as a prop and then pass on the `onItemClicked` prop into `ListItem` without touching it. This is a code smell, signaling that the component is dealing with something not directly relevant to its function.

Then, the `onItemClick` prop is passed from the `List` component's parent `SearchableList` component, as shown here:

```
const SearchableList = ({
  items,
  onSearch,
  onItemClicked,
}: SearchableListProps) => {
  const [filteredItems, setFilteredItems] = useState<Item[]>(items);

  const handleSearch = (keyword: string) => {
    setFilteredItems(items.filter((item) => item.name.
      includes(keyword)));
  };

  return (
    <div>
      <SearchInput onSearch={handleSearch} />
      <List items={filteredItems} onItemClicked={onItemClicked} />
    </div>
  );
};
```

Observe how we transfer the `onItemClicked` prop to the `ListItem` component. First, it goes through the `List` component, which directly passes it down to `ListItem` without using it for anything. This is a classic example of prop drilling. The same could happen with `SearchInput`. As we continue to add more and more props from the outside and drill them down through the component tree, the entire structure could soon become unmanageable.

Fortunately, the Context API provides an elegant solution to the prop drilling issue, which we will review in the next section (we covered the fundamentals of using the Context API in *Chapter 2*; you can revisit that chapter if you'd like a refresher).

Using the Context API to resolve prop drilling

The concept behind using the Context API to address prop drilling is to create a shared container for all sub-components under a common parent. This eliminates the need for explicitly passing down props from parent to child. Sub-components can directly access the shared context whenever necessary. Another advantage of using the Context API is that it triggers automatic re-rendering of components whenever the data within the context changes.

Returning to our searchable list example, which has already got the *props drilling* issue, `onItemClicked` in the `List` component isn't necessary as `List` doesn't use the prop. This scenario involves just one layer and one prop. Now, envision a situation where we need to insert additional elements between the `List` and `ListItem` components; we would have to pass the `onItemClicked` prop down to where it's utilized. The complexity is amplified if we have multiple props to relay.

The first step is to define a context with an appropriate type:

```
import { createContext } from "react";
import { Item } from "./types";

type SearchableListContextType = {
  onSearch: (keyword: string) => void;
  onItemClicked: (item: Item) => void;
};

const noop = () => {};

const SearchableListContext =
createContext<SearchableListContextType>({
  onSearch: noop,
  onItemClicked: noop,
});

export { SearchableListContext };
```

This code defines a React context called `SearchableListContext`. It specifies the types of the `onSearch` and `onItemClicked` functions that the context will hold. It also initializes these functions with a no-operation (`noop`) function by default.

Now, we can use the context as a wrapper in the searchable list to provide the context to all its child components:

```
const SearchableList = ({
  items,
  onSearch,
  onItemClicked,
}: SearchableListProps) => {
  const [filteredItems, setFilteredItems] = useState<Item[]>(items);

  const handleSearch = (keyword: string) => {
    setFilteredItems(items.filter((item) => item.name.
      includes(keyword)));
  };

  return (
    <SearchableListContext.Provider value={{ onSearch, onItemClicked
}}>
```

```
      <SearchInput onSearch={handleSearch} />
      <List items={filteredItems} />
    </SearchableListContext.Provider>
  );
};
```

The `SearchableList` component wraps its children, `SearchInput` and `List`, inside `SearchableListContext.Provider`. This allows these child components to access the `onSearch` and `onItemClicked` functions from the context without passing them down explicitly as props. The `handleSearch` function filters items based on the search keyword.

This means our `List` component can be reverted to the simple version before we introduce `onItemClicked`:

```
const List = ({ items }: { items: Item[] }) => {
  return (
    <section data-testid="searchable-list">
      <ul>
        {items.map((item) => (
          <ListItem item={item} />
        ))}
      </ul>
      <footer>Total items: {items.length}</footer>
    </section>
  );
};
```

For `ListItem`, we can directly access `onItemClicked` from the context:

```
const ListItem = ({ item }: { item: Item }) => {
  const { onItemClicked } = useContext(SearchableListContext);

  return (
    <li onClick={() => onItemClicked(item)}>
      <h2>{item.name}</h2>
      <p>{item.description}</p>
    </li>
  );
};
```

The `ListItem` component now uses `useContext` to access the `onItemClicked` function from `SearchableListContext`. When a list item is clicked, `onItemClicked` is called with the clicked item as an argument.

Likewise, for the `SearchInput` component, there's no need to pass down extra props from `SearchableList`. Instead, we can directly access what we need from the context:

```
const SearchInput = ({ onSearch }: { onSearch: (keyword: string) =>
  void }) => {
  const { onSearch: providedOnSearch } =
   useContext(SearchableListContext);

  const handleChange = (e: ChangeEvent<HTMLInputElement>) => {
    onSearch(e.target.value);
    providedOnSearch(e.target.value);
  };

  return <input type="text" onChange={handleChange} />;
};
```

The `SearchInput` component uses the `useContext` Hook to access the `onSearch` function from `SearchableListContext`. When the input changes, it calls both the local `onSearch` function and the one from the context, effectively merging external and internal behaviors.

As demonstrated, the Context API results in a much cleaner structure. It allows you to make additional structural adjustments to sub-components without the concern of continually passing props down the hierarchy. This simplifies the component interface, making it easier to read and understand.

Summary

In this chapter, we delved into some of the most pressing challenges that are often encountered in React development, such as the leakage of business logic, the complexities associated with prop drilling, and the difficulties of managing shared state. To counter these issues, we introduced robust solutions such as the ACL and the Context API. These strategies aim to streamline your code, making it both more maintainable and effective for long-term projects.

Next up, we'll dive into common React design patterns that you can use to further refine your coding skills. Stay tuned.

9

Applying Design Principles in React

Design principles are like the cardinal rules that guide software development, ensuring that code remains maintainable, scalable, and readable over time. In the ever-changing landscape of technology, adhering to these principles can be the difference between a project's long-term success and its descent into "code hell," where changes become increasingly arduous and bugs frequent.

For React applications, the importance of design principles escalates due to the library's declarative nature and component-based architecture. React empowers developers to build complex UIs from small, isolated pieces of code known as components. While this modular approach is one of React's strongest features, it can also lead to a messy and unmanageable code base if design principles are ignored.

In a typical React project, components often share state and behavior, get nested within each other, and are reused across different parts of an application. Without following design principles, you might find yourself entangled in a web of dependencies, making it difficult to change or even understand the code. For instance, neglecting the **Single Responsibility Principle** (**SRP**) could result in components that are difficult to test and refactor, while ignoring the **Interface Segregation Principle** (**ISP**) could make your components less reusable and more coupled to specific use cases.

Furthermore, as React continues to evolve, with new features such as Hooks and concurrent mode, having a design principle-centered approach ensures that you can adapt to these changes without significant rewrites. This allows you to focus on building features, fixing bugs, and delivering value, instead of grappling with technical debt.

Adhering to design principles in React development is not just a best practice but a necessity. It serves as a proactive measure to counteract complexity, making your React code easier to read, test, and maintain.

In this chapter, we commence by revisiting the SRP, a core concept that often serves as the bedrock of clean, maintainable code. From the humble beginnings of a simple string-transforming function, we'll explore how this principle scales up to the complexities of render props, enriching the structure and readability of your React components.

Transitioning from there, we introduce the **Dependency Inversion Principle (DIP)**, a transformative approach to component design. This section emphasizes that focusing on the interface – not the nitty-gritty details of implementation – is the pathway to reusable and easily understandable components.

Concluding the chapter, we delve into **Command and Query Responsibility Segregation (CQRS)**, a pattern that gains importance as your React applications grow in size and complexity. Through a discussion on CQRS, you'll discover strategies to separate your application's command and query responsibilities, thereby making it more manageable and scalable.

This chapter aims to equip you with a holistic understanding of key design principles, which in turn will lay a strong foundation for the rest of your journey in mastering React.

In this chapter, we will cover the following topics:

- Revisiting the Single Responsibility Principle
- Embracing the Dependency Inversion Principle
- Understanding Command and Query Responsibility Segregation in React

Technical requirements

A GitHub repository has been created to host all the code we discuss in the book. For this chapter, you can find the recommended structure at `https://github.com/PacktPublishing/ React-Anti-Patterns/tree/main/code/src/ch9`.

Revisiting the Single Responsibility Principle

In *Chapter 4*, we delved into the SRP within the context of designing React components. Yet this principle is more universal, acting as the bedrock for various other programming tenets. To bring this idea to life, let's work through some hands-on examples.

Identifying the core responsibility of a component is key to adhering to the SRP. Once you isolate what the component is fundamentally meant to do, it becomes easier to refactor and abstract out auxiliary functionalities.

The SRP, being a high-level guideline, is advantageous when applied directly at the code level. There are numerous ways to implement this principle, but recognizing when to apply it is crucial, especially as complexity increases.

The most common two techniques we'll use are *render props* and *composition*. Render props refer to a technique in React for sharing code between components using a prop whose value is a function. A component with a render prop takes a function that returns a React element and calls it instead of implementing its own render logic. On the other hand, composition in React is a development pattern where you build components as small, reusable pieces and then compose them together to create more complex UIs.

In the following section, we'll explore two specific examples, demonstrating how we use render props and composition respectively to adhere to this principle in practice.

Exploring the render props pattern

Let's start simple with a basic function component called `Title`:

```
const Title = () => <div>Title | This is a title</div>
```

As it stands, this component merely outputs a static string. To give it the ability to render different titles, we introduce a `title` prop:

```
const Title = ({ title }: { title: string }) => <div>Title |
{title}</div>;
```

With this change, the component becomes more versatile, appending a fixed prefix, `Title |`, to any title we pass in. But what if we want to further manipulate the title, perhaps to capitalize it?

By utilizing a higher-order function – the `transformer` parameter in the following code snippet – we can modify our `Title` component as follows:

```
const Title = ({
  title,
  transformer,
}: {
  title: string;
  transformer: (s: string) => string;
}) => <div>Title | {transformer(title)}</div>;
```

> **Note**
>
> In many programming languages (including JavaScript), a **higher-order function** is one that either takes another function as an argument, returns a function, or both. These functions are foundational in functional programming, enabling you to write modular and reusable code. They are commonly used for operations such as `map`, `filter`, and `reduce` on arrays, function composition, currying, and event handling. Higher-order functions simplify code structure, improve maintainability, and allow for more advanced programming techniques.

Great – our title is now fully customizable. But let's stretch this even further. What if we want the title to be inside an `h3` tag rather than a simple `div` tag? React has got us covered – we can pass a function that returns JSX elements:

```
const Title = ({
  title,
  render,
```

```
    }: {
      title: string;
      render: (s: string) => React.ReactNode;
    }) => <div>{render(title)}</div>;
```

Notice the use of the render prop – we call it as a function and pass in `title`.

To use the render prop, we can pass an anonymous function (inside the curly braces) into it, as in the following code:

```
<Title
  title="This is a title"
  render={(s: string) => {
    const formatted = s.toUpperCase();
    return <h3>{formatted}</h3>;
  }}
/>
```

In React, this higher-order function doesn't necessarily have to be named `render`. We could just as easily use the `children` prop for a more intuitive design, like so:

```
const Title = ({
  title,
  children,
}: {
  title: string;
  children: (s: string) => React.ReactNode;
}) => <div>{children(title)}</div>;
```

This allows us to invoke `children` as if it were a regular function:

```
<Title title="This is a title">
  {(s: string) => {
    const formatted = s.toUpperCase();
    return <h3>{formatted}</h3>;
  }}
</Title>
```

The `Title` component receives a `title` prop and a child function (the latter of which is called a **render prop**). The child function takes a string, s, converts it to uppercase, and renders it within an h3 tag. The `Title` component calls this child function with the provided title prop for custom rendering.

In React, the render prop pattern involves passing a function as a prop to a component. This function returns JSX that the component will render as part of its output. The pattern allows for more flexible and reusable components by giving the parent component control over a part of the child component's rendering logic. It's particularly useful for sharing behavior across multiple components.

Take note of the overarching pattern at play here: abstraction. Initially, we might think of h2 or h3 as specific instances of headings. However, upon zooming out a bit, we start to understand that they're part of a broader abstraction: a React component or, more technically, ReactNode.

This realization allows us to see the utility of using render props or children as higher-order functions. They're not just features; they represent the level of abstraction we've achieved. Now, instead of being limited to a specific HTML tag such as h3, we can pass any JSX element as an argument, from headings to fully styled components.

With our newly crafted generic component that uses a render prop, we've essentially created a reusable framework. The beauty lies in the fact that we only need to write this general-purpose code once.

Render props and composition are excellent techniques for this. They allow you to extend or customize the behavior of a component without altering its core logic. This keeps your components clean, modular, and easy to test, as each component does one thing and does it well. We have already seen how render props work in the evolution of Title, so let's now have a look at composition.

Using composition to apply the SRP

Composition is a term we have used in many places throughout the book, and at its core is the SRP. If each part of the system can do its job well, it's then possible to compose them together. Let's inspect a concrete example of this.

Assume we have an Avatar component in a design system with a handy feature: if a user passes in a name prop to the component, then when the mouse hovers over the avatar, a tooltip will show up at the bottom of the avatar with the name as its content:

Figure 9.1: Avatar component with Tooltip

Internally, `Avatar` utilizes another component, `Tooltip`, to make it happen:

```
import Tooltip from "@xui/tooltip";

type AvatarProps = {
  name?: string;
  url: string;
};

const Avatar = ({ name, url }: AvatarProps) => {
  if (name) {
    return (
      <Tooltip content={name}>
        <div className="rounded">
          <img src={url} alt={name} />
        </div>
      </Tooltip>
    );
  }
  return (
    <div className="rounded">
      <img src={url} alt="" />
    </div>
  );
};
```

The `Avatar` component takes two optional props, `name` and `url`, and displays an image using the URL provided. If the `name` prop is also provided, it wraps the image in a `Tooltip` component that shows the name when hovered over. The `div` tag is styled with a `rounded` class, which will present the avatar in a circle.

The original code for the `Avatar` component tightly coupled it to a `Tooltip` feature. As users demanded more customization options for the tooltip, maintaining this coupling became challenging. Adding more props to handle tooltip customization can bloat the `Avatar` component and create a ripple effect: any change in `Tooltip` may necessitate changes in `Avatar`, making it hard to manage.

Instead of forcing `Tooltip` into `Avatar`, we can simplify `Avatar` to focus solely on its primary function—displaying an image. This stripped-down version excludes the tooltip, reducing its bundle size and making it more maintainable. Here's how the simplified `Avatar` component looks:

```
const Avatar = ({ name = "", url }: AvatarProps) => (
  <div className="rounded">
    <img src={url} alt={name} title={name} />
  </div>
);
```

By doing so, we make the `Avatar` and `Tooltip` components composable, meaning they can work independently of each other. The consumer can then choose to wrap `Avatar` with `Tooltip` if desired, as shown in the following code snippet:

```
import Avatar from "@xui/avatar";
import Tooltip from "@xui/tooltip";

const MyAvatar = (props) => (
  <Tooltip
    content="Juntao Qiu"
  >
    <Avatar
      name="Juntao Qiu"
      url="https://avatars.githubusercontent.com/u/122324"
    />
  </Tooltip>
);
```

The code imports `Avatar` and `Tooltip` components from the `"@xui"` library. It then defines a `MyAvatar` component that displays an avatar for `"Juntao Qiu"` (if there isn't a name needed here, we don't use the `Tooltip` component). When you hover over the avatar, a tooltip appears on top with the name **Juntao Qiu** in a design customized with a white font color on a blue background.

The benefit of this approach is twofold:

- The `Avatar` component remains lean, reducing its bundle size

- The consumer has the freedom to customize `Tooltip` or even use different tooltip libraries without affecting `Avatar`

In short, the separation makes the code more modular, and users only have to "pay" in terms of code and complexity for the features they actually use.

In both the render props and composition examples, we underlined the essence of the SRP in modern web development. The SRP advocates for building components that do one thing and do it well, making them more maintainable, reusable, and flexible.

Next, let's pivot to discussing the DIP, another crucial perspective that complements these design principles.

Embracing the Dependency Inversion Principle

The **DIP** is one of the five principles that make up SOLID, a set of guidelines aimed at helping developers create more maintainable, flexible, and scalable software. Specifically, the DIP encourages developers to depend on abstractions, not on concrete implementations.

The DIP addresses several challenges that developers face when building and maintaining large systems. One such problem is the rigidity that comes from tightly coupled modules. When high-level modules are dependent on low-level modules, even small changes to the low-level code can have a broad impact, necessitating changes across the system.

Understanding how the DIP works

In terms of high-level modules and low-level modules, let's think of a notification feature in a system. Here, we want to send out a notification in a form that the user prefers, either an email, an SMS message, or both:

```
class EmailNotification {
  send(message: string, type: string) {
    console.log(`Sending email with message: ${message}, type:
${type}`);
  }
}

class Application {
  private emailNotification: EmailNotification;

  constructor(emailNotification: EmailNotification) {
    this.emailNotification = emailNotification;
  }

  process() {
    // perform some actions to response user interaction
    this.emailNotification.send("Some events happened", "info");
  }
}

const app = new Application(new EmailNotification());
app.process();
```

In the code, the `EmailNotification` class has a method called `send` that takes `message` and `type` as parameters. It then prints out a log to indicate that an email with this `message` and `type` is being sent. The `Application` class, on the other hand, has a `process` method that simulates some kind of user interaction. Inside this method, `Application` uses an instance of `EmailNotification` to send an email whenever `process` is invoked.

One important thing to note here is that Application is tightly coupled to EmailNotification. This means that if you wanted to change how notifications are sent, perhaps by using SMS instead of email, you'd have to modify the Application class directly, thereby violating the SRP and making the system less flexible.

So, to resolve the problem, we can introduce a Notification interface and let EmailNotification implement the interface. That means we could have multiple implementations of the interface. Plus, instead of Application depending on the EmailNotification class, Application depends on the Notification interface. Because we rely on the interface, from Application's view, it doesn't matter which concrete implementation is passed in, as long as it implements the Notification interface – that means we could easily swap it to an SMSNotification class if we like. Here's what the code for all of this will look like:

```
interface Notification {
  send(message: string, type: string): void;
}

class EmailNotification implements Notification {
  send(message: string, type: string) {
    console.log(`Sending email with message: ${message}, type:
      ${type}`);
  }
}

class Application {
  private notifier: Notification;

  constructor(notifier: Notification) {
    this.notifier = notifier;
  }

  process() {
    // perform some actions to response user interaction
    this.notifier.send("Some event happened", "info");
  }
}
```

The code defines a Notification interface with a send method, which is then implemented by the EmailNotification class. The Application class is now constructed with any object that adheres to the Notification interface. Within its process method, Application uses this object to send a notification. This setup decouples the Application class from the specific notification mechanism, making it more flexible and easier to change or extend.

For instance, if we decide to replace `EmailNotification` with `SMSNotification`, the `Application` class won't need any modifications; we would simply provide a different instance that implements the `Notification` interface:

```
const app = new Application(new EmailNotification());
app.process();

// or
const app = new Application(new SMSNotification());
app.process();
```

All right – that's briefly about how the DIP works. Let's look at another example to find out how to apply the same principle inside a React application.

Applying the DIP in an analytics button

Now, imagine you have a generic button component that's used across various parts of your application. You want to send analytics events when the button is clicked, but how exactly those events are sent should be abstracted away from the button component itself.

The problem is that generic buttons are widely used in many products already, and not all of them need the analytics functionality. So, if you simply change the `onClick` handler in the shared `Button` component, it will annoy many innocent users.

Let's have a look at the current `Button` implementation:

```
const Button = ({ onClick: provided, name, ...rest }: ButtonProps) =>
{
  const onClick = (e) => {
    // emit an event to the analytic server
    return provided(e);
  };

  return <button onClick={onClick} {...rest} />;
};
```

Instead, we could define a new component that wraps the original button around and hijacks the click handler for the analysis:

```
import { Button } from "@xui/button";

const FancyButton = ({
  onClick: originalOnClick,
  ...rest
}: FancyButtonProps) => {
  const onClick = (e) => {
```

```
    //emit an event to the analytic server
    console.log('sending analytics event to a remote server');
    return originalOnClick(e);
  };

  return <Button onClick={onClick} {...rest} />;
};
```

The new code defines a `FancyButton` component that wraps around a basic `Button` component. When clicked, `FancyButton` first sends an analytics event to a remote server and then proceeds to execute the original `onClick` function passed to it. All other props are passed down directly to the underlying `Button` component.

The issue here is that many instances where the `Button` component is used might contain similar analytics code, leading to repetitive logic across the code base. This redundancy is undesirable, as any changes to the analytics logic would require updates in multiple locations, increasing the risk of errors.

So, let's consider the DIP. We will make some changes in the original `Button` component, but instead of sending analytics events directly, we'll first extract an interface and make the button rely on the interface (keep in mind there could be multiple implementations of that interface).

Just as with the previous `Notification` example, `EmailNotification` is one of the notification channels that send email. In this button example, one of the implementations sends an event, whereas for products that don't use analytics at all, they just pass in an empty implementation.

To make the change, we'll need to define a new interface type, and we need a context for the implementation of the interface to live in:

```
import { createContext } from "react";

export interface InteractionMeasurement {
  measure(name: string | undefined, timestamp?: number): void;
}

export default createContext<InteractionMeasurement | null>(null);
```

This code creates a React context named `InteractionMeasurement` with an interface that specifies a `measure` method. This method takes a name (either a string or undefined) and an optional timestamp, while the context is initialized as `null`.

Inside the `Button` component, we can use `useContext` to access the context we defined:

```
import InteractionContext, {
  InteractionMeasurement
} from "./InteractionContext";

const Button = ({ name, onClick: providedOnClick, children }:
```

```
ButtonType) => {
  const interactionContext = useContext<InteractionMeasurement |
   null>(
    InteractionContext
  );

  const handleClick = useCallback(
    (e) => {
      interactionContext &&
      interactionContext.measure(name, e.timeStamp);
      providedOnClick(e);
    },
    [providedOnClick, interactionContext, name]
  );

  return <button onClick={handleClick}>{children}</button>;
};
```

The code defines a Button component that uses InteractionContext to track clicks. When the button is clicked, it calls the measure method from the context, passing in the button's name and the click event's timestamp. Then, it proceeds to execute any additional onClick logic provided. This way, click tracking is abstracted away into the context, making the Button component more reusable and maintainable.

If interactionContext is null, the measure function won't be called, and the component will proceed to execute only the providedOnClick function passed in as a prop. This allows for optional analytics tracking based on the availability of InteractionContext.

That would perfectly resolve the problem we have – if a product wants to enable the analytics, they can use Button within a context that contains an InteractionMeasurement implementation.

Having said that, let's say we have a FormApp application that uses Button inside an InteractionContext instance:

```
import InteractionContext from "./InteractionContext";
import { Button } from "@xui/button";

const FormApp = () => {
  const context = {
    measure: (e, t) => {
      //send event and timestamp to remote
      console.log(`sending to remote server  ${e}: ${t}`);
    },
  };

  const onClick = () => {
```

```
      console.log("submit");
   };

   return (
     <InteractionContext.Provider value={context}>
       <form>
         <Button name="submit-button" onClick={onClick}>
           Submit
         </Button>
       </form>
     </InteractionContext.Provider>
   );
};
```

The `FormApp` component defines its own analytics logic in the `measure` function inside the `context` object. It then passes this function to child components through `InteractionContext.Provider`. When a button inside the form is clicked, not only will the button's specific `onClick` logic be executed, but the `measure` function will also send event and timestamp data to a remote server for analytics. This setup allows for context-based analytics without tying the `Button` component to a specific implementation.

For users who don't want the analytics functionality, they can just use the `Button` component as usual:

```
import { Button } from "@xui/button";

const App = () => {
  const onClick = () => {
    console.log("checkout");
  };

  return (
    <Button name="checkout-button" onClick={onClick}>
      Checkout
    </Button>
  );
};
```

This methodology offers exceptional flexibility and dynamism, making it invaluable for designing common components. It enhances both code reusability and system maintainability while also reducing the overall bundle size.

Be aware that adding an extra `context` object in such scenarios may initially seem excessive. However, in large code bases where different teams work on distinct parts, this approach becomes more relevant. For instance, a product team focused on analysis might have different objectives compared to a design system team, whose aim is to develop generic and atomic components. The design system team may not be concerned with analytical aspects. Consequently, directly modifying the Button component in this environment can be impractical or challenging.

Having that said, I would like to introduce another design principle I constantly use in my code; you can think of it as a special form of the SRP at its core. This principle is CQRS.

Understanding Command and Query Responsibility Segregation in React

The **Command and Query Responsibility Segregation** (**CQRS**) principle (also known as the **Separation of Command and Query Principle**) is a software design principle that suggests that methods or functions should either be commands that modify the system's state or queries that return information about the system's state, but not both.

Commands (or **modifiers**) are methods that perform an action or change the state of an object without returning a value. **Queries**, on the other hand, are methods to read an object's state without any changes. Separating commands and queries can help reduce coupling between components, making testing, maintaining, and modifying code easier. It also makes it easier to reason about the behavior of code and can improve the overall design of a system.

Although this pattern is widely used on a large scale, such as in designing the architecture of systems, it works well at the code level as well. I will demonstrate this in a ShoppingCart component:

```
type Item = {
  id: string;
  name: string;
  price: number;
}

const ShoppingApplication = () => {
  const [cart, setCart] = useState<Item[]>([]);

  const addItemToCart = (item: Item) => {
    setCart([...cart, item]);
  };

  const removeItemFromCart = (id: string) => {
    setCart(cart.filter((item) => item.id !== id));
  };

  const totalPrice = cart.reduce((total, item) => total + item.price,
    0);

  return (
```

```
    <div>
      <ProductList addToCart={addItemToCart} />

      <h2>Shopping Cart</h2>
      <ul>
        {cart.map((item) => (
          <li key={item.id}>
            {item.name} - {item.price}
            <button onClick={() => removeItemFromCart(item.
              id)}>Remove</button>
          </li>
        ))}
      </ul>
      <p>Total Price: {totalPrice}</p>
    </div>
  );
};
```

The ShoppingApplication component maintains a shopping cart using the useState Hook with an array of items of type Item. The addItemToCart function adds new items to the cart, and removeItemFromCart removes items based on their id value. totalPrice is calculated as the sum of all item prices in the cart.

The component renders a list of items in the cart, along with their total price. Each item has a **Remove** button that calls removeItemFromCart when clicked. A ProductList component is also rendered, and it receives addItemToCart as a prop for adding products to the cart.

The previous code appears to be okay at first glance, but it contains some subtle issues. One problem is that when multiple identical products are added to the cart, the keys will overlap, triggering React's warning about unique keys. Additionally, if you click the **Remove** button in this situation, it will delete all instances of that product from the cart, which is far from ideal and leads to a poor user experience.

To fix these issues, we need to introduce a new uniqKey field to the Item type. We also need to generate a unique key before an item is inserted into the cart array. With that unique ID, we are finally able to remove items by uniqKey instead of by id. This is what the code will look like:

```
const addItemToCart = (item: Item) => {
  setCart([...cart, { ...item, uniqKey: `${item.id}-${Date.now()}`
}]);
};

const removeItemFromCart = (key: string) => {
  setCart(cart.filter((item) => item.uniqKey !== key));
};
```

We also need to update how the cart is rendered in JSX:

```
<h2>Shopping Cart</h2>
<ul>
  {cart.map((item) => (
    <li key={item.uniqKey}>
      {item.name} - {item.price}
      <button onClick={() => removeItemFromCart(item.uniqKey)}>
        Remove
      </button>
    </li>
  ))}
</ul>
```

While the code is technically sound and sufficiently straightforward for its current scope, as we expand the `ShoppingApplication` component with more states and calculations, applying the CQRS principle could provide a structured way to keep everything organized.

We'll use the React Context API and the `useReducer` Hook to implement CQRS for the `ShoppingApplication` component. Let's take a look at them now.

Introducing useReducer

The `useReducer` Hook in React is used for state management in functional components; it is particularly useful when the next state depends on the previous one or when you have complex state logic. The `useReducer` Hook takes two arguments: a reducer function and an initial state, and it returns the current state and a `dispatch` method to trigger updates.

For the first parameter, a reducer function receives the current state and an `action` object, which contains information on how to update the state. The function should return the new state based on the action type and payload. The second parameter is the initial state you want to pass in and will be used as the default value when invoked.

Let's define a reducer function for our `ShoppingApplication` component:

```
type ShoppingCartState = {
  items: Item[];
  totalPrice: number;
};

type ActionType = {
  type: string;
  payload: Item;
};

const shoppingCartReducer = (
```

```
    state: ShoppingCartState = initState,
    action: ActionType
  ) => {
    switch (action.type) {
      case "ADD_ITEM": {
        const item = {
          ...action.payload,
          uniqKey: `${action.payload.id}-${Date.now()}`,
        };
        return { ...state, items: [...state.items, item] };
      }

      case "REMOVE_ITEM":
        const newItems = state.items.filter(
          (item) => item.uniqKey !== action.payload.uniqKey
        );
        return { ...state, items: newItems };
      default:
        return state;
    }
  };
```

So, shoppingCartReducer is a function that takes two arguments – the current state and an action:

- The state is of type ShoppingCartState, which includes an array of items and totalPrice

- The action is of type ActionType, which includes a string type to identify the action and a payload containing an Item object

Inside the reducer function, a switch statement is used to determine which action is being dispatched. The "ADD_ITEM" case adds a new item to the state's items array. This item is given a unique key, uniqKey, to differentiate it from identical items. The "REMOVE_ITEM" case removes an item from the items array based on this unique key.

By using this structure, the reducer function provides a predictable way to manage the shopping cart's state in response to different actions. Note there is nothing fancy here in this reducer function; it's just a regular JavaScript function. To see how it works, we could test the reducer function with the following code:

```
const item = {
  id: "p1",
  name: "iPad",
  price: 666,
};

let x = shoppingCartReducer(initState, {
```

```
    type: "ADD_ITEM",
    payload: item,
  });
```

```
  console.log(x);
```

And we would get something like this (obviously, your `uniqKey` value would be different from mine as it's generated by the time an item is added):

```
{
    "items": [
        {
            "id": "p1",
            "name": "iPad",
            "price": 666,
            "uniqKey": "p1-1696059737801"
        }
    ],
    "totalPrice": 0
}
```

All right – that should give a taste of what a reducer function is and how it works with any given input. Now, let's see how we can connect it with our application.

Using a reducer function in a context

Let's see how we can use a reducer function to implement CQRS to simplify our shopping cart example. Firstly, we'll need a context to manage the cart state, and also expose query functions for components to use:

```
import React, { createContext, useContext, useReducer } from "react";
import { Item } from "./type";

type ShoppingCartContextType = {
  items: Item[];
  addItem: (item: Item) => void;
  removeItem: (item: Item) => void;
};

const ShoppingCartContext = createContext<ShoppingCartContextType |
null>(null);

export const ShoppingCartProvider = ({
  children,
```

```
}: {
  children: React.ReactNode;
}) => {
  const [state, dispatch] = useReducer(shoppingCartReducer, {
    items: [],
    totalPrice: 0,
  });

  const addItem = (item: Item) => {
    dispatch({type: ADD_ITEM, payload: item});
  };

  const removeItem = (item: Item) => {
    dispatch({type: REMOVE_ITEM, payload: item});
  };

  return (
    <ShoppingCartContext.Provider value={{items: state.items, addItem,
    removeItem}}>
      {children}
    </ShoppingCartContext.Provider>
  );
};
```

This code creates a React context for managing a shopping cart. Inside `ShoppingCartProvider`, it uses the `useReducer` Hook to handle cart actions. Two functions, `addItem` and `removeItem`, dispatch actions to modify the cart. The `Provider` component makes the cart state and these functions available to its child components via `ShoppingCartContext`. This allows any nested components to interact with the shopping cart.

Note that `addItem` and `removeItem` are two command functions in the CQRS principle that only change the state without returning any data. If we want to get the data, we can define a query function, like so:

```
export const useTotalPrice = () => {
  const context = useContext<ShoppingCartContextType>(
    ShoppingCartContext
  );

  const {items} = context;

  return items.reduce((acc, item) => acc + item.price, 0);
};
```

Here, we define a custom Hook called `useTotalPrice` that calculates the total price of items in a shopping cart. It uses the React `useContext` Hook to access the shopping cart data from `ShoppingCartContext`. It then uses the `reduce` method to sum up the prices of all items in the cart, starting with an initial value of 0.

For the `ShoppingApplication` component, we can simply wrap `ProductList` and `ShoppingCart` inside the `ShoppingCartContext` instance we just created:

```
const ShoppingApplication = () => {
  const context = useContext(ShoppingCartContext);
  const { items, addItem, removeItem } = context;
  const totalPrice = useTotalPrice();

  return (
    <div>
      <ProductList addToCart={addItem} />

      <h2>Shopping Cart</h2>
      <ul>
        {items.map((item) => (
          <li key={item.uniqKey}>
            {item.name} - {item.price}
            <button onClick={() => removeItem(item)}>Remove</button>
          </li>
        ))}
      </ul>
      <p>Total Price: {totalPrice}</p>
    </div>
  );
};
```

The `ShoppingApplication` component serves as the main interface for the shopping application. It uses React's `useContext` Hook to access the shopping cart context, which provides a list of items in the cart (`items`), a function to add items (`addItem`), and a function to remove items (`removeItem`). The component also uses a `useTotalPrice` custom Hook to calculate the total price of items in the cart.

And in the outmost App component, we can encapsulate the `ShoppingApplication` component:

```
<ShoppingCartProvider>
  <ShoppingApplication />
</ShoppingCartProvider>
```

So, CQRS is a design pattern that separates the modification and query aspects of a system to enhance scalability, maintainability, and simplicity. We demonstrated this principle by implementing a shopping cart feature – commands to modify the cart's state, such as adding or removing items, were segregated from the queries, which included fetching a list of items and calculating the total price; this separation was made clear through the use of React's Context API and custom Hooks, which isolated each responsibility effectively. This not only improves code readability but also makes it easier to manage and scale the application in the future.

Summary

In this chapter, we've unpacked three crucial design principles: the SRP for focused, easy-to-understand components, the DIP for modular, testable code, and CQRS for a distinct separation between commands and queries, enhancing maintainability. These principles offer a robust foundation for building scalable and high-quality software.

In the next chapter, we'll dive deeper into composition principles to further refine our approach to React application design.

10

Diving Deep into
Composition Patterns

The journey of building scalable and maintainable user interfaces is riddled with challenges. One primary challenge faced by developers is ensuring that components remain modular, reusable, and easy to understand as a code base grows. The more intertwined and tightly coupled our components become, the harder it is to maintain, test, or even onboard new team members.

Composition has emerged as a powerful technique to address this challenge, enabling developers to build more organized, scalable, and cleaner code bases. Instead of creating large, monolithic components that carry out numerous tasks, we break them down into smaller, more manageable pieces that can be combined in versatile ways. This offers us a clear path to streamline logic, enhance reusability, and maintain a clear separation of concerns.

This chapter is dedicated to understanding and mastering composition in React. We'll delve into foundational techniques such as higher-order functions before transitioning into higher-order components and Hooks. You'll learn how these tools seamlessly align with the principles of composition, allowing you to build more robust applications with React. Our journey will culminate with a deep dive into headless components, a paradigm that encapsulates logic without dictating the UI, offering unparalleled flexibility.

By the chapter's end, you'll appreciate the benefits of employing composition techniques. You'll be equipped to create UIs that are not just scalable and maintainable but also a pleasure to work with. Let's embark on this enlightening exploration of composition in React.

In this chapter, we will cover the following topics:

- Understanding composition through higher-order components
- Diving deep into custom Hooks
- Developing a drop-down list component
- Exploring a headless component pattern

Technical requirements

A GitHub repository has been created to host all the code we discuss in the book. For this chapter, you can find the recommended structure at `https://github.com/PacktPublishing/React-Anti-Patterns/tree/main/code/src/ch10`.

Understanding composition through higher-order components

Composition might be the most important technique in software design overall, and like many other fundamental design principles, it applies on many different levels. In this section, we'll review how we can use higher-order functions and their variation in the React world – higher-order components – to implement composition.

Reviewing higher-order functions

We discussed some examples of higher-order functions in *Chapter 9*, but it's such an important concept that I would like to review it a bit more here. A **higher-order function** (**HOF**) is a function that either takes another function as its argument, returns a function, or both. The ability to accept a function as a parameter has a lot of advantages, especially when it comes to composition.

Consider the following example:

```
const report = (content: string) => {
    const header = "=== Header ===";
    const footer = "=== Footer ===";

    return [header, content, footer].join("\n");
};
```

Here, the `report` function generates a formatted report containing a header, the provided content, and a footer. For instance, given the input `hello world`, the output would be as follows:

```
=== Header ===
hello world
=== Footer ===
```

Now, imagine a scenario where some users wish to print the content in uppercase. While we could achieve this with `content.toUpperCase()`, other users might prefer the content as-is. Introducing conditions within our report function is one approach to pleasing both sets of users. Drawing inspiration from our previous discussion about the title example in *Chapter 9*, we can allow a `transformer` function to be passed.

This enables clients to format the string as they desire, like so:

```
const report = (content: string, transformer: (s: string) => string)
=> {
  const header = "=== Header ===";
  const footer = "=== Footer ===";


  return [header, transformer(content), footer].join("\n");
};
```

For flexibility, we can provide a default transformer, ensuring that those who don't wish to customize the format can use the function without changes:

```
const report = (
  content: string,
  transformer: (s: string) => string = (s) => s
) => {
  const header = "=== Header ===";
  const footer = "=== Footer ===";


  return [header, transformer(content), footer].join("\n");
};
```

The report function generates a string with a defined header and footer, and the main content in between. It accepts a content string and an optional transformer function. If the transformer is provided, it modifies the content; otherwise, the content remains unchanged. The result is a formatted report with the modified or original content placed between the header and footer. That's essentially how powerful HOFs can be, helping us to write more composable code.

Reflecting upon this, an interesting thought emerges – can we incorporate this composable and functional approach into our React applications? Indeed, we can. The ability to augment components isn't just limited to standard functions. In React, we have **higher-order components (HOCs)**.

Introducing HOCs

An HOC is essentially a function that accepts a component and returns a new, enhanced version of it. The principle behind HOCs is straightforward – they allow you to inject additional functionality into an existing component. This pattern is especially beneficial when you want to reuse certain behaviors across multiple components.

Let's delve into an example:

```
const checkAuthorization = () => {
    // Perform authorization check, e.g., check local storage or send
        a request to a remote server
```

```
  }

  const withAuthorization = (Component: React.FC): React.FC => {
    return (props: any) => {
      const isAuthorized = checkAuthorization();
      return isAuthorized ? <Component {...props} /> : <Login />;
    };
  };
```

In this snippet, we define a function, checkAuthorization, to handle the authorization check. Then, we create a HOC, withAuthorization. This HOC takes a component (Component) as its argument and returns a new function. This returned function, when rendered, will either render the original Component (if the user is authorized) or a Login component (if the user is not authorized).

Now, suppose we have a ProfileComponent that we want to secure. We can use withAuthorization to create a new, secured version of ProfileComponent:

```
  const Profile = withAuthorization(ProfileComponent);
```

This means that whenever Profile is rendered, it will first check whether a user is authorized. If so, it renders ProfileComponent; otherwise, it redirects the user to the Login component.

Now that we've seen how HOCs can control access with withAuthorization, let's shift our focus to enhancing user interactions. We'll delve into an ExpandablePanel component, showcasing how HOCs can also manage interactive UI elements and state transitions.

Implementing an ExpandablePanel component

Let's kick things off with a basic ExpandablePanel component. This component, as the name suggests, consists of a title and a content area. Initially, the content area is collapsed, but a click on the title expands it to reveal the content.

ExpandablePanel

Figure 10.1: An expandable panel

The code for such a component is straightforward:

```
export type PanelProps = {
  heading: string;
  content: ReactNode;
};

const ExpandablePanel = ({ heading, content }: PanelProps) => {
  const [isOpen, setIsOpen] = useState<boolean>(false);

  return (
    <article>
      <header onClick={() => setIsOpen((isOpen) =>
        !isOpen)}>{heading}</header>
      {isOpen && <section>{content}</section>}
    </article>
  );
};
```

Now, suppose we want to jazz it up a bit, making the panel expand automatically when rendered and then collapse after a few seconds. Here's how we could adjust the code to achieve that:

```
const AutoCloseExpandablePanel = ({ heading, content }: PanelProps) =>
{
  const [isOpen, setIsOpen] = useState<boolean>(true);

  useEffect(() => {
    const id = setTimeout(() => {
      setIsOpen(false);
    }, 3000);

    return () => {
      clearTimeout(id);
    };
  }, []);

  return (
    <article>
      <header onClick={() => setIsOpen((isOpen) =>
        !isOpen)}>{heading}</header>
      {isOpen && <section>{content}</section>}
    </article>
  );
};
```

In this revised version, we initialize `isOpen` to `true` so that the panel starts as expanded. Then, we utilize `useEffect` to set a timer that collapses the panel after 3,000 milliseconds (3 seconds).

This pattern of auto-collapsing components is quite common in UI development – think of notifications, alerts, or tooltips that disappear after a while. To promote code reusability, let's extract this auto-collapsing logic into a HOC:

```
interface Toggleable {
  isOpen: boolean;
  toggle: () => void;
}


const withAutoClose = <T extends Partial<Toggleable>>(
  Component: React.FC<T>,
  duration: number = 2000
) => (props: T) => {
  const [show, setShow] = useState<boolean>(true);

  useEffect(() => {
    if (show) {
      const timerId = setTimeout(() => setShow(false), duration);
      return () => clearTimeout(timerId);
    }
  }, [show]);

  return (
    <Component
      {...props}
      isOpen={show}
      toggle={() => setShow((show) => !show)}
    />
  );
};
```

In `withAutoClose`, we define a generic HOC that adds auto-closing functionality to any component. This HOC accepts a duration parameter to customize the auto-close delay, defaulting to 2,000 milliseconds (2 seconds).

To ensure a smooth integration, we can also extend `PanelProps` to include optional `Toggleable` properties:

```
type PanelProps = {
  heading: string;
  content: ReactNode;
} & Partial<Toggleable>;
```

Now, we can refactor ExpandablePanel to accept isOpen and toggle props from withAutoClose:

```
const ExpandablePanel = ({
  isOpen,
  toggle,
  heading,
  content,
}: PanelProps) => {
  return (
    <article>
      <header onClick={toggle}>{heading}</header>
      {isOpen && <section>{content}</section>}
    </article>
  );
};
```

With this setup, creating an auto-closing version of ExpandablePanel is a breeze:

```
export default withAutoClose(ExpandablePanel, 3000);
```

And guess what? The auto-closing logic we've encapsulated in withAutoClose can be reused across various components:

```
const AutoDismissToast = withAutoClose(Toast, 3000);
const TimedTooltip = withAutoClose(Tooltip, 3000);
```

The versatility of HOCs shines when it comes to composition – the ability to apply one HOC to the result of another. This capability aligns well with the principle of function composition in functional programming.

Let's consider another HOC, withKeyboardToggle, which augments a panel's behavior to respond to keyboard inputs to toggle the panel's expanded/collapsed state. Here's the code for withKeyboardToggle:

```
const noop = () => {};

const withKeyboardToggle =
  <T extends Partial<Toggleable>>(Component: React.FC<T>) =>
  (props: T) => {
    const divRef = useRef<HTMLDivElement>(null);

    const handleKeyDown = (event: KeyboardEvent<HTMLDivElement>) => {
      if (event.key === "Enter" || event.key === " ") {
        event.preventDefault();
        (props.toggle ?? noop)();
```

```
    }

    if (event.key === "Escape" && divRef.current) {
      divRef.current.blur();
    }
  };

  return (
    <div onKeyDown={handleKeyDown} tabIndex={0} ref={divRef}>
      <Component {...props} />
    </div>
  );
};

export default withKeyboardToggle;
```

In the withKeyboardToggle HOC, a reference (divRef) is created for the wrapping div to enable keyboard interactions. The handleKeyDown function defines the behavior for the *Enter*, *Space*, and *Escape* keys – the *Enter* or *Space* keys toggle the panel's state, while the *Escape* key removes focus from the panel. These keyboard event handlers allow the wrapped component to respond to keyboard navigation.

Now, let's compose withKeyboardToggle and withAutoClose together to create a new component, AccessibleAutoClosePanel:

```
const AccessibleAutoClosePanel =
  withAutoClose(withKeyboardToggle(ExpandablePanel), 2000);
```

In the withAutoClose(withKeyboardToggle(ExpandablePanel), 2000); expression, withKeyboardToggle is first applied to ExpandablePanel, enhancing it with keyboard toggle capability. The result is then fed into withAutoClose, which further enhances the component to auto-close after a 2,000-millisecond delay. This chaining of HOCs results in a new component, AccessibleAutoClosePanel, which inherits both the keyboard toggle and auto-close behaviors.

This is a vivid example of how HOCs can be nested and composed to build more complex behavior from simpler, single-responsibility components, which is illustrated further in *Figure 10.2*:

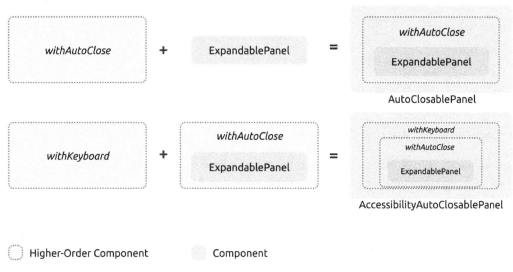

Figure 10.2: A Higher-Order Component

If you have some background in object-oriented programming, this concept might resonate with you, as it aligns with the **Decorator** design pattern. If you're not familiar, it dynamically adds behaviors to objects by wrapping them in additional objects, rather than altering their structure. This allows for greater flexibility than subclassing, as it extends functionality without modifying the original object.

Now, while HOCs remain beneficial in various scenarios for both class components and functional components, React Hooks offer a more lightweight approach to achieving composition. Let's look at Hooks next.

Exploring React Hooks

Hooks provide a means to extract stateful logic from a component, enabling its independent testing and reuse. They pave the way for reutilizing stateful logic without altering your component hierarchy. Essentially, Hooks let you "hook into" React state and other life cycle features from function components.

Following on from the `ExpandablePanel` component example, let's look at this code:

```
const useAutoClose = (duration: number) => {
  const [isOpen, setIsOpen] = useState<boolean>(true);

  useEffect(() => {
    if (isOpen) {
      const timerId = setTimeout(() => setIsOpen(false), duration);
      return () => clearTimeout(timerId);
    }
```

```
  }, [duration, isOpen]);

  const toggle = () => setIsOpen((show) => !show);

  return { isOpen, toggle };
};


export default useAutoClose;
```

In this useAutoClose Hook, we create an isOpen state and a function toggle to switch the state. The useEffect function sets a timer to change isOpen to false after a specified duration, but only if isOpen is true. It also cleans up the timer to prevent memory leaks.

Now, to integrate this Hook into our ExpandablePanel, minimal amendments are needed:

```
const ExpandablePanel = ({ heading, content }: PanelProps) => {
  const { isOpen, toggle } = useAutoClose(2000);

  return (
    <article>
      <header onClick={toggle}>{heading}</header>
      {isOpen && <section>{content}</section>}
    </article>
  );
};
```

Here, we deleted the passed-in isOpen and toggle props and utilized the return value from the useAutoClose Hook, seamlessly incorporating the auto-close functionality.

Next, to incorporate keyboard navigation, we define another Hook, useKeyboard, which captures key events to toggle the panel:

```
const useKeyboard = (toggle: () => void) => {
  const handleKeyDown = (event: KeyboardEvent) => {
    if (event.key === "Enter" || event.key === " ") {
      event.preventDefault();
      toggle();
    }
  };

  return { handleKeyDown };
};
```

Then, embedding `useKeyboard` within `ExpandablePanel` is straightforward:

```
const ExpandablePanel = ({ heading, content }: PanelProps) => {
  const { isOpen, toggle } = useAutoClose(2000);
  const { handleKeyDown } = useKeyboard(toggle);

  return (
    <article onKeyDown={handleKeyDown} tabIndex={0}>
      <header onClick={toggle}>{heading}</header>
      {isOpen && <section>{content}</section>}
    </article>
  );
};
```

Here, `handleKeyDown` from `useKeyboard` is employed to detect key presses, enhancing our component with keyboard interactivity.

In *Figure 10.3*, you can observe how the Hooks link with the underlying `ExpandablePanel`, contrasting the HOC scenario where the component is wrapped:

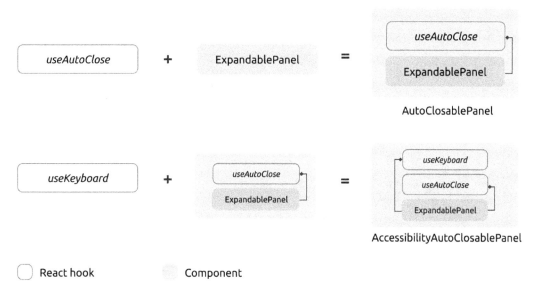

Figure 10.3: Using alternative Hooks

Hooks embody a neat package of reusable logic, isolated from the component yet easily integrated. Unlike the wrapping approach of HOCs, Hooks offer a plugin mechanism, making them lightweight and well-managed by React. This characteristic of Hooks not only promotes code modularity but also facilitates a cleaner and more intuitive way to enrich our components with additional functionalities.

However, be aware that Hooks offer more versatility than initially apparent. They're not just for managing UI-related state but are also effective for handling UI side effects, such as data fetching and global event handling (such as page-level keyboard shortcuts). We have seen how to use them for keyboard event handlers, so now, let's explore how Hooks can streamline network requests.

Unveiling remote data fetching

In previous chapters, we leveraged `useEffect` for data fetching, a prevalent approach. When retrieving data from a remote server, it typically necessitates the introduction of three distinct states – `loading`, `error`, and `data`.

Here's a method to implement these states:

```
//...
  const [loading, setLoading] = useState<boolean>(false);
  const [data, setData] = useState<Item[] | null>(null);
  const [error, setError] = useState<Error | undefined>(undefined);

  useEffect(() => {
    const fetchData = async () => {
      setLoading(true);

      try {
        const response = await fetch("/api/users");

        if (!response.ok) {
          const error = await response.json();
          throw new Error(`Error: ${error.error || response.status}`);
        }

        const data = await response.json();
        setData(data);
      } catch (e) {
        setError(e as Error);
      } finally {
        setLoading(false);
      }
    };

    fetchData();
  }, []);

//...
```

In the preceding code, we use React Hooks to manage asynchronous data fetching, initializing states for `loading`, `data`, and `error`. Inside `useEffect`, the `fetchData` function attempts to retrieve user data from the `"/api/users"` endpoint. If successful, the data is stored; if not, an error is recorded. Regardless of the outcome, the loading state is updated to reflect completion. `useEffect` runs only once, similar to the component's initial mounting phase.

Refactoring for elegance and reusability

Incorporating fetching logic directly within our component can work, but it's not the most elegant or reusable approach. Let's refactor this by extracting the fetching logic into a separate function:

```
const fetchUsers = async () => {
  const response = await fetch("/api/users");

  if (!response.ok) {
    const error = await response.json();
    throw new Error('Something went wrong');
  }

  return await response.json();
};
```

With the `fetchUsers` function in place, we can take a step further by abstracting our fetching logic into a generic Hook. This Hook will accept a fetch function and manage the associated `loading`, `error`, and `data` states:

```
const useService = <T>(fetch: () => Promise<T>) => {
  const [loading, setLoading] = useState<boolean>(false);
  const [data, setData] = useState<T | null>(null);
  const [error, setError] = useState<Error | undefined>(undefined);

  useEffect(() => {
    const fetchData = async () => {
      setLoading(true);

      try {
        const data = await fetch();
        setData(data);
      } catch(e) {
        setError(e as Error);
      } finally {
        setLoading(false);
      }
```

```
    };

    fetchData();
  }, [fetch]);

  return {
    loading,
    error,
    data,
  };
}
```

Now, the useService Hook emerges as a reusable solution to fetch data across our application. It's a neat abstraction that we can employ to fetch various types of data, as seen here:

```
const { loading, error, data } = useService(fetchProducts);
//or
const { loading, error, data } = useService(fetchTickets);
```

With this refactoring, we've not only simplified our data fetching logic but also made it reusable across different scenarios in our application. This sets a solid foundation as we continue to enhance our drop-down component and delve deeper into more advanced features and optimizations.

As we have explored Hooks and their capabilities in managing state and logic, let's apply this knowledge to build a more complex UI component from scratch — a drop-down list. This exercise will not only reinforce our understanding of Hooks but also demonstrate their practical application in creating interactive UI elements.

We'll start with a basic version of a drop-down list and then gradually introduce more features to make it functional and user-friendly. This process will also set the stage for a later discussion on headless components, showcasing a design pattern that further abstracts and manages state and logic in UI components.

Developing a drop-down list component

A drop-down list is a common component used in many places. Although there's a native select component for basic use cases, a more advanced version offering more control over each option provides a better user experience.

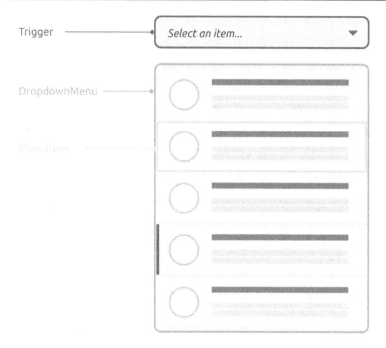

Figure 10.4: A drop-down list component

When creating one from scratch, a complete implementation requires more effort than it appears at first glance. It's essential to consider keyboard navigation, accessibility (for instance, screen reader compatibility), and usability on mobile devices, among others.

We'll begin with a simple, desktop version that only supports mouse clicks, gradually building in more features to make it realistic. Note that the goal here is to reveal a few software design patterns rather than teach you how to build a drop-down list for production use (actually, I don't recommend doing this from scratch and would instead suggest using more mature libraries).

Basically, we need an element (let's call it a trigger) for the user to click, and a state to control the show and hide actions of the list panel. Initially, we hide the panel, and when the trigger is clicked, we show the list panel. Here is the code:

```
import { useState } from "react";

interface Item {
   icon: string;
   text: string;
   id: string;
   description: string;
```

```
}

type DropdownProps = {
  items: Item[];
};

const Dropdown = ({ items }: DropdownProps) => {
  const [isOpen, setIsOpen] = useState(false);
  const [selectedItem, setSelectedItem] = useState<Item | null>(null);

  return (
    <div className="dropdown">
      <div className="trigger" tabIndex={0} onClick={() =>
      setIsOpen(!isOpen)}>
        <span className="selection">
          {selectedItem ? selectedItem.text : "Select an item..."}
        </span>
      </div>
      {isOpen && (
        <div className="dropdown-menu">
          {items.map((item) => (
            <div
              key={item.id}
              onClick={() => setSelectedItem(item)}
              className="item-container"
            >
              <img src={item.icon} alt={item.text} />
              <div className="details">
                <div>{item.text}</div>
                <small>{item.description}</small>
              </div>
            </div>
          ))}
        </div>
      )}
    </div>
  );
};
```

In the code, we've set up the basic structure for our drop-down component. Using the useState Hook, we manage the isOpen and selectedItem states to control the dropdown's behavior. A simple click on the trigger toggles the drop-down menu, while selecting an item updates the selectedItem state.

Let's break down the component into smaller, manageable pieces to see it more clearly. We'll start by extracting a `Trigger` component to handle user clicks:

```
const Trigger = ({
  label,
  onClick,
}: {
  label: string;
  onClick: () => void;
}) => {
  return (
    <div className="trigger" tabIndex={0} onClick={onClick}>
      <span className="selection">{label}</span>
    </div>
  );
};
```

Similarly, we'll extract a `DropdownMenu` component to render the list of items:

```
const DropdownMenu = ({
  items,
  onItemClick,
}: {
  items: Item[];
  onItemClick: (item: Item) => void;
}) => {
  return (
    <div className="dropdown-menu">
      {items.map((item) => (
        <div
          key={item.id}
          onClick={() => onItemClick(item)}
          className="item-container"
        >
          <img src={item.icon} alt={item.text} />
          <div className="details">
            <div>{item.text}</div>
            <small>{item.description}</small>
          </div>
        </div>
      ))}
    </div>
  );
};
```

Now, in the `Dropdown` component, we simply use these two components, passing in the corresponding state, turning them into purely controlled components (stateless components):

```
const Dropdown = ({ items }: DropdownProps) => {
  const [isOpen, setIsOpen] = useState(false);
  const [selectedItem, setSelectedItem] = useState<Item | null>(null);

  return (
    <div className="dropdown">
      <Trigger
        label={selectedItem ? selectedItem.text : "Select an item..."}
        onClick={() => setIsOpen(!isOpen)}
      />
      {isOpen && <DropdownMenu items={items}
        onItemClick={setSelectedItem} />}
    </div>
  );
};
```

In this updated code structure, we've separated concerns by creating specialized components for different parts of the dropdown, making the code more organized and easier to manage. We can see the result here:

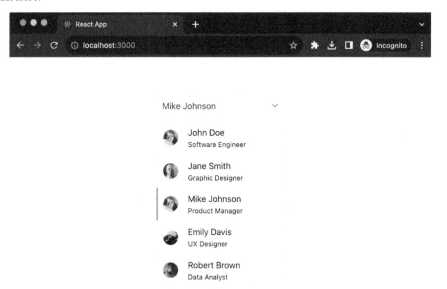

Figure 10.5: A native implementation list

As you can see in *Figure 10.5*, the basic drop-down list appears, but that's only a small part of the whole drop-down list features. Keyboard navigation, for example, is a necessary feature for an accessible component, which we will implement next.

Implementing keyboard navigation

Incorporating keyboard navigation within our drop-down list enhances the user experience by providing an alternative to mouse interactions. This is particularly important for accessibility and offers a seamless navigation experience on a web page. Let's explore how we can achieve this using the onKeyDown event handler.

Initially, we'll attach a handleKeyDown function to the onKeyDown event in our Dropdown component. Here, we utilize a switch statement to determine the specific key pressed and perform actions accordingly. For instance, when the Enter or Space key is pressed, the dropdown is toggled. Similarly, the ArrowDown and ArrowUp keys allow navigation through the list items, cycling back to the start or end of the list when necessary:

```
const Dropdown = ({ items }: DropdownProps) => {
  // ... previous state variables ...

  const handleKeyDown = (e: React.KeyboardEvent) => {
    switch (e.key) {
      // ... case blocks ...
    }
  };

  return (
    <div className="dropdown" onKeyDown={handleKeyDown}>
      {/* ... rest of the JSX ... */}
    </div>
  );
};
```

Additionally, we have updated our DropdownMenu component to accept a selectedIndex prop. This prop is used to apply a highlighted style and set the aria-selected attribute to the currently selected item, enhancing the visual feedback and accessibility:

```
const DropdownMenu = ({
  items,
  selectedIndex,
  onItemClick,
}: {
  items: Item[];
  selectedIndex: number;
  onItemClick: (item: Item) => void;
}) => {
  return (
    <div className="dropdown-menu" role="listbox">
```

```
    {/* ... rest of the JSX ... */}
  </div>
 );
};
```

Moving forward, we can encapsulate the state and keyboard event handling logic within a custom Hook named `useDropdown`. This Hook returns an object containing the necessary states and functions, which can be destructured and used within our `Dropdown` component, keeping it clean and maintainable:

```
const useDropdown = (items: Item[]) => {
  // ... state variables ...

  const handleKeyDown = (e: React.KeyboardEvent) => {
    // ... switch statement ...
  };

  const toggleDropdown = () => setIsOpen((isOpen) => !isOpen);

  return {
    isOpen,
    toggleDropdown,
    handleKeyDown,
    selectedItem,
    setSelectedItem,
    selectedIndex,
  };
};
```

Now, our `Dropdown` component is simplified and more readable; it leverages the `useDropdown` Hook to manage its state and handle keyboard interactions, demonstrating a clear separation of concerns and making the code easier to understand and manage:

```
const Dropdown = ({ items }: DropdownProps) => {
  const {
    isOpen,
    selectedItem,
    selectedIndex,
    toggleDropdown,
    handleKeyDown,
    setSelectedItem,
  } = useDropdown(items);

  return (
```

```
    <div className="dropdown" onKeyDown={handleKeyDown}>
      <Trigger
        onClick={toggleDropdown}
        label={selectedItem ? selectedItem.text : "Select an item..."}
      />
      {isOpen && (
        <DropdownMenu
          items={items}
          onItemClick={setSelectedItem}
          selectedIndex={selectedIndex}
        />
      )}
    </div>
  );
};
```

Through these modifications, we have successfully implemented keyboard navigation in our drop-down list, making it more accessible and user-friendly. This example also illustrates how Hooks can be utilized to manage complex state and logic in a structured and modular manner, paving the way for further enhancements and feature additions to our UI components.

We can visualize the code a bit better with the React DevTools. Note that in the **hooks** section, all the states are listed:

Figure 10.6: Chrome DevTools to inspect what's in the hooks section

The power of extracting our logic into a Hook comes into full play when we need to implement a different UI while maintaining the same underlying functionality. By doing so, we've segregated our state management and interaction logic from the UI rendering, making it a breeze to change the UI without touching the logic.

We've explored how utilizing small components with custom Hooks can enhance our code structure. However, what happens when we're faced with managing more complex states? Consider a scenario where the drop-down data comes from a service API, requiring us to handle asynchronous service calls along with additional state management. In such cases, does this structure still hold up effectively?

The scenario of fetching data from a remote source brings forth the necessity to manage a few more states – specifically, we need to handle loading, error, and data states. As illustrated in *Figure 10.7*, besides displaying a regular list, we also aim to manage scenarios where the data is not immediately accessible – either when it's still loading from a remote API or it isn't available.

Figure 10.7: Different statuses

Such states, while common, are crucial for the user experience. Take, for instance, a drop-down list featuring country names. It's a common feature, yet when we open the list, the names might still be loading, during which a loading indicator is displayed. Additionally, in situations where the downstream service is unavailable or other errors arise, an error message is presented instead.

When extending our existing code, it's crucial to deliberate on the additional states that will be introduced. Let's explore strategies to preserve simplicity as we integrate new features.

Maintaining simplicity in the Dropdown component

Incorporating remote data fetching has not complicated our Dropdown component, thanks to the abstracted logic in the useService and useDropdown Hooks. Our component code remains in its simplest form, effectively managing the fetching states and rendering the content based on the data received:

```
const Dropdown = () => {
    const { data, loading, error } = useService(fetchUsers);

    const {
```

```
      toggleDropdown,
      dropdownRef,
      isOpen,
      selectedItem,
      selectedIndex,
      updateSelectedItem,
      getAriaAttributes,
    } = useDropdown<Item>(data || []);

    const renderContent = useCallback(() => {
      if (loading) return <Loading />;
      if (error) return <Error />;
      if (data) {
        return (
          <DropdownMenu
            items={data}
            updateSelectedItem={updateSelectedItem}
            selectedIndex={selectedIndex}
          />
        );
      }
      return null;
    }, [loading, error, data, updateSelectedItem, selectedIndex]);

    return (
      <div
        className="dropdown"
        ref={dropdownRef as RefObject<HTMLDivElement>}
        {...getAriaAttributes()}
      >
        <Trigger
          onClick={toggleDropdown}
          text={selectedItem ? selectedItem.text : "Select an item..."}
        />
        {isOpen && renderContent()}
      </div>
    );
  };
```

In this updated Dropdown component, we utilize the useService Hook to manage the data fetching states and the useDropdown Hook to manage the drop-down-specific states and interactions. The renderContent function elegantly handles the rendering logic based on the fetching states, ensuring that the correct content is displayed, whether it's loading, an error, or data.

Through the separation of concerns and the use of Hooks, our Dropdown component remains clean and straightforward, showcasing the power of composable logic in React. Now, this pattern actually has a particular name in building UI – the Headless Component pattern. Let's look at it in more detail.

Introducing the Headless Component pattern

The **Headless Component pattern** unveils a robust avenue to cleanly segregate our JSX code from the underlying logic. While composing a declarative UI with JSX comes naturally, the real challenge lies in managing state. This is where headless components come into play, by shouldering all the state management intricacies and propelling us toward a new horizon of abstraction.

In essence, a **Headless Component** is a function or object that encapsulates logic but doesn't render anything itself. It leaves the rendering part to the consumer, thus offering a high degree of flexibility in how the UI is rendered. This pattern can be exceedingly useful when we have complex logic that we want to reuse across different visual representations.

As shown in the following code, the useDropdownLogic Hook has all the logic but no UI elements, while MyDropdown uses the headless component and only has to deal with rendering logic:

```
function useDropdownLogic() {
  // ... all the dropdown logic
  return {
    // ... exposed logic
  };
}

function MyDropdown() {
  const dropdownLogic = useDropdownLogic();
  return (
    // ... render the UI using the logic from dropdownLogic
  );
}
```

In a visual representation, the headless component acts as a thin interface layer. On one side, it interacts with JSX views, and on the other, it communicates with underlying data models. We touched upon data modeling in *Chapter 8* and will revisit it in *Chapter 11*. This pattern is particularly beneficial for individuals seeking solely the behavior or state management aspect of the UI, as it conveniently segregates it from the visual representation.

Let's see a visual illustration in *Figure 10.8*. You can think of your code as having a few layers – the JSX is on the top and is response for the look and feel part of the application, the headless component (Hooks in this case) manages all the stateful logic, and beneath them is the domain layer, which has the logic to handle data mapping and transformation (we will go into more detail on this in *Chapter 11* and *Chapter 12*).

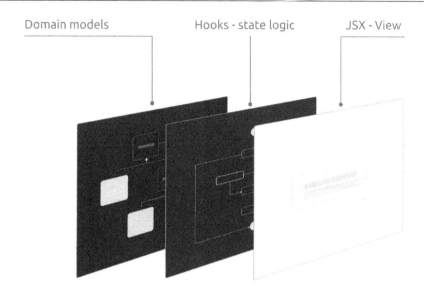

Using hooks as the headless component

Figure 10.8: The Headless Component pattern

In summarizing the Headless Component pattern, it's worth mentioning that although it can be realized through HOCs or render props, its implementation as a React Hook is more prevalent. Within the Headless Component pattern, all shareable logic is encapsulated, allowing for a seamless transition to other UIs without necessitating any modifications to the stateful logic.

The advantages and drawbacks of Headless Component pattern

The advantages of the Headless Component pattern include the following:

- **Reusability**: The logic encapsulated in Headless Component pattern can be reused across multiple components. This fosters **Don't Repeat Yourself** (**DRY**) principles in your codebase.

- **Separation of concerns**: By decoupling logic from rendering, headless components promote a clear separation of concerns, which is a cornerstone of maintainable code.

- **Flexibility**: They allow for varying UI implementations while sharing the same core logic, making it easier to adapt to different design requirements or frameworks.

The drawbacks of Headless Component pattern include the following:

- **Learning curve**: The pattern may introduce a learning curve for developers unfamiliar with it, potentially slowing down development initially.
- **Over-abstraction**: If not managed judiciously, the abstraction created by headless components can lead to a level of indirection that might make the code harder to follow.

Libraries and further learnings

The Headless Component pattern has been embraced by various libraries to facilitate the creation of accessible, customizable, and reusable components. Here are some notable libraries along with a brief description of each:

- **React Aria**: A library from Adobe that provides accessibility primitives and Hooks to build inclusive React applications. It offers a collection of Hooks to manage keyboard interactions, focus management, and Aria annotations, making it easier to create accessible UI components.
- **Headless UI**: A completely unstyled, fully accessible UI component library, designed to integrate beautifully with Tailwind CSS. It provides the behavior and accessibility foundation upon which you can build your own styled components.
- **React Table**: A headless utility for building fast and extendable tables and data grids for React. It provides a flexible Hook that allows you to create complex tables with ease, leaving the UI representation up to you.
- **Downshift**: A minimalist library to help you create accessible and customizable dropdowns, comboboxes, and so on. It handles all the logic while letting you define the rendering aspect.

These libraries embody the essence of the Headless Component pattern by encapsulating complex logic and behaviors, making it straightforward to create highly interactive and accessible UI components. While the provided example serves as a learning stepping stone, it's prudent to leverage these production-ready libraries to build robust, accessible, and customizable components in a real-world scenario.

This pattern not only educates us on managing complex logic and state but also encourages us to explore production-ready libraries that have honed the Headless Component approach, delivering robust, accessible, and customizable components for real-world use.

Summary

In this chapter, we delved into the world of HOCs and Hooks in React, exploring their utility in enhancing component logic while maintaining a clean, readable code base. Through the lens of creating an expandable panel and a drop-down list, we illustrated the composability of HOCs and the encapsulation of stateful logic that Hooks offer. Transitioning to a more intricate drop-down list, we introduced asynchronous data fetching, demonstrating how Hooks can simplify state management in data-loading scenarios.

We then transitioned into the realm of Headless Component, a powerful pattern that separates logic from the JSX code, providing a robust framework to manage state while leaving the UI representation to the developer. Through examples, we demonstrated how this separation facilitates the creation of reusable, accessible, and customizable components. The discussion was enriched with a review of notable libraries, such as React Table, Downshift, React Aria, and Headless UI, that embody the Headless Component pattern, providing ready-to-use solutions to build interactive and accessible UI components.

In the upcoming chapter, we'll implement the patterns we've discussed and delve into architectural strategies to enhance modularity. We'll also address the challenges posed by larger applications.

Part 4: Engaging in Practical Implementation

In the final part of this book, you will apply your accumulated knowledge in a hands-on manner by employing a layered architecture in React and journeying through an end-to-end project implementation. This part aims to encapsulate the essence of all the principles, patterns, and practices discussed throughout the book.

This part contains the following chapters:

11

Introducing Layered Architecture in React

As React applications grow in size and complexity, managing code efficiently becomes a challenge. The linear growth of features can lead to an exponential increase in complexity, making the code base difficult to understand, test, and maintain. Enter **Layered Architecture**, a design approach that's not just confined to backend systems but is equally beneficial for client-side applications.

Structuring your React application in a layered manner solves several key problems:

- **Separation of concerns**: Different layers handle different responsibilities, making the code base easier to navigate and understand

- **Reusability**: Business logic and data models become easily reusable across different parts of the application

- **Testability**: A layered architecture makes it simpler to write unit and integration tests, leading to a more robust application

- **Maintainability**: As the application scales, making changes or adding features becomes significantly easier when following a layered structure

In this chapter, we will explore the concept of layered architecture in the context of a React application, delving into the extraction of application concern layers, defining precise data models, and illustrating the use of strategy patterns. Through a step-by-step example, we'll see how to practically implement these concepts and why they are indispensable for large-scale applications.

In this chapter, we will cover the following topics:

- Understanding the evolution of a React application

- Enhancing the Code Oven application

- Implementing the ShoppingCart component

- Delving into layered architecture

Technical requirements

A GitHub repository has been created to host all the code we discuss in the book. For this chapter, you can find the recommended structure at `https://github.com/PacktPublishing/React-Anti-Patterns/tree/main/code/src/ch11`.

Understanding the evolution of a React application

Applications with different sizes require different strategies. For small or one-off projects, you might find that all logic is just written inside React components. You may see one or only a few components in total. The code looks pretty much like HTML, with only some variables or states used to make the page "dynamic," but overall, the code is easy to understand and change.

As the application grows, and more and more code is added to the code base, without a proper way to organize it, the code base will soon get into an unmaintainable state. This means that even adding small features will be time-consuming as developers need more time to read the code.

In this section, I'll list several different ways we can structure our React application to make sure our code always remains in a healthy state, making it effortless to add new features and easy to extend or fix existing defects. We'll start with a simple structure and gradually evolve it to handle scale problems. Let's have a quick review of the steps to build frontend applications that scale.

Single-component applications

To start, let's talk about the simplest possible approach to writing a React application – a single-component application.

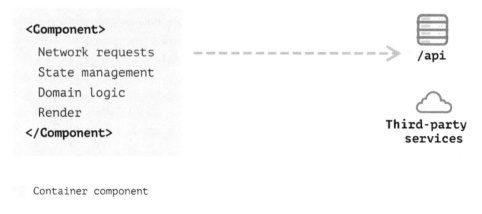

Figure 11.1: Single-component application

The mono-component undertakes a variety of tasks, ranging from fetching data from a remote server, managing its internal state, and handling domain logic, to rendering. This approach may be suitable for small applications with a single form or for those looking to understand the process of transitioning their application from another framework to React.

However, you'll soon realize that consolidating everything into a single component can make the code difficult to understand and manage. Everything being housed in one component can quickly become overwhelming, particularly when dealing with logic such as iterating over item lists to create individual components. This complexity highlights the need to decompose the mono-component into smaller, responsibility-focused components.

Multiple-component applications

Deciding to split the component into several components, with these structures reflecting what's happening on the resulting HTML, is a good idea and it helps you to focus on one component at a time.

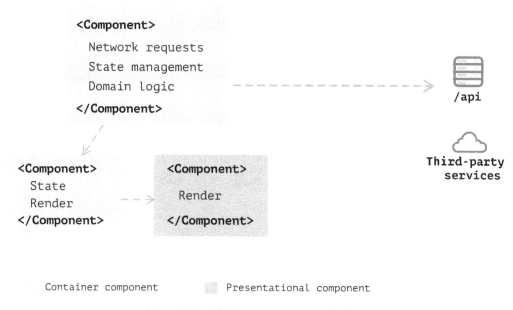

Figure 11.2: Multiple-component application

Essentially, you'll transition from a monolithic component to multiple components, each with a specific purpose. For example, one component may be dedicated to rendering a list, another to rendering a list item, and another solely for fetching data and passing data down to its children.

It's better to have clear responsibilities. However, as your application expands, responsibilities extend beyond the view layer to include tasks such as sending network requests, reshaping data for the view to consume, and collecting data to send back to the server. Additionally, there might be logic to transform data once it's fetched. Housing this calculation logic within views doesn't seem appropriate as it's not directly related to user interfaces. Moreover, some components may become cluttered with excessive internal states.

State management with Hooks

It's a better idea to split this logic into separate places. Luckily, in React, you can define your own Hooks. This is a great way to share this state and the logic whenever state changes.

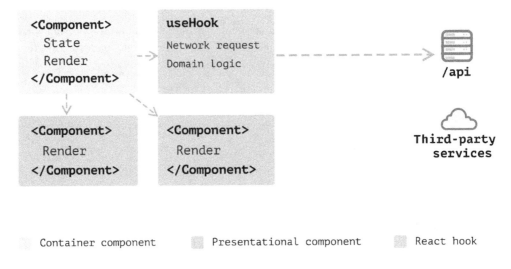

Figure 11.3: State management with Hooks

Now you have a bunch of elements extracted from components. You have a few pure presentational components, some reusable Hooks that make other components stateful, and some container components (for data fetching, for example).

At this stage, it's common to find calculations scattered across views, Hooks, or various utility functions. The lack of structure can make further modifications quite challenging and prone to errors. For instance, if you've fetched some data for rendering, but the data schema differs in views, you'll need to transform the data. However, the location for placing this transforming logic may not be clear.

Extracting business models

So, you've started to become aware that extracting this logic into yet another place can bring you many benefits. For example, with that split, the logic can be cohesive and independent of any views. Then, you extract a few domain objects.

These simple objects can handle data mapping (from one format to another), check nulls, and use fallback values as required. As the amount of these domain objects grows, you will find you need some inheritance or polymorphism to make things even cleaner. Thus you apply many design patterns you find helpful from other places to the frontend application:

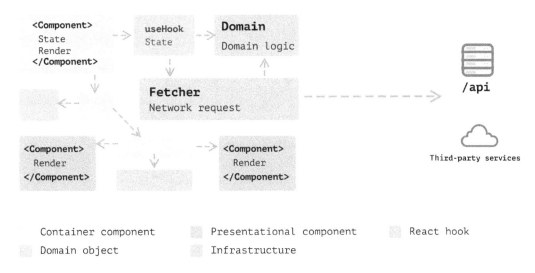

Figure 11.4: Extracting business models

Now, your code base has expanded with more elements, each having a clear boundary regarding their responsibilities. Hooks are employed for state management, while domain objects represent domain concepts, such as a user object encompassing an avatar, or a `PaymentMethod` object representing the details of a payment method.

As we segregate different elements from the views, the code base scales accordingly. Eventually, it reaches a point where we need to structure the application to respond to changes more efficiently.

Layered frontend application

As the application continues to evolve, certain patterns begin to emerge. You'll notice a collection of objects that don't belong to any user interface, and they remain indifferent to whether the underlying data originates from a remote service, local storage, or cache. Consequently, you'll want to segregate them into distinct layers. We'll need to introduce a better approach for these different parts of the application.

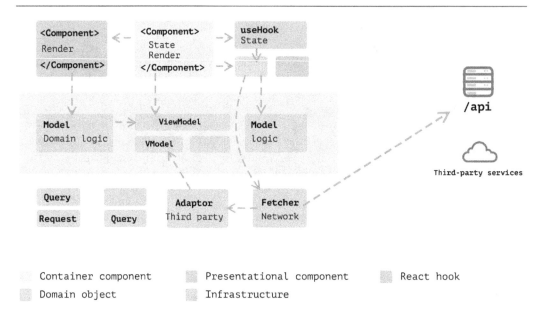

Figure 11.5: Layered frontend application

As illustrated in *Figure 11.5*, we can allocate different parts to separate folders, each distinctly and physically isolated from the others. This way, if there's a need to modify models, you won't need to navigate through the views folder, and vice versa.

That was a high-level overview of the evolution process, and you should have a taste of how you should structure your code or at least what the direction should be. In larger-scale applications, you'll likely encounter a variety of modules and functions, each tailored to different aspects of the app. This could include a request module for handling network requests, or adapters designed to interface with various data vendors, such as Google's login API or payment gateway clients.

However, there will be many details, such as how to define a model, how to access a model from views or Hooks, and so on. You need to consider this before applying the theory to your application.

> **Read more**
>
> You can find a detailed explanation of Presentation Domain Data Layering here: `https://martinfowler.com/bliki/PresentationDomainDataLayering.html`.

In the following sections, I'll guide you through expanding the Code Oven application we introduced in *Chapter 7*, to showcase essential patterns and design principles for large frontend applications.

Enhancing the Code Oven application

Recall that at the end of *Chapter 7*, we developed the basic structure of a pizza store application named Code Oven, leveraging test-driven development to establish a solid foundation for the app.

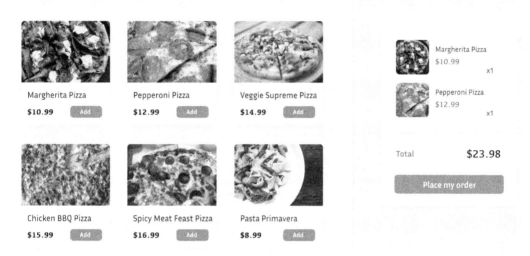

Figure 11.6: The Code Oven application

> **Note**
>
> Remember that we employed the design mockup as a guide, not to implement all the details exhaustively. The primary goal remains to illustrate how to refactor the code while preserving its maintainability.

Although we didn't delve much into feature implementation in that chapter, in this chapter, we'll extend our setup further. We'll explore how different architectural types can assist us in managing complexity.

As a refresher, by the end of *Chapter 7*, our structure looked like this:

```
export function PizzaShopApp() {
  const [cartItems, setCartItems] = useState<string[]>([]);

  const addItem = (item: string) => {
    setCartItems([...cartItems, item]);
  };

  return (
```

```
    <>
      <h1>The Code Oven</h1>
      <MenuList onAddMenuItem={addItem} />
      <ShoppingCart cartItems={cartItems} />
    </>
  );
}
```

And we assumed the data to be in this shape:

```
const pizzas = [
  "Margherita Pizza",
  "Pepperoni Pizza",
  "Veggie Supreme Pizza"
];
```

While this setup allows consumers to browse what the restaurant offers, it would be significantly more useful if we enabled online ordering. However, one immediate issue is that the pizzas lack prices and descriptions, crucial for supporting online orders. Descriptions are also vital as they list the ingredients, informing consumers of what's included.

Saying that, it's actually not practical to define menu data within the JavaScript code. Typically, we'd have a service hosting such data, providing more detailed information.

To show this, suppose we have data hosted on the `https://api.code-oven.com/menus` remote service, defined as follows:

```
[
  {
    "id": "p1",
    "name": "Margherita Pizza",
    "price": 10.99,
    "description": "Classic pizza with tomato sauce and mozzarella",
    "ingredients": ["Tomato Sauce", "Mozzarella Cheese", "Basil",
     "Olive Oil"],
    "allergyTags": ["Dairy"],
    "calories": 250,
    "category": "Pizza"
  },
  //...
]
```

To bridge the gap between our app and this data, we need to define a type for the remote data, like so:

```
type RemoteMenuItem = {
  id: string;
```

```
    name: string;
    price: number;
    description: string;
    ingredients: string[];
    allergyTags: string[];
    category: string;
    calories: number
}
```

Now, to integrate this remote menu data, we'll utilize useEffect to fetch the data, and then display the items once fetched. We'll make these changes within the MenuList component:

```
const MenuList = ({
  onAddMenuItem,
}: {
  onAddMenuItem: (item: string) => void;
}) => {
  const [menuItems, setMenuItems] = useState<string[]>([]);

  useEffect(() => {
    const fetchMenuItems = async () => {
      const result = await fetch('https://api.code-oven.com/menus');
      const menuItems = await result.json();

      setMenuItems(menuItems.map((item: RemoteMenuItem) => item.
        name));
    }

    fetchMenuItems();
  }, [])

  return (
    <div data-testid="menu-list">
      <ol>
        {menuItems.map((item) => (
          <li key={item}>
            {item}
            <button onClick={() => onAddMenuItem(item)}>Add</button>
          </li>
        ))}
      </ol>
    </div>
  );
};
```

Here, the MenuList component fetches a list of menu items from an external API upon the initial render and displays this list. Each item comes with an **Add** button, and clicking this button triggers the onAddMenuItem function, passed as a prop to MenuList, with the item name as its argument.

By mapping RemoteMenuItem to a string after fetching the data, we ensure our tests continue to pass.

Now, we aim to reveal the price and display the ingredients from the data to the UI components. However, given the potentially long list of ingredients, we'll only show the first three to avoid occupying too much screen space. Also, we want to use lowercase category and rename it to type.

Initially, we define a new type to better structure our data:

```
type MenuItem = {
  id: string;
  name: string;
  price: number;
  ingredients: string[];
  type: string;
}
```

Here, the MenuItem type includes the item's id, name, price, ingredients, and type properties.

Now, it's time to update our MenuList component to use this new type:

```
const MenuList = ({
  onAddMenuItem,
}: {
  onAddMenuItem: (item: string) => void;
}) => {
  const [menuItems, setMenuItems] = useState<MenuItem[]>([]);

  useEffect(() => {
    const fetchMenuItems = async () => {
      const result = await fetch("http://api.code-oven.com/menus");
      const menuItems = await result.json();

      setMenuItems(
        menuItems.map((item: RemoteMenuItem) => {
          return {
            id: item.id,
            name: item.name,
            price: item.price,
            type: item.category.toUpperCase(),
            ingredients: item.ingredients.slice(0, 3),
          };
        })
```

```
        );
      };

    fetchMenuItems();
  }, []);

  return (
    <div data-testid="menu-list">
      <ol>
        {menuItems.map((item) => (
          <li key={item.id}>
            <h3>{item.name}</h3>
            <span>${item.price}</span>
            <div>
              {item.ingredients.map((ingredient) => (
                <span>{ingredient}</span>
              ))}
            </div>
            <button onClick={() => onAddMenuItem(item.name)}>Add
              </button>
          </li>
        ))}
      </ol>
    </div>
  );
};
```

In the MenuList component, we've now made use of the MenuItem type in our useState Hook. The fetchMenuItems function, triggered within useEffect, reaches out to the API, fetches the menu items, and maps over them to transform the data into the desired MenuItem format. This transformation includes retaining only the first three items from the ingredients array for each item.

Each MenuItem component is then rendered as a list item within the component. We display the item's name, price, and iterate over the ingredients array to render each ingredient.

While the code is functional, there's a concern: we've intertwined network requests, data mapping, and rendering logic within a single component. It's a sound practice to separate view-related code from non-view code, ensuring cleaner, more maintainable code.

Refactoring the MenuList through a custom Hook

We're no strangers to using custom Hooks for data fetching – it's a practice that enhances readability and organizes logic neatly. In our scenario, extracting the menuItems state and the fetching logic into a separate Hook will declutter the MenuList component.

So, let's create a Hook named `useMenuItems`:

```
const useMenuItems = () => {
  const [menuItems, setMenuItems] = useState<MenuItem[]>([]);

  useEffect(() => {
    const fetchMenuItems = async () => {
      const result = await fetch(
        "https://api.code-oven.com/menus"
      );
      const menuItems = await result.json();

      setMenuItems(
        menuItems.map((item: RemoteMenuItem) => {
          // ... transform RemoteMenuItem to MenuItem
        })
      );
    };

    fetchMenuItems();
  }, []);

  return { menuItems };
};
```

Within the `useMenuItems` Hook, we initialize the `menuItems` state with an empty array. When the Hook mounts, it triggers the `fetchMenuItems` function that fetches data from the specified URL. Following the fetch, a mapping operation is performed to convert each `RemoteMenuItem` object to a `MenuItem` object. The transformation details are omitted here, but it's where we adapt the fetched data to the desired format. Subsequently, the transformed menu items are set to the `menuItems` state.

Now, in our `MenuList` component, we can simply call `useMenuItems` to obtain the `menuItems` array:

```
const MenuList = ({
  onAddMenuItem,
}: {
  onAddMenuItem: (item: string) => void;
}) => {
  const { menuItems } = useMenuItems();
  //...
}
```

This refactoring is quite beneficial, redirecting `MenuList` back to a streamlined state and reinstating its single responsibility. However, when we shift our focus to the `useMenuItems` Hook, particularly the data mapping segment, a few operations occur. It fetches data and trims off some unused fields such as `description` and `calories` from the remote data. It also encapsulates the logic to retain only the first three ingredients. Ideally, we'd like to centralize this transformation logic into a common location, ensuring a tidy and manageable code structure.

Transitioning to a class-based model

As touched upon in *Chapter 8*, employing the **Anti-Corruption Layer** (**ACL**) pattern can be a strategic move for managing our data effectively. We'll employ classes in TypeScript to encapsulate data and logic in a unified location, referred to as a model. A significant step in this direction would be transitioning our `MenuItem` type definition into a class, hence centralizing all mapping logic within this class. This setup will serve as a dedicated hub for any future data shape alterations and related logic.

Transitioning `MenuItem` from a type to a class is straightforward. We require a constructor to accept `RemoteMenuItem` and some getter functions to access the data:

```
export class MenuItem {
  private readonly _id: string;
  private readonly _name: string;
  private readonly _type: string;
  private readonly _price: number;
  private readonly _ingredients: string[];

  constructor(item: RemoteMenuItem) {
    this._id = item.id;
    this._name = item.name;
    this._price = item.price;
    this._type = item.category;
    this._ingredients = item.ingredients;
  }

  // ... getter functions for id, name, price just returns the private
        fields

  get type() {
    return this._type.toLowerCase();
  }

  get ingredients() {
    return this._ingredients.slice(0, 3);
  }
}
```

In the `MenuItem` class, we define private `readonly` properties for `id`, `name`, `type`, `price`, and `ingredients`. The constructor initializes these properties using values from a `RemoteMenuItem` object passed to it. We then have getter methods for each property to provide read-only access to their values. Particularly, the `ingredients` getter returns only the first three items from the `ingredients` array.

Though, at a glance, this setup seems to have more code compared to a simple type definition, it effectively encapsulates the data and exposes it in a controlled manner. This aligns with the principles of immutability and encapsulation. The class structure's beauty is its capability to house behaviors – in our case, the slicing logic for ingredients is tucked neatly within the class.

With this new class in place, our `useMenuItems` Hook becomes more streamlined:

```
export const useMenuItems = () => {
  //...

  useEffect(() => {
    const fetchMenuItems = async () => {
      //...
      setMenuItems(
        menuItems.map((item: RemoteMenuItem) => {
          return new MenuItem(item);
        })
      );
    };

    fetchMenuItems();
  }, []);

  return { menuItems };
};
```

Now, the `useMenuItems` Hook merely maps over the fetched menu items, creating a new instance of `MenuItem` for each, which significantly tidies up the transformation logic previously housed within the Hook.

The benefits of a class-based model

Transitioning to a class-based model from a simple type comes with a set of advantages that could serve our application well in the long run:

- **Encapsulation**: A class brings related properties and methods under one roof, thus promoting clear structure and organization. It also restricts direct data access, fostering better control and data integrity.

- **Method behavior**: For complex behaviors or operations associated with a menu item, a class provides a structured platform to define these methods, whether they relate to data manipulation or other business logic.

- **Inheritance and polymorphism**: In the case of a hierarchy or polymorphic behavior among menu items, a class structure is indispensable. It allows different menu item types to inherit from a common base class, overriding or extending behavior as needed.

- **Consistent interface**: Classes ensure a consistent interface to the data, which is invaluable when multiple application parts interact with menu items.

- **Read-only properties**: Classes enable the definition of read-only properties, thereby controlling data mutation. This is a crucial aspect of maintaining data integrity and working with immutable data structures.

Now, as we transition into expanding our application's functionality with a shopping cart, it's crucial to approach this new section with the lessons learned from our data modeling exercise. This will ensure a structured and effective implementation, paving the way for a user-friendly online ordering experience.

Implementing the ShoppingCart component

As we venture into the implementation of the ShoppingCart component, we will aim to provide a seamless interface for users to review their selected items before proceeding to the checkout. Besides displaying the items, we also intend to reward our customers with some appealing discount policies.

In *Chapter 7*, we defined a rudimentary ShoppingCart component, as shown here:

```
export const ShoppingCart = ({ cartItems }: { cartItems: string[] })
=> {
  return (
    <div data-testid="shopping-cart">
      <ol>
        {cartItems.map((item) => (
          <li key={item}>{item}</li>
        ))}
      </ol>
      <button disabled={cartItems.length === 0}>Place My Order
        </button>
    </div>
  );
};
```

The ShoppingCart component accepts a cartItems prop, which is an array of strings. It returns a div tag containing an ordered list (<ol>), where each item in the cartItems array is rendered as a list item (<li>). Below the list, a **Place My Order** button is rendered, which is disabled if the cartItems array is empty.

However, to enhance the user experience, it's crucial to display the price for each item and the total amount beneath the item list, yet above the **Place My Order** button. Here's how we can augment our component to fulfill these requirements:

```
export const ShoppingCart = ({ cartItems }: { cartItems: MenuItem[] })
=> {
  const totalPrice = cartItems.reduce((acc, item) => (acc += item.
price), 0);

  return (
    <div data-testid="shopping-cart" className="shopping-cart">
      <ol>
        {cartItems.map((item) => (
          <li key={item.id}>
            <h3>{item.name}</h3>
            <span>${item.price}</span>
          </li>
        ))}
      </ol>
      <div>Total: ${totalPrice}</div>
      <button disabled={cartItems.length === 0}>Place My Order
      </button>
    </div>
  );
};
```

The ShoppingCart component is now equipped to accept a cartItems prop, which comprises an array of MenuItem objects (instead of a simple string). To compute the total price of items in the cart, we employ the reduce method. This method iterates over each item, accumulating their prices to present a total. The component then returns a JSX markup that renders a list of cart items, each displaying its name and price.

This revamped ShoppingCart component not only enhances the clarity of the order for users but also lays down a foundation for introducing discount policies, which we can explore as we continue refining our application.

Applying discounts to Items

Let's assume we have different discount policies for different types of menu items. For instance, pizzas with more than three toppings receive a 10 percent discount, while large pasta dishes enjoy a 15 percent discount.

To incorporate this, we initially attempt to extend the `MenuItem` class with a new field called `calculateDiscount`:

```
export class MenuItem {
  //... the private fields

  constructor(item: RemoteMenuItem) {
    //... assignment
  }

  get calculateDiscount() {
    return this.type === 'pizza' && this.toppings >= 3 ? this.price *
    0.1 : 0;
  }
}
```

However, we encounter a problem – since pasta dishes don't have toppings, this leads to a type error.

To resolve this, we first extract an interface named `IMenuItem`, and then have `PizzaMenuItem` and `PastaMenuItem` classes implement this interface:

```
export interface IMenuItem {
  id: string;
  name: string;
  type: string;
  price: number;
  ingredients: string[];

  calculateDiscount(): number;
}
```

Next, we define an abstract class to implement the interface, allowing `PizzaMenuItem` and `PastaMenuItem` to extend the abstract class respectively:

```
export abstract class AbstractMenuItem implements IMenuItem {
  private readonly _id: string;
  private readonly _name: string;
  private readonly _price: number;
```

```
private readonly _ingredients: string[];

protected constructor(item: RemoteMenuItem) {
  this._id = item.id;
  this._name = item.name;
  this._price = item.price;
  this._ingredients = item.ingredients;
}

static from(item: IMenuItem): RemoteMenuItem {
  return {
    id: item.id,
    name: item.name,
    price: item.price,
    category: item.type,
    ingredients: item.ingredients,
  };
}

//... the getter functions

abstract calculateDiscount(): number;
}
```

In the `AbstractMenuItem` class, we introduced a static `from` method. This method takes an `IMenuItem` instance and transforms it into a `RemoteMenuItem` instance, preserving the necessary fields for our application.

The `calculateDiscount` method is declared as an abstract method, requiring its child classes to implement the actual discount calculation.

> **Note**
>
> An **abstract class** serves as a base class for other classes and cannot be instantiated on its own. It's a way to define a common interface and/or implementation for a set of derived classes. Abstract classes often contain abstract methods, which are declared without implementations, leaving it to derived classes to provide specific implementations. By doing so, abstract classes enable a common structure while ensuring that certain methods are implemented in derived classes, promoting a consistent behavior across all derived types. They are a key feature in object-oriented programming, supporting polymorphism and encapsulation.

We need to override and put the actual `calculateDiscount` logic in sub-classes. For `PizzaMenuItem`, it simply extends `AbstractMenuItem` and implements `calculateDiscount`:

```
export class PizzaMenuItem extends AbstractMenuItem {
  private readonly toppings: number;

  constructor(item: RemoteMenuItem, toppings: number) {
    super(item);
    this.toppings = toppings;
  }

  calculateDiscount(): number {
    return this.toppings >= 3 ? this.price * 0.1 : 0;
  }
}
```

The `PizzaMenuItem` class extends `AbstractMenuItem`, inheriting its properties and methods. It defines a private `readonly` property, `toppings`, to hold the number of toppings. In the constructor, it takes two arguments: `RemoteMenuItem` and `toppings` (which indicates the number of toppings). It calls the constructor of `AbstractMenuItem` with `item` using `super(item)` and initializes `this.toppings` with the passed-in `toppings` argument.

The `calculateDiscount` method is implemented to return a 10% discount if the number of toppings is 3 or more. This method overrides the abstract `calculateDiscount` method from `AbstractMenuItem`.

Similarly, we can create a `PastaMenuItem` class like so:

```
export class PastaItem extends AbstractMenuItem {
  private readonly servingSize: string;

  constructor(item: RemoteMenuItem, servingSize: string) {
    super(item);
    this.servingSize = servingSize;
  }

  calculateDiscount(): number {
    return this.servingSize === "large" ? this.price * 0.15 : 0;
  }
}
```

The relationship of these classes can be visualized as in *Figure 11.7*:

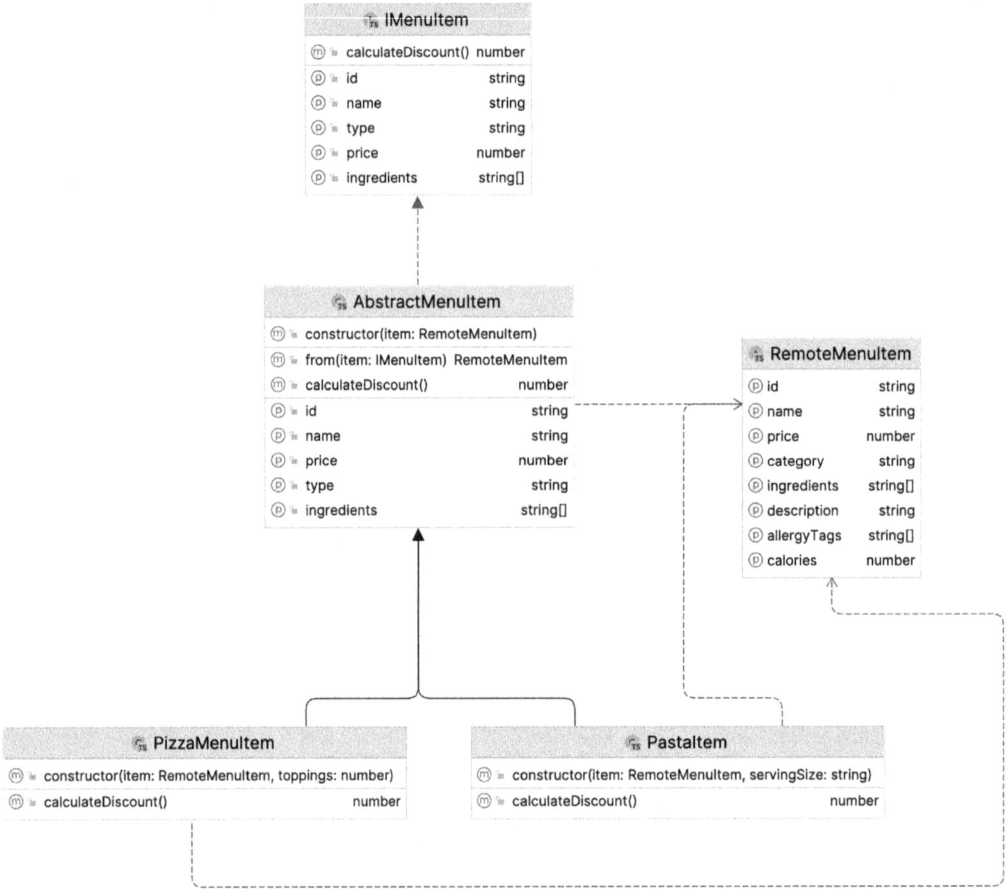

Figure 11.7: Model classes

The `AbstractMenuItem` abstract class implements the `IMenuItem` interface and uses `RemoteMenuItem`. Both `PizzaItem` and `PastaItem` are extending `AbstractMenuItem` and have their own logic for calculating the discount.

Next, in the `MenuList` component, when adding items to the shopping cart, we create instances of the right class based on the item type:

```
export const MenuList = ({}) => {
  //...
  const [toppings, setToppings] = useState([]);
  const [size, setSize] = useState<string>("small");

  const handleAddMenuItem = (item: IMenuItem) => {
```

```
    const remoteItem = AbstractMenuItem.from(item);
    if (item.type === "pizza") {
      onAddMenuItem(new PizzaMenuItem(remoteItem, toppings.length));
    } else if (item.type === "pasta") {
      onAddMenuItem(new PastaItem(remoteItem, size));
    } else {
      onAddMenuItem(item);
    }
  };

  return (
    //...
  );
};
```

The `handleAddMenuItem` function transforms the `IMenuItem` object item into a `RemoteMenuItem` object using the `AbstractMenuItem.from(item)` method. Following this, it checks the type property of the item to determine whether it's a pizza or pasta. If it's a pizza, a new `PizzaMenuItem` instance is created using `remoteItem` and the selected number of toppings, and this new item is added to the cart via the `onAddMenuItem` function. If the item is neither a pizza nor pasta, the original item is added to the cart directly through the `onAddMenuItem` function.

Lastly, within the `ShoppingCart` component, we calculate the total discount value similarly to how we calculated the total price, and use it for rendering:

```
export const ShoppingCart = ({ cartItems }: { cartItems: IMenuItem[]
}) => {
  const totalPrice = cartItems.reduce((acc, item) => (acc += item.
price), 0);
  const totalDiscount = cartItems.reduce(
    (acc, item) => (acc += item.calculateDiscount()),
    0
  );

  return (
    <div data-testid="shopping-cart">
      {/* rendering the list */}
      <div>Total Discount: ${totalDiscount}</div>
      <div>Total: ${totalPrice - totalDiscount}</div>
      <button disabled={cartItems.length === 0}>Place My Order
      </button>
    </div>
  );
};
```

The `ShoppingCart` component calculates `totalPrice` by iterating over the `cartItems` array and summing up the price of each item. Similarly, it calculates `totalDiscount` by summing up the discounts for each item, obtained by calling the `calculateDiscount()` method on each item. In the returned JSX, it renders a list and displays `totalDiscount` and the final total price (which is `totalPrice` minus `totalDiscount`) below the list.

At this juncture, the function operates effectively. Nonetheless, there are several factors to contemplate – the discount is currently specified on each product: for instance, pizza has its own discount rule while pasta has its own. What would be our approach if we need to implement a store-wide discount, such as a discount for a public holiday?

Exploring the Strategy pattern

Suppose it's a bustling Friday night, and we wish to offer a special discount on all pizzas and drinks. However, we don't intend to apply additional discounts on items already discounted — for instance, a pizza with four toppings should only receive this specific special discount.

Handling such arbitrary discounts can be complex, necessitating a decoupling of the calculation logic from the item type. Moreover, we'd like the flexibility to remove these discounts after Friday or after a certain period.

We can use a design pattern called the **Strategy pattern** to achieve flexibility here. The Strategy pattern is a behavioral design pattern that enables selecting an algorithm's implementation at runtime. It encapsulates a family of algorithms and makes them interchangeable, allowing the client to choose the most suitable one without modifying the code.

We'll extract the logic into a separate entity, defining a strategy interface as follows:

```
export interface IDiscountStrategy {
  calculate(price: number): number;
}
```

This interface provides a blueprint for different discount strategies. For example, we could have a strategy with no discount:

```
class NoDiscountStrategy implements IDiscountStrategy {
  calculate(price: number): number {
    return 0;
  }
}
```

The `NoDiscountStrategy` class implements the `IDiscountStrategy` interface with a `calculate` method that takes a price as input and returns zero, meaning no discount is applied.

And for `SpecialDiscountStrategy` component, a special discount strategy offering a 15% discount will be applied:

```
class SpecialDiscountStrategy implements IDiscountStrategy {
  calculate(price: number): number {
    return price * 0.15;
  }
}
```

To utilize these strategies, we need to slightly modify the `IMenuItem` interface:

```
export interface IMenuItem {
  // ... other fields
  discountStrategy: IDiscountStrategy;
}
```

We added `discountStrategy` with type `IDiscountStrategy` in the `IMenuItem` interface. And because we moved the logic of calculating discount into strategy, we don't need the `calculateDiscount` abstract method in `AbstractMenuItem` anymore and the class will no longer remain abstract, so we renamed it to `BaseMenuItem` instead. Instead, it will incorporate a setter for the discount strategy and implement the discount calculation:

```
export class BaseMenuItem implements IMenuItem {
  // ... other fields
  private _discountStrategy: IDiscountStrategy;

  constructor(item: RemoteMenuItem) {
    // ... other fields
    this._discountStrategy = new NoDiscountStrategy();
  }

  // ... other getters

  set discountStrategy(strategy: IDiscountStrategy) {
    this._discountStrategy = strategy;
  }

  calculateDiscount() {
    return this._discountStrategy.calculate(this.price);
  }
}
```

The `BaseMenuItem` class now implements the `IMenuItem` interface and encapsulates a discount strategy, initially set to `NoDiscountStrategy`. It defines a setter to update the discount strategy, and a `calculateDiscount` method, which delegates the discount calculation to the encapsulated discount strategy's `calculate` method, passing the item's price as an argument.

Figure 11.8 should now give you a much clearer idea of what the relationships are:

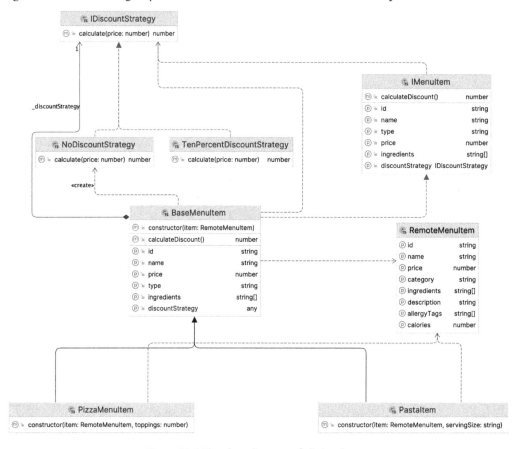

Figure 11.8: The class diagram of all the classes

As observed, `BaseMenuItem` implements the `IMenuItem` interface and utilizes `IDiscountStrategy`. There are multiple implementations of the `IDiscountStrategy` interface for specific discount algorithms, and several classes extend the `BaseMenuItem` class.

Note that the `RemoteMenuItem` type is used by all the classes implementing the `IMenuItem` interface.

Now, when we need to apply a particular strategy, it can be done effortlessly, like so:

```
export const MenuList = ({
  onAddMenuItem,
}: {
  onAddMenuItem: (item: IMenuItem) => void;
}) => {
  // ...
  const handleAddMenuItem = (item: IMenuItem) => {
    if (isTodayFriday()) {
      item.discountStrategy = new SpecialDiscountStrategy();
    }

    onAddMenuItem(item);
  };
```

In the `MenuList` component, the `handleAddMenuItem` function checks if today is Friday using the `isTodayFriday` function. If it is, it sets `discountStrategy` of the item to a new instance of `SpecialDiscountStrategy` before passing the item to the `onAddMenuItem` function, which is received as a prop. This way, a special discount is applied to the menu item on Fridays.

This setup grants us the desired flexibility. For instance, in the `handleAddMenuItem` function, depending on whether it's Friday or the item is a pizza, we can easily switch the discount strategy:

```
const handleAddMenuItem = (item: IMenuItem) => {
  if (isTodayFriday()) {
    item.discountStrategy = new SpecialDiscountStrategy();
  }

  if(item.type === 'pizza') {
    item.discountStrategy = new PizzaDiscountStrategy();
  }

  onAddMenuItem(item);
};
```

In this `handleAddMenuItem` function, depending on certain conditions, a different discount strategy is applied to the item before it's passed to the `onAddMenuItem` function. Initially, it checks if today is Friday using `isTodayFriday()` and, if true, it assigns a new instance of `SpecialDiscountStrategy` to `item.discountStrategy`. However, if the item is of type `pizza`, irrespective of the day, it overwrites `item.discountStrategy` with a new instance of `PizzaDiscountStrategy`.

This approach keeps our discount logic modular and easy to adjust, catering to different scenarios with minimal code modification. As we're extracting new logic components – Hooks, data models, domain logic (discount strategies), and views – out of the application code, it's evolving into a layered frontend application.

Delving into layered architecture

Our application has transitioned wonderfully to a more robust state, with clear, understandable, and modifiable logic, which is now also more test-friendly.

A further refinement I envision is relocating the logic present in ShoppingCart to a custom Hook. We can do this like so:

```
export const useShoppingCart = (items: IMenuItem[]) => {
  const totalPrice = useMemo(
    () => items.reduce((acc, item) => (acc += item.price), 0),
    [items]
  );

  const totalDiscount = useMemo(
    () => items.reduce((acc, item) => (acc += item.
     calculateDiscount()), 0),
    [items]
  );

  return {
    totalPrice,
    totalDiscount,
  };
};
```

The useShoppingCart Hook accepts an array of IMenuItem objects and computes two values – totalPrice and totalDiscount:

- totalPrice is calculated by reducing the items, summing up their price property
- totalDiscount is calculated by reducing the items, summing up the discount for each item obtained by calling item.calculateDiscount()

Both calculations are wrapped in useMemo to ensure they are only recomputed when the items array changes.

With this modification, `ShoppingCart` becomes elegantly simplified and can easily utilize these values:

```
export const ShoppingCart = ({ cartItems }: { cartItems: IMenuItem[]
}) => {
  const { totalPrice, totalDiscount } = useShoppingCart(cartItems);

  return (
    {/* JSX for the rendering logic */}
  );
};
```

An alternative approach would be employing the context and `useReducer` Hook to manage all logic within context and Hooks, however, since we explored that in *Chapter 8*, I'll leave further exploration to you (you can use both code examples provided in *Chapter 8* and this chapter and try to use `context` and `useReducer` to simplify `ShoppingCart`).

The layered structure of the application

We've delved into organizing components and models into separate files; it's equally vital to continue refining our project structure. Functions with distinct responsibilities should reside in different folders, streamlining navigation through the application and saving time. Our application now exhibits a fresh structural anatomy:

```
src
├── App.tsx
├── hooks
│   ├── useMenuItems.ts
│   └── useShoppingCart.ts
├── models
│   ├── BaseMenuItem.ts
│   ├── IMenuItem.ts
│   ├── PastaItem.ts
│   ├── PizzaMenuItem.ts
│   ├── RemoteMenuItem.ts
│   └── strategy
│       ├── IDiscountStrategy.ts
│       ├── NoDiscountStrategy.ts
│       ├── SpecialDiscountStrategy.ts
│       └── TenPercentageDiscountStrategy.ts
└── views
    ├── MenuList.tsx
    └── ShoppingCart.tsx
```

And that's how the layers formed. Within the view layer, we have primarily pure TSX rendering straightforward tags. These views leverage Hooks for state and side effect management. Meanwhile, in the model layer, model objects encompass business logic, algorithms for toggling between different discount strategies, and data shape transformations, among other functionalities. This structure promotes separation of concerns, making the code organized, reusable, and easier to maintain.

It's important to note the one-directional link here; the upper layer accesses the lower layer, but not vice versa. TSX uses Hooks for state management, and Hooks employ models for calculations. However, we can't use JSX or Hooks in the model layer. This layering technique facilitates change or replacement in the underlying layers without impacting the upper layers, promoting a clean and maintainable structure.

In our Code Oven application, as illustrated in *Figure 11.9*, the layout features a menu items list on the left and a shopping cart on the right. Within the shopping cart, each item displays detailed discount and price information on the page.

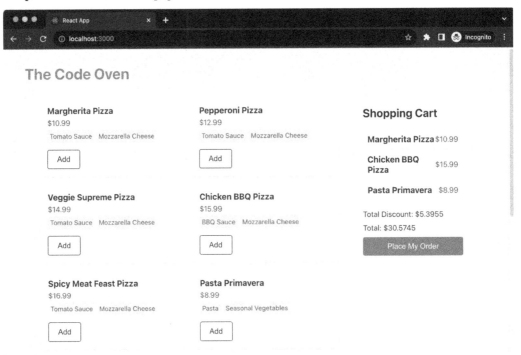

Figure 11.9: Final look and feel of the application

Advantages of layered architecture

The layered architecture confers numerous benefits:

- **Enhanced maintainability**: The division of a component into distinct segments facilitates easier identification and rectification of defects in specific code sections, thus minimizing time spent and reducing the likelihood of engendering new bugs during modifications.

- **Increased modularity**: This architecture is inherently more modular, promoting code reuse and simplifying the addition of new features. Even within each layer, such as views, the code tends to be more composable.

- **Enhanced readability**: The logic within the code becomes significantly more understandable and navigable, an asset not only for the original developer but also for others who may interact with the code base. This clarity is central to effecting changes in the code.

- **Improved scalability**: The reduced complexity within each module renders the application more scalable, making it easier to introduce new features or alterations without impacting the entire system—a critical advantage for large, complex applications projected to evolve over time.

- **Tech-stack migration**: Albeit unlikely in most projects, should the need arise, the view layer can be replaced without altering the underlying models and logic, thanks to the encapsulation of domain logic in pure JavaScript (or TypeScript) code, oblivious to the views' existence.

Summary

In this chapter, we implemented layered architecture in our application, enhancing its maintainability, modularity, readability, scalability, and potential for tech-stack migration. By segregating logic, refining the `ShoppingCart` component through a custom Hook, and organizing the application into distinct layers, we've significantly bolstered the code's structure and ease of management. This architectural approach not only streamlines the current code base but also lays a solid foundation for future expansions and refinements.

In the next chapter, we'll look at the end-to-end journey of implementing an application from scratch, using the user acceptance test-driven development approach, doing refactoring, cleaning up along the way, and always keeping our code as clean as we can.

12

Implementing an End-To-End Project

In the previous chapters, we delved into a variety of topics, including testing, **test-driven development** (**TDD**), design patterns, and design principles. These concepts are invaluable as they pave the way toward a more resilient and maintainable codebase. Now, I'd like to embark on a journey of constructing an application from the ground up, applying the knowledge we've acquired to tackle an end-to-end scenario.

The aim is to illustrate how we can dissect requirements into actionable tasks, and subsequently test and implement them. We'll also explore how to stub network requests, thereby eliminating dependencies on remote systems during development, and how to confidently refactor code without fear of breaking existing functionality.

We'll venture into building a functional weather application from scratch, interfacing with a genuine weather API server to fetch and display a list of weather data. Along the way, we'll implement accessibility features such as keyboard interactions, revisit the **Anti-Corruption Layer** (**ACL**) and single responsibility principle, and much more.

The overarching goal is to showcase the end-to-end process of crafting a functioning software solution, all while keeping the code in a maintainable, understandable, and extensible state.

The following topics will be covered:

- Reviewing the requirements for the weather application
- Crafting our initial acceptance test
- Implementing the City Search feature
- Implementing an ACL
- Implementing an Add to Favorite feature
- Fetching previous weather data when the application relaunches

Technical requirements

A GitHub repository has been created to host all the code we'll discuss in this book. For this chapter, you can find the recommended structure at `https://github.com/PacktPublishing/React-Anti-Patterns/tree/main/code/src/ch12`.

We need to complete a few more steps before we proceed. Please follow the next section to set up the necessary API keys.

Getting the OpenWeatherMap API key

To utilize OpenWeatherMap, you'll need to create an account at `https://openweathermap.org/`. Although various plans are available based on usage, the free plan suffices for our purposes. After registering, navigate to **My API keys** to find your API key, as displayed in *Figure 12.1*:

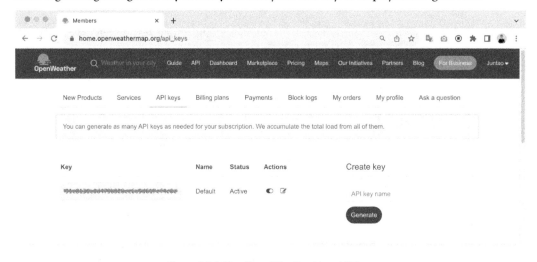

Figure 12.1: The OpenWeatherMap API key

Keep a copy of this key handy as we'll use it to make calls to the weather API so that we can fetch data.

Preparing the project's code base

If you prefer to follow along with me, you will need to install a few packages before we start. However, if you want to see the final results, they're already in the repository mentioned earlier. I recommend that you follow along to see how we evolve our application into the final state.

To kick things off, we'll create a new React app using the following commands:

```
npx create-react-app weather-app --template typescript
cd weather-app
yarn add cypress jest-fetch-mock -D
yarn install
```

These commands are used to set up a new React project with TypeScript and Cypress:

- `npx create-react-app weather-app --template typescript`: This command utilizes `npx` to run the `create-react-app` utility, which scaffolds out a new React application in a directory named `weather-app`. The `--template typescript` option specifies that this project should be configured to use TypeScript.

- `yarn add cypress jest-fetch-mock -D`: This command installs Cypress, a testing framework, as a development dependency in the project, and `jest-fetch-mock`, for mocking the `fetch` function in jest tests. The `-D` flag indicates that this is a development dependency, meaning it's not required for the production version of the application.

- `yarn install`: This command installs all the dependencies listed in the `package.json` file of the project, ensuring that all the necessary libraries and tools are available.

Finally, we can start the template application by running the following command:

```
yarn start
```

This will launch the application on port 3000. You can leave the application running on 3000 open and open another terminal window for running tests.

Reviewing the requirements for the weather application

Our envisioned weather application is designed to be a fully functional platform with the following capabilities:

- Enables users to search for cities of interest, be it their hometown, current residence, or a future travel destination

- Allows users to add cities to a favorite list, with the selection persisting locally for easy access during future visits

- Supports the addition of multiple cities to the user's list

- Ensures the site is thoroughly navigable via keyboard, facilitating ease of access for all users

The result will resemble what's illustrated in *Figure 12.2*:

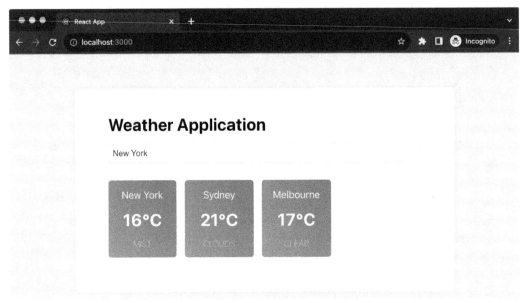

Figure 12.2: The weather application

While it's not an overly complex application, it encompasses several intriguing elements. For instance, we'll navigate through the hurdles of applying TDD in a UI application, testing Hooks, and making informed decisions on when to employ user acceptance tests versus lower-level tests.

We will commence with an initial acceptance test to ensure the application operates end-to-end, albeit it is merely verifying a single text element's appearance.

Crafting our initial acceptance test

Chapter 7 familiarized us with the notion of starting with an acceptance test – a test that's approached from an end user's standpoint, as opposed to a developer's perspective. Essentially, we aim for our test to validate aspects a user would perceive or interact with on the web page, rather than technicalities such as function calls or class initializations.

Within the folder you created in the *Technical requirements* section (that is, `weather-app`), create a Cypress test within `cypress/e2e/weather.spec.cy.ts`:

```
describe('weather application', () => {
  it('displays the application title', () => {
    cy.visit('http://localhost:3000/');
    cy.contains('Weather Application');
  });
});
```

In this code snippet, we defined a test suite named `weather application`. It uses the describe function in the Cypress testing framework. This test case comprises two main actions: navigating to the local development server at `http://localhost:3000/` using `cy.visit`, and then checking the page to ensure it contains the `Weather Application` text using `cy.contains`. If `Weather Application` is found on the page, the test will pass; if not, it will fail.

Executing the test using `npx cypress run` will, as expected, yield an error on the console due to our yet unmodified app:

```
1) weather application
      displays the application title:
    AssertionError: Timed out retrying after 4000ms: Expected to find
      content: 'Weather Application' but never did.
    at Context.eval (webpack://tdd-weather/./cypress/e2e/weather.
      spec.cy.ts:4:7)
```

This error reveals that it was anticipating the `Weather Application` text but didn't locate it within the default 4-second timeout specified by Cypress. To rectify this, we'll need to tweak `App.tsx` so that it includes this text.

After clearing the current content in `App.tsx` (generated by `create-react-app`), we'll insert a simple `h1` tag to display the text:

```
import React from 'react';

function App() {
  return (
    <div className="App">
      <h1>Weather Application</h1>
    </div>
  );
}
```

This code defines a functional component named App in React, which renders a `div` element containing an `h1` element with the `Weather Application` text. With this heading defined, our Cypress test will pass.

Now, let's move on to the first meaningful feature – allowing users to search by a city name.

Implementing a City Search feature

Let's commence the development of our first feature – City Search. Users will be able to enter a city name into a search box, which triggers a request to a remote server. Upon receiving the data, we'll render it into a list for user selection. Throughout this chapter, we'll utilize the OpenWeatherMap API for city searches as well as retrieving weather information.

Introducing the OpenWeatherMap API

OpenWeatherMap is a service that offers global weather data via an API, allowing users to access current, forecasted, and historical weather data for any location worldwide. It's a popular choice among developers for embedding real-time weather updates into apps and websites.

We're going to use two APIs in our weather application – one for searching the city by name and another for getting the actual real-time weather. To use the API, you'll need the API key you received when following the instructions in the *Technical requirements* section.

You can try sending the request to OpenWeatherMap either in your browser or with a command-line tool such as `curl` or `http` (from `https://httpie.io/`):

```
http https://api.openweathermap.org/geo/1.0/direct?q="Melbourne"&limit
=5&appid=<your-app-key>
```

This line utilizes the `http` command to send an HTTP request to the OpenWeatherMap API, specifically to its geocoding endpoint (`geo/1.0/direct`), looking up cities named `Melbourne`, with a limit of 5 results. The `appid` (as specified in the preceding URL) parameter is where you need to insert *your* OpenWeatherMap API key to authenticate the request.

So, the command fetches basic geocoding information about cities named Melbourne, which can later be used to get weather data for those locations. You will get the result in JSON format, like so:

```
[
    {
        "country": "AU",
        "lat": -37.8142176,
        "local_names": {},
        "lon": 144.9631608,
        "name": "Melbourne",
        "state": "Victoria"
    },
    {
        "country": "US",
        "lat": 28.106471,
        "local_names": {
        },
        "lon": -80.6371513,
        "name": "Melbourne",
        "state": "Florida"
    }
]
```

Be aware that the OpenWeatherMap free plan comes with a rate limit, restricting us to a maximum of 60 requests per minute and 1,000,000 requests per month. While these limits may seem high, the number of requests can accumulate quickly during development through testing and debugging. To conserve our request allowance, we'll avoid making requests to the real server and instead stub these requests, returning predefined values. For a refresher on stubbing, refer to *Chapter 5*.

Let's save the resultant data into a text file named `search-results.json`, located under `cypress/fixtures/search-result.json`.

Stubbing the search results

With the file in place, we can write a test for the **Search city by name** feature. As we don't send the real request to OpenWeatherMap, we'll intercept network requests that are sent to the API and return the file content we created previously – that is, `fixtures/search-result.json`:

```
import searchResults from '../fixtures/search-result.json';

describe('weather application', () => {
  //...

  it('searches for a city', () => {
    cy.intercept("GET", "https://api.openweathermap.org/geo/1.0/
     direct?q=*", {
       statusCode: 200,
       body: searchResults,
    });

    cy.visit('http://localhost:3000/');

    cy.get('[data-testid="search-input"]').type('Melbourne');
    cy.get('[data-testid="search-input"]').type('{enter}');

    cy.get('[data-testid="search-results"] .search-result')
      .should('have.length', 5);
  });
});
```

Here, we created a test case called `'searches for a city'`. The test case does the following:

1. First, it sets up an interception for a GET request that goes to the OpenWeatherMap API for city searches. Whenever a request matching the criteria is made, it responds with a 200 status code and the body content from a predefined `searchResults` file, essentially mocking the API response.

2. Then, it navigates to the application running on `http://localhost:3000/`.

3. Next, it simulates a user typing `Melbourne` into an input field with a `data-testid` value of `search-input` and pressing the *Enter* key.

4. Lastly, it checks that a container with a `data-testid` value of `"search-results"` contains exactly five elements with a class of `search-result`, which are the search results that are returned from the stubbed API request. This verifies that the application correctly displays the search results.

We're in the red step in TDD (the first step, which indicates that a test is failing), so let's go to our application code, `App.tsx`, to fix the test:

```
function App() {
  const [query, setQuery] = useState<string>("");
  const [searchResults, setSearchResults] = useState<any[]>([]);

  const handleKeyDown = (e: KeyboardEvent<HTMLInputElement>) => {
    if (e.key === "Enter") {
      fetchCities();
    }
  };

  const handleChange = (e: ChangeEvent<HTMLInputElement>) => {
    setQuery(e.target.value);
  };

  const fetchCities = () => {
    fetch(
      `https://api.openweathermap.org/geo/1.0/direct?q=${query}&limit=
      5&appid=<app-key>`
    )
      .then((r) => r.json())
      .then((cities) => {
        setSearchResults(
          cities.map((city: any) => ({
            name: city.name,
          }))
        );
      });
  };

  return (
    <div className="app">
```

```
    <h1>Weather Application</h1>

    <div className="search-bar">
      <input
        type="text"
        data-testid="search-input"
        onKeyDown={handleKeyDown}
        onChange={handleChange}
        placeholder="Enter city name (e.g. Melbourne, New York)"
      />
    </div>

    <div className="search-results-popup">
      {searchResults.length > 0 && (
        <ul data-testid="search-results">
          {searchResults.map((city, index) => (
            <li key={index} className="search-result">
              {city.name}
            </li>
          ))}
        </ul>
      )}
    </div>
  </div>
  );
}
```

The App function in this code sets up a simple weather application using React. It initializes the `query` and `searchResults` state variables to handle user input and display search results, respectively. The `handleKeyDown` and `handleChange` event handlers are set up to update the search query and trigger a city search when the user presses *Enter*. The `fetchCities` function sends a request to the OpenWeatherMap API, processes the response to extract the city names, and updates `searchResults`.

In the TSX part, an input field is provided for the user to type a city name, and a list displays the search results whenever there are any available.

The tests are now passing with these changes, and we can launch our browser to access the application. As depicted in *Figure 12.3*, our implementation now displays a drop-down list of cities upon conducting a search:

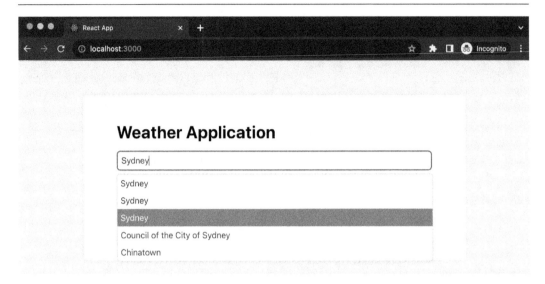

Figure 12.3: The search result dropdown

> **Note**
>
> I've incorporated some CSS to enhance the visual appeal. However, to maintain focus on the core content, the CSS has not been included here. For a complete understanding, you can refer to the repository mentioned in the *Technical requirements* section to see the full implementation.

Enhancing the search result list

As we utilize city names for search queries, it's common to encounter multiple matches in the search results. To refine this, we could enrich each item with additional details such as the state name, country name, or even coordinates to make the results more distinctive.

Following the TDD approach, we'll start with a test. Although a Cypress test could be crafted, detailing such aspects is better suited for lower-level tests such as unit tests. Cypress tests are end-to-end, encompassing all the parts – pages, network (even with interceptors) – and from its standpoint, it perceives no components, just HTML, CSS, and JavaScript. This makes them more costly to run, extending the feedback loop compared to lower-level tests, which generally operate in an in-memory browser and focus on isolated areas.

For this enhancement, we'll employ Jest tests, which are more lightweight, faster, and offer specificity in test case writing.

In the following snippet, we aim to test if an item displays the city name:

```
it("shows a city name", () => {
  render(<SearchResultItem item={{ city: "Melbourne" }} />);
  expect(screen.getByText("Melbourne")).toBeInTheDocument();
});
```

Here, we invoke the `render` method from the React Testing Library on a `SearchResultItem` component, passing a prop item with a `city` field. Then, we assert that the `Melbourne` text is present in the document.

At this point, we lack a `SearchResultItem` component ready for testing. However, a slight refactoring can help us extract one. Let's create a `SearchResultItem.tsx` file and define the component as follows:

```
export const SearchResultItem = ({ item }: { item: { city: string } })
=> {
  return <li className="search-result">{item.city}</li>;
};
```

Now, integrate the component in `App.tsx`:

```
function App() {
  //...
  <div className="search-results-popup">
    {searchResults.length > 0 && (
      <ul data-testid="search-results" className="search-results">
        {searchResults.map((city, index) => (
          <SearchResultItem key={index} item={{ city }} />
        ))}
      </ul>
    )}
  </div>
  //...
}
```

In this part of `App.tsx`, we map through `searchResults`, rendering `SearchResultItem` for each city, and passing the city data as a prop.

Now, let's extend our tests to check for the city name, state, and country:

```
it("shows a city name, the state, and the country", () => {
  render(
    <SearchResultItem
      item={{ city: "Melbourne", state: "Victoria", country:
        "Australia" }}
    />
  );
  expect(screen.getByText("Melbourne")).toBeInTheDocument();
  expect(screen.getByText("Victoria")).toBeInTheDocument();
  expect(screen.getByText("Australia")).toBeInTheDocument();
});
```

Next, to accommodate these new fields, we'll tweak the type definition of `SearchResultItem` and render the passed props:

```
type SearchResultItemProps = {
  city: string;
  state: string;
  country: string;
};

export const SearchResultItem = ({ item }: { item:
SearchResultItemProps }) => {
  return (
    <li className="search-result">
      <span>{item.city}</span>
      <span>{item.state}</span>
      <span>{item.country}</span>
    </li>
  );
};
```

Here, we define a `SearchResultItemProps` type to specify the shape of the item prop, ensuring it contains the `city`, `state`, and `country` fields. Our `SearchResultItem` component then renders these fields within a list item, each in a separate `span` element.

As you can see, now, the list item provides more details to help users distinguish between the results:

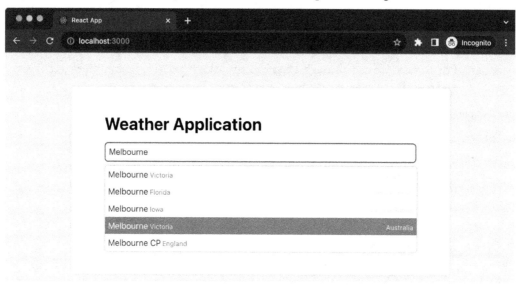

Figure 12.4: Enhanced city drop-down list

Before we proceed to the next major feature, let's tackle some housekeeping tasks. While we've been focused on delivering the feature, we haven't given much attention to code quality so far, so let's do that.

Implementing an ACL

Within our application, the `SearchResultItem` component serves its purpose well. However, the challenge arises from the discrepancy between the data shape we require and the data shape we receive from the remote server.

Consider the server's response:

```
[
    {
    "country": "US",
    "lat": 28.106471,
    "local_names": {
      "en": "Melbourne",
      "ja": "メルボーン",
      "ru": "Мельбурн",
      "uk": "Мелборн"
    },
    "lon": -80.6371513,
    "name": "Melbourne",
    "state": "Florida"
  }
]
```

The server's response includes many elements we don't need. Moreover, we want to shield our `SearchResultItem` component from any future changes to the data shape from the server.

As we discussed in *Chapter 8*, we can employ an ACL to address this issue. Using this, we aim to map the city name and state directly, but for the country, we want to display its full name to avoid any ambiguity in the UI.

To do this, first, we must define a `RemoteSearchResultItem` type to represent the remote data shape:

```
interface RemoteSearchResultItem {
  city: string;
  state: string;
  country: string;

  lon: number;
  lat: number;

  local_names: {
```

```
    [key: string]: string
  }
}
```

Next, we must change the `SearchResultItemProps` type to a class, enabling its initialization within the TypeScript code:

```
const countryMap = {
  "AU": "Australia",
  "US": "United States",
  "GB": "United Kingdom"
  //...
}

class SearchResultItemType {
  private readonly _city: string;
  private readonly _state: string;
  private readonly _country: string;

  constructor(item: RemoteSearchResultItem) {
    this._city = item.city;
    this._state = item.state;
    this._country = item.country
  }

  get city() {
    return this._city
  }

  get state() {
    return this._state
  }

  get country() {
    return countryMap[this._country] || this._country;
  }
}
```

This segment of code defines a class, `SearchResultItemType`, that accepts a `RemoteSearchResultItem` object in its `constructor` and initializes its properties accordingly. It also provides getter methods to access these properties, with a special handler for the country property to the map country code to its full name.

Now, our `SearchResultItem` component can utilize this newly defined class:

```
import React from "react";
import { SearchResultItemType } from "./models/SearchResultItemType";

export const SearchResultItem = ({ item }: { item:
SearchResultItemType }) => {
  return (
    <li className="search-result">
      <span>{item.city}</span>
      <span>{item.state}</span>
      <span>{item.country}</span>
    </li>
  );
};
```

Note how we use the `item.city` and `item.state` getter functions, just like a regular JavaScript object.

Then, in our Jest tests, we can verify the transformation logic straightforwardly, as seen here:

```
it("converts the remote type to local", () => {
  const remote = {
    country: "US",
    lat: 28.106471,
    local_names: {
      en: "Melbourne",
      ja: "メルボーン",
      ru: "Мельбурн",
      uk: "Мелборн",
    },
    lon: -80.6371513,
    name: "Melbourne",
    state: "Florida",
  };

  const model = new SearchResultItemType(remote);

  expect(model.city).toEqual('Melbourne');
  expect(model.state).toEqual('Florida');
  expect(model.country).toEqual('United States');
});
```

In this test, we create an instance of `SearchResultItemType` using a mock `RemoteSearchResultItem` object and verify that the transformation logic works as intended – the fields are correctly mapped and the country has its full name too.

Once the tests confirm the expected behavior, we can apply this new class within our application code, as follows:

```
const fetchCities = () => {
  fetch(
    `https://api.openweathermap.org/geo/1.0/direct?q=${query}&limit=5&
    appid=<api-key>`
  )
    .then((r) => r.json())
    .then((cities) => {
      setSearchResults(
        cities.map(
          (item: RemoteSearchResultItem) => new
          SearchResultItemType(item)
        )
      );
    });
};
```

This function fetches city data from the remote server, transforms the received data into instances of `SearchResultItemType`, and then updates the `searchResults` state.

With enriched details in the dropdown, users can identify their desired city. Having achieved this, we can proceed to allow users to add cities to their favorite list, paving the way to display weather information for these selected cities.

Given our Cypress feature tests, there's a safeguard against inadvertently breaking functionality. Additionally, with the newly incorporated unit tests, any discrepancies between remote and local data shapes will be automatically detected. We are now well-positioned to embark on developing the next feature.

Implementing an Add to Favorite feature

Let's investigate implementing our next feature: `'adds city to favorite list'`. Because this is a feature that is critical in the weather application, we want to make sure users can see the city being added and that the dropdown is closed.

First, we'll start with another Cypress test:

```
it('adds city to favorite list', () => {
  cy.intercept("GET", "https://api.openweathermap.org/geo/1.0/
direct?q=*", {
    statusCode: 200,
    body: searchResults,
  });
```

```
cy.visit('http://localhost:3000/');

cy.get('[data-testid="search-input"]').type('Melbourne');
cy.get('[data-testid="search-input"]').type('{enter}');

cy.get('[data-testid="search-results"] .search-result')
  .first()
  .click();

cy.get('[data-testid="favorite-cities"] .city')
  .should('have.length', 1);

cy.get('[data-testid="favorite-cities"]
  .city:contains("Melbourne")').should('exist');
cy.get('[data-testid="favorite-cities"] .city:contains("20°C")').
  should('exist');
})
```

In the test, we set up an intercept to mock a GET request to the OpenWeatherMap API and then visit the app running on localhost. From here, it simulates typing Melbourne into a search input and hitting *Enter*. After that, it clicks on the first search result and checks if the favorite cities list now contains one city. Finally, it verifies that the favorite cities list contains a city element with Melbourne and 20°C.

Please note that there are a few things that need a bit more explanation in the last two lines:

- `cy.get(selector)`: This Cypress command is used to query DOM elements on a page. It's similar to `document.querySelector`. Here, it's being used to select elements with specific text content inside a particular part of the DOM. Cypress supports not only the basic CSS selectors, such as class and ID selectors, but also advanced selectors such as `.city:contains("Melbourne")`, so we can use a selector for a more specific selection.

- `.city:contains(text)`: This is a jQuery-style selector that Cypress supports. It allows you to select an element containing specific text. In this case, it's being used to find elements within `[data-testid="favorite-cities"]` that have a class of `city` and contain Melbourne or 20°C.

- `.should('exist')`: This is a Cypress command that asserts that the selected elements should exist in the DOM. If the element does not exist, the test will fail.

Now, to get the weather for the city, we need another API endpoint:

```
http https://api.openweathermap.org/data/2.5/weather?lat=-
37.8142176&lon=144.9631608&appid=<api-key>&units=metric
```

The API requires two parameters: the latitude and longitude.

Then, it returns the current weather in this format:

```
{
  //...
  "main": {
      "feels_like": 20.75,
      "humidity": 56,
      "pressure": 1009,
      "temp": 20.00,
      "temp_max": 23.46,
      "temp_min": 18.71
  },
  "name": "Melbourne",
  "timezone": 39600,
  "visibility": 10000,
  "weather": [
      {
          "description": "clear sky",
          "icon": "01d",
          "id": 800,
          "main": "Clear"
      }
  ],
  //...
}
```

There are many fields in the response but we only need some of them for now. We can intercept the request and serve the response in the Cypress test, just like we did for the city search API:

```
cy.intercept('GET', 'https://api.openweathermap.org/data/2.5/
weather*', {
  fixture: 'melbourne.json'
}).as('getWeather')
```

Transitioning to the implementation, we'll weave an onClick event handler into SearchResultItem; upon clicking an item, an API call will be triggered, followed by the addition of a city to a list designated for rendering:

```
export const SearchResultItem = ({
  item,
  onItemClick,
}: {
  item: SearchResultItemType;
```

```
  onItemClick: (item: SearchResultItemType) => void;
}) => {
  return (
    <li className="search-result" onClick={() => onItemClick(item)}>
    { /* JSX for rendering the item details */ }
    </li>
  );
};
```

Now, let's dive into the application code to interlace the data-fetching logic:

```
const onItemClick = (item: SearchResultItemType) => {
  fetch(
    `http https://api.openweathermap.org/data/2.5/weather?lat=${item.
latitude}&lon=${item.longitude}&appid=<api-key>&units=metric`
  )
    .then((r) => r.json())
    .then((cityWeather) => {
      setCity({
        name: cityWeather.name,
        degree: cityWeather.main.temp,
      });
    });
};
```

The onItemClick function is triggered upon clicking a city item. It makes a network request to the OpenWeatherMap API using the item's latitude and longitude, fetching the current weather data for the selected city. Then, it parses the response to JSON, extracts the city name and temperature from the parsed data, and updates the city state using the setCity function, which will cause the component to re-render and display the selected city's name and current temperature.

Note the SearchResultItemType parameter in the previous snippet. We'll need to extend this type so that it encompasses latitude and longitude. We can achieve this by revisiting the ACL layer in the SearchResultItemType class:

```
class SearchResultItemType {
  //... the city, state, country as before
  private readonly _lat: number;
  private readonly _long: number;

  constructor(item: RemoteSearchResultItem) {
    //... the city, state, country as before
    this._lat = item.lat;
    this._long = item.lon;
```

```
  }

  get latitude() {
    return this._lat;
  }

  get longitude() {
    return this._long;
  }
}
```

With that, we have extended `SearchResultItemType` with two new fields, `latitude` and `longitude`, which will be used in the API query.

Finally, upon successfully retrieving the city data, it's time for rendering:

```
function App() {
  const [city, setCity] = useState(undefined);

  const onItemClick = (item: SearchResultItemType) => {
    //...
  }

  return (
      <div className="search-results-popup">
        {searchResults.length > 0 && (
          <ul data-testid="search-results">
            {searchResults.map((item, index) => (
              <SearchResultItem
                key={index}
                item={item}
                onItemClick={onItemClick}
              />
            ))}
          </ul>
        )}
      </div>

      <div data-testid="favorite-cities">
        {city && (
          <div className="city">
            <span>{city.name}</span>
            <span>{city.degree}°C</span>
          </div>
        )}
```

```
      </div>
  );
}
```

In this block of code, the onItemClick function is assigned as the onClick event handler for each SearchResultItem. When a city is clicked, the onItemClick function is invoked, triggering a fetch request to retrieve the weather data for the selected city. Once the data is obtained, the setCity function updates the city state, which then triggers a re-render, displaying the selected city in the **Favorite Cities** section.

Now that all the tests have passed, it signifies that our implementation aligns with the expectations up to this point. However, before we proceed to the next enhancement, it's essential to undertake some refactoring to ensure our code base remains robust and easily maintainable.

Modeling the weather

Just as we modeled the city search result, it's necessary to model the weather for similar reasons – to isolate our implementation from the remote data shape, and to centralize data shape conversion, fallback logic, and so on.

Several areas require refinement. We must do the following:

- Ensure all the relevant data is typed
- Create a data model for the weather to centralize all formatting logic
- Utilize fallback values within the data model when certain data is unavailable

Let's begin with the remote data type, RemoteCityWeather:

```
interface RemoteCityWeather {
  name: string;
  main: {
    temp: number;
    humidity: number;
  };
  weather: [{
    main: string;
    description: string;
  }];
  wind: {
    deg: number;
    speed: number;
  };
}

export type { RemoteCityWeather };
```

Here, we defined a type called `RemoteCityWeather` to reflect the remote data shape (and have also filtered out a few fields that we don't use).

Then, we must define a new type called `CityWeather` for our UI to use CityWeather:

```
import { RemoteCityWeather } from "./RemoteCityWeather";

export class CityWeather {
  private readonly _name: string;
  private readonly _main: string;
  private readonly _temp: number;

  constructor(weather: RemoteCityWeather) {
    this._name = weather.name;
    this._temp = weather.main.temp;
    this._main = weather.weather[0].main;
  }

  get name() {
    return this._name;
  }

  get degree() {
    return Math.ceil(this._temp);
  }

  get temperature() {
    if (this._temp == null) {
      return "-/-";
    }
    return `${Math.ceil(this._temp)}°C`;
  }

  get main() {
    return this._main.toLowerCase();
  }
}
```

This code defines a `CityWeather` class to model city weather data. It takes a `RemoteCityWeather` object as a constructor argument and initializes private fields from it – that is, _name, _temp, and _main. The class provides getter methods to access a city's name, rounded temperature in degrees, formatted temperature string, and the weather description in lowercase.

For the temperature's `getter` method, if _temp is null or undefined, it returns a string, -/-. Otherwise, it proceeds to calculate the ceiling (rounding up to the nearest whole number) of _temp using `Math.ceil(this._temp)`, appends a degree symbol to it, and returns this formatted string. This way, the method provides a fallback value of `-/-` when `_temp` is not set while formatting the temperature value when `_temp` is set.

Now, in `App`, we can use the calculated logic:

```
const onItemClick = (item: SearchResultItemType) => {
  fetch(
    `https://api.openweathermap.org/data/2.5/weather?lat=${item.
latitude}&lon=${item.longitude}&appid=<api-key>&units=metric`
  )
    .then((r) => r.json())
    .then((cityWeather: RemoteCityWeather) => {
      setCity(new CityWeather(cityWeather));
      setDropdownOpen(false);
    });
};
```

The `onItemClick` function is triggered when a city item is clicked. It makes a `fetch` request to the OpenWeatherMap API using the latitude and longitude of the clicked city item. Upon receiving the response, it converts the response into JSON, then creates a new `CityWeather` instance with the received data, and updates the city state using `setCity`.

Additionally, it closes the drop-down menu by setting the `setDropdownOpen` state to `false`. If we don't close it off, the Cypress test will not be able to "see" the underlying weather information, which will cause the test to fail, as shown in the following screenshot:

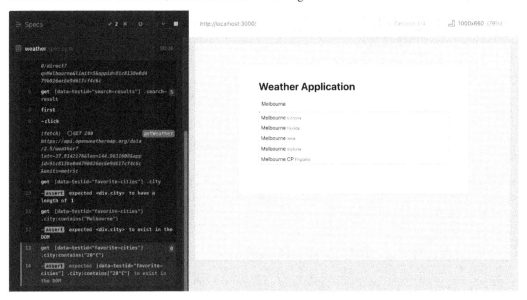

Figure 12.5: The Cypress test failed because the weather is covered

Then, we must render the selected city details correspondingly:

```
<div data-testid="favorite-cities">
  {city && (
    <div className="city">
      <span>{city.name}</span>
      <span>{city.temperature}</span>
    </div>
  )}
</div>
```

For rendering the city part, if the city state is defined (that is, a city has been selected), it displays a `div` element with a class name of `city`. Inside this `div` element, we can see the city's name and temperature using the `city.name` and `city.temperature` properties, respectively.

Now, with some additional styling, our application looks like this:

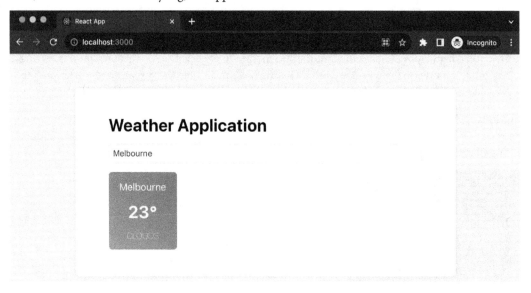

Figure 12.6: Adding a city to the favorite list

We've done an excellent job with data modeling and have set up a solid ACL to bolster our UI's robustness and ease of maintenance. Nonetheless, upon examining the root App component, we'll undoubtedly find areas that require improvement.

Refactoring the current implementation

Our current App component has grown too lengthy for easy readability and feature additions, indicating a need for some refactoring to tidy things up. It doesn't adhere well to the single responsibility principle as it takes on multiple responsibilities: handling network requests for city search and weather queries, managing the state of the dropdown's open and closed status, and several event handlers.

One approach to realigning with better design principles is to break the UI into smaller components. Another is utilizing custom Hooks for state management. Given that a significant portion of the logic here revolves around managing the state for the city search dropdown, it's sensible to start by isolating this part.

Let's start by extracting all city search-related logic into a custom Hook:

```
const useSearchCity = () => {
  const [query, setQuery] = useState<string>("");
  const [searchResults, setSearchResults] =
   useState<SearchResultItemType[]>(
     []
  );
  const [isDropdownOpen, setDropdownOpen] = useState<boolean>(false);

  const fetchCities = () => {
    fetch(
      `https://api.openweathermap.org/geo/1.0/direct?q=${query}&limit=
      5&appid=<api-key>`
    )
      .then((r) => r.json())
      .then((cities) => {
        setSearchResults(
          cities.map(
            (item: RemoteSearchResultItem) => new
            SearchResultItemType(item)
          )
        );
        openDropdownList();
      });
  };

  const openDropdownList = () => setDropdownOpen(true);
  const closeDropdownList = () => setDropdownOpen(false);

  return {
    fetchCities,
    setQuery,
    searchResults,
    isDropdownOpen,
    openDropdownList,
    closeDropdownList,
```

```
    };
  };


  export { useSearchCity };
```

The useSearchCity Hook manages the city search functionality. It initializes states for query, search results, and dropdown open status using useState. The fetchCities function triggers a network request to fetch cities based on the query, processes the response to create SearchResultItemType instances, updates the search results state, and opens the drop-down list. Two functions, openDropdownList and closeDropdownList, are defined to toggle the dropdown's open status. The Hook returns an object containing these functionalities, which can be used by components that import and invoke useSearchCity.

Next, we extract a component, SearchCityInput, to handle all the search input-related work: to handle the *Enter* key for performing the search, open the drop-down list, and handle users clicking on each item:

```
  export const SearchCityInput = ({
    onItemClick,
  }: {
    onItemClick: (item: SearchResultItemType) => void;
  }) => {
    const {
      fetchCities,
      setQuery,
      isDropdownOpen,
      closeDropdownList,
      searchResults,
    } = useSearchCity();

    const handleKeyDown = (e: KeyboardEvent<HTMLInputElement>) => {
      if (e.key === "Enter") {
        fetchCities();
      }
    };

    const handleChange = (e: ChangeEvent<HTMLInputElement>) =>
      setQuery(e.target.value);

    const handleItemClick = (item: SearchResultItemType) => {
      onItemClick(item);
      closeDropdownList();
    };

    return (
```

```
    <>
      <div className="search-bar">
        <input
          type="text"
          data-testid="search-input"
          onKeyDown={handleKeyDown}
          onChange={handleChange}
          placeholder="Enter city name (e.g. Melbourne, New York)"
        />
      </div>

      {isDropdownOpen && (
        //... render the dropdown
      )}
    </>
  );
};
```

The `SearchCityInput` component is responsible for rendering and managing the user input for searching cities, utilizing the `useSearchCity` Hook to access search-related functionalities.

The `handleKeyDown` and `handleChange` functions are defined to handle user interactions, triggering a search upon pressing *Enter* and updating the query on input change, respectively. Then, the `handleItemClick` function is defined to handle the action when a search result item is clicked, which triggers the `onItemClick` prop function and closes the drop-down list.

In the `render` method, an input field is provided for the user to type the search query, and the drop-down list is conditionally rendered based on the `isDropdownOpen` state. If the dropdown is open and there are search results, a list of `SearchResultItem` components is rendered, each being passed the current item data and the `handleItemClick` function.

For all the logic of the weather for a city, we can extract another Hook, `useCityWeather`:

```
const useFetchCityWeather = () => {
  const [cityWeather, setCityWeather] = useState<CityWeather |
    undefined>(undefined);

  const fetchCityWeather = (item: SearchResultItemType) => {
    fetch(
      `https://api.openweathermap.org/data/2.5/weather?lat=${item.
latitude}&lon=${item.longitude}&appid=<api-key>&units=metric`
    )
      .then((r) => r.json())
      .then((cityWeather: RemoteCityWeather) => {
        setCityWeather(new CityWeather(cityWeather));
```

```
        });
    };

    return {
      cityWeather,
      fetchCityWeather,
    };
  };
```

The useFetchCityWeather custom Hook is designed to manage the fetching and storing of weather data for a specified city. It maintains a state, cityWeather, to hold the weather data. The Hook provides a function, fetchCityWeather, which takes a SearchResultItemType object as an argument to get the latitude and longitude values for the API call.

Upon receiving the response, it processes the JSON data, creates a new CityWeather object from the RemoteCityWeather data, and updates the cityWeather state with it. The Hook returns the cityWeather state and the fetchCityWeather function for use in other components (Weather, for example).

We could extract a Weather component to accept cityWeather and render it:

```
const Weather = ({ cityWeather }: { cityWeather: CityWeather |
undefined }) => {
  if (cityWeather) {
    return (
      <div className="city">
        <span>{cityWeather.name}</span>
        <span>{cityWeather.degree}°C</span>
      </div>
    );
  }

  return null;
};
```

The Weather component accepts a prop, cityWeather. If cityWeather is defined, the component renders a div element with the city class name, displaying the city's name and temperature in degrees Celsius. If cityWeather is undefined, it returns null.

With the extracted Hook and component, our App.tsx is simplified into something like this:

```
function App() {
  const { cityWeather, fetchCityWeather } = useFetchCityWeather();

  const onItemClick = (item: SearchResultItemType) =>
```

```
    fetchCityWeather(item);

  return (
    <div className="app">
      <h1>Weather Application</h1>

      <SearchCityInput onItemClick={onItemClick} />

      <div data-testid="favorite-cities">
        <Weather cityWeather={cityWeather} />
      </div>
    </div>
  );
}
```

In the App function, we're utilizing the useFetchCityWeather custom Hook to obtain cityWeather and fetchCityWeather values. The onItemClick function is defined to call fetchCityWeather with an item of the SearchResultItemType type. In the rendering part, we can now simply use the component and functions we extracted.

If we open the project folder to examine the current folder structure, we will see that we have different elements defined in distinct modules:

```
src
├── App.tsx
├── index.tsx
├── models
│   ├── CityWeather.ts
│   ├── RemoteCityWeather.ts
│   ├── RemoteSearchResultItem.ts
│   ├── SearchResultItemType.test.ts
│   └── SearchResultItemType.ts
├── search
│   ├── SearchCityInput.tsx
│   ├── SearchResultItem.test.tsx
│   ├── SearchResultItem.tsx
│   └── useSearchCity.ts
└── weather
    ├── Weather.tsx
    ├── useFetchCityWeather.test.ts
    ├── useFetchCityWeather.ts
    └── weather.css
```

Now, after all that work, each module possesses a clearer boundary and defined responsibility. If you wish to delve into the search functionality, `SearchCityInput` is your starting point. For insights on the actual search execution, the `useSearchCity` Hook is where you'd look. Each level maintains its own abstraction and distinct responsibility, simplifying code comprehension and maintenance significantly.

Since our code is in a great state and is ready for us to add more features on top of it, we can look into enhancing the current feature.

Enabling multiple cities in the favorite list

Now, let's examine a specific example to illustrate the ease with which we can expand the existing code with a simple feature upgrade. A user may have several cities they're interested in, but at present, we can only display one city.

To allow multiple cities in the favorite list, which component should we modify to implement this change? Correct – the `useFetchCityWeather` Hook. To enable it so that it can manage a list of cities, we'll need to display this list within `App`. There's no need to delve into the city search-related files, indicating that this structure has halved the time we would spend sifting through files.

As we're performing TDD, let's write a test for the Hook first:

```
const weatherAPIResponse = JSON.stringify({
  main: {
    temp: 20.0,
  },
  name: "Melbourne",
  weather: [
    {
      description: "clear sky",
      main: "Clear",
    },
  ],
});

const searchResultItem = new SearchResultItemType({
  country: "AU",
  lat: -37.8141705,
  lon: 144.9655616,
  name: "Melbourne",
  state: "Victoria",
});
```

Firstly, let's define some data we want to test against. We can initialize data with `weatherAPIResponse`, which contains a mock response from a weather API in JSON string format, and `searchResultItem`, which holds an instance of `SearchResultItemType` with location details for Melbourne, Australia.

For the actual test case, we'll need to use `fetchMock` from `jest-fetch-mock`; we installed it in the *Technical requirements* section:

```
describe("fetchCityWeather function", () => {
  beforeEach(() => {
    fetchMock.resetMocks();
  });

  it("returns a list of cities", async () => {
    fetchMock.mockResponseOnce(weatherAPIResponse);

    const { result } = renderHook(() => useFetchCityWeather());

    await act(async () => {
      await result.current.fetchCityWeather(searchResultItem);
    });

    await waitFor(() => {
      expect(result.current.cities.length).toEqual(1);
      expect(result.current.cities[0].name).toEqual("Melbourne");
    });
  });
});
```

The preceding code sets up a test suite for the `fetchCityWeather` function. Before each test, it resets any mocked fetch calls. The test case aims to verify that the function returns a list of cities. It mocks an API response using `fetchMock.mockResponseOnce`, then invokes the `useFetchCityWeather` custom Hook. The `fetchCityWeather` function is called within an `act` block to handle state updates. Finally, the test asserts that the returned list of cities contains one city, **Melbourne**.

This setup helps test the `fetchCityWeather` function in isolation, ensuring it behaves as expected when provided with a specific input and when receiving a specific API response.

Correspondingly, we need to update the `useFetchCityWeather` Hook to enable multiple items:

```
const useFetchCityWeather = () => {
  const [cities, setCities] = useState<CityWeather[]>([]);

  const fetchCityWeather = (item: SearchResultItemType) => {
    //... fetch
      .then((cityWeather: RemoteCityWeather) => {
```

```
        setCities([new CityWeather(cityWeather), ...cities]);
      });
  };

  return {
    cities,
    fetchCityWeather,
  };
};
```

The useFetchCityWeather Hook now maintains a state of an array of CityWeather objects called cities. We still send requests to the OpenWeatherMap API and then we make sure the new item is inserted at the start of the list when it's fetched. It returns an object containing the cities array to the calling place.

Finally, in App, we can iterate over cities to generate the Weather component for each one:

```
function App() {
  //...
  const { cities, fetchCityWeather } = useFetchCityWeather();

  return (
    <div className="app">
      {/* other jsx */}
      <div data-testid="favorite-cities">
        {cities.map((city) => (
          <Weather key={city.name} cityWeather={city} />
        ))}
      </div>
    </div>
  );
}
```

The cities array is mapped over, and for each CityWeather object in the array, a Weather component is rendered. The key prop for each Weather component is set to the city's name, and the cityWeather prop is set to the CityWeather object itself, which will display the weather information for each city in the list.

Now, we will be able to see something like this in the UI:

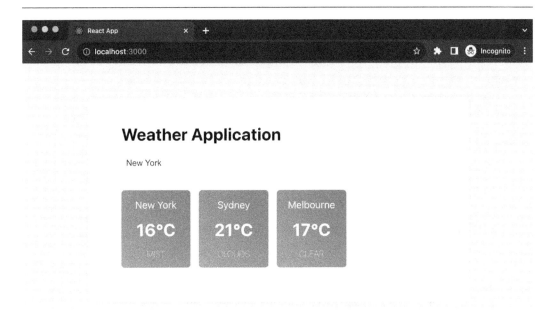

Figure 12.7: Showing multiple cities in the favorite list

Before diving into our next and final feature, it's essential to make one more straightforward improvement to the existing code – ensuring adherence to the single responsibility principle.

Refactoring the weather list

The functionality is operational and all tests have passed; the subsequent focus is on enhancing code quality. Keep the TDD approach in mind: tackle one task at a time and make incremental improvements. Then, we can extract a `WeatherList` component that renders the whole city list:

```
const WeatherList = ({ cities }: { cities: CityWeather[] }) => {
  return (
    <div data-testid="favorite-cities" className="favorite-cities">
      {cities.map((city) => (
        <Weather key={city.name} cityWeather={city} />
      ))}
    </div>
  );
};
```

The `WeatherList` component receives a cities prop, which is an array of `CityWeather` objects. It iterates through this array using `map`, rendering a `Weather` component for each city.

With the new `WeatherList` component in place, `App.tsx` will be simplified to something like this:

```
function App() {
  const { cities, fetchCityWeather } = useFetchCityWeather();
  const onItemClick = (item: SearchResultItemType) =>
   fetchCityWeather(item);

  return (
    <div className="app">
      <h1>Weather Application</h1>
      <SearchCityInput onItemClick={onItemClick} />
      <WeatherList cities={cities} />
    </div>
  );
}
```

Fantastic! Now that our application structure is clean and each component has a single responsibility, this is an opportune time to dive into implementing a new (and the last one) feature to enhance our weather application further.

Fetching previous weather data when the application relaunches

For the final feature in our weather application, we aim to retain the user's selections so that upon their next visit to the application, instead of encountering an empty list, they see the cities they selected previously. This feature is likely to be highly utilized – users will only need to add a few cities initially, and afterward, they may merely open the application to have the weather for their cities loaded automatically.

So, let's start the feature with a user acceptance test using Cypress:

```
const items = [
  {
    name: "Melbourne",
    lat: -37.8142,
    lon: 144.9632,
  },
];

it("fetches data when initializing when possible", () => {
  cy.window().then((window: any) => {
    window.localStorage.setItem(
      "favoriteItems",
      JSON.stringify(items, null, 2)
    );
```

```
  });

  cy.intercept("GET", "https://api.openweathermap.org/data/2.5/
    weather*", {
    fixture: "melbourne.json",
  }).as("getWeather");

  cy.visit("http://localhost:3000/");

  cy.get('[data-testid="favorite-cities"] .city').should("have.
    length", 1);

  cy.get(
    '[data-testid="favorite-cities"] .city:contains("Melbourne")'
  ).should("exist");
  cy.get('[data-testid="favorite-cities"] .city:contains("20°C")').
    should(
      "exist"
    );
});
```

The cy.window() command accesses the global window object and sets a favoriteItems item in localStorage with the items array. Following that, cy.intercept() stubs the network request to the OpenWeatherMap API, using a fixture file called melbourne.json for the mock response. The cy.visit() command navigates to the application on http://localhost:3000/. Once on the page, the test checks for one city item in the favorite cities list, verifies the presence of a city item for Melbourne, and confirms it displays a temperature of 20°C.

In other words, we set up one item in localStorage so that when the page loads, it can read localStorage and make a request to the remote server, just like what we do in onItemClick.

Next, we'll need to extract a data fetching function within useFetchCityWeather. Currently, the fetchCityWeather function is handling two tasks – fetching data and updating the cities' state. To adhere to the single responsibility principle, we should create a new function solely for fetching data, leaving fetchCityWeather to handle updating the state:

```
export const fetchCityWeatherData = async (item: SearchResultItemType)
=> {
  const response = await fetch(
    `https://api.openweathermap.org/data/2.5/weather?lat=${item.
latitude}&lon=${item.longitude}&appid=<api-key>&units=metric`
  );
  const json = await response.json();
  return new CityWeather(json);
};
```

The `fetchCityWeatherData` function takes a `SearchResultItemType` object as an argument, constructs a URL with the latitude and longitude of the item, and sends a `fetch` request to the OpenWeatherMap API. Upon receiving the response, it converts the response into JSON, creates a new `CityWeather` object with the JSON data, and returns it.

Now, `fetchCityWeather` can be updated as follows:

```
const useFetchCityWeather = () => {
  //...
  const fetchCityWeather = (item: SearchResultItemType) => {
    return fetchCityWeatherData(item).then((cityWeather) => {
      setCities([cityWeather, ...cities]);
    });
  };
  //...
}
```

The `useFetchCityWeather` Hook now contains a `fetchCityWeather` function that calls `fetchCityWeatherData` with a given `SearchResultItemType` item. When the promise resolves, it receives a `CityWeather` object and then updates the state cities by adding the new `CityWeather` object at the beginning of the existing cities array.

Next, in the App component, we can use `useEffect` to hydrate the `localStorage` data and send requests for the actual weather data:

```
useEffect(() => {
  const hydrate = async () => {
    const items = JSON.parse(localStorage.getItem("favoriteItems") ||
      "[]");

    const promises = items.map((item: any) => {
      const searchResultItem = new SearchResultItemType(item);
      return fetchCityWeatherData(searchResultItem);
    });

    const cities = await Promise.all(promises);
    setCities(cities);
  };

  hydrate();
}, []);
```

In this code snippet, a `useEffect` Hook triggers a function named `hydrate` when the component mounts thanks to the empty dependency array, `[]`.

Inside `hydrate`, firstly, it retrieves a stringified array from `localStorage` under the `favoriteItems` key, parsing it back to a JavaScript array, or defaulting to an empty array if the key doesn't exist. Then, it maps through this items array, creating a new instance of `SearchResultItemType` for each item, which it passes to the `fetchCityWeatherData` function. This function returns a promise, which is collected into an array of promises.

Using `Promise.all`, it waits for all these promises to resolve before updating the state with `setCities`, populating it with the fetched city weather data. Finally, `hydrate` is called within the `useEffect` to execute this logic upon component mounting.

Finally, to save an item in `localStorage` when a user clicks an item, we need a bit more code:

```
const onItemClick = (item: SearchResultItemType) => {
  setTimeout(() => {
    const items = JSON.parse(localStorage.getItem("favoriteItems") ||
"[]");

    const newItem = {
      name: item.city,
      lon: item.longitude,
      lat: item.latitude,
    };

    localStorage.setItem(
      "favoriteItems",
      JSON.stringify([newItem, ...items], null, 2)
    );
  }, 0);

  return fetchCityWeather(item);
};
```

Here, the `onItemClick` function accepts an argument item of the `SearchResultItemType` type. Inside the function, `setTimeout` is utilized with a delay of 0 milliseconds, essentially deferring the execution of its contents until after the current call stack has cleared – so, the UI will not be blocked.

Within this deferred block, it retrieves a stringified array from `localStorage` under the `favoriteItems` key, parsing it back to a JavaScript array, or defaulting to an empty array if the key doesn't exist. Then, it creates a new object, `newItem`, from the item argument, extracting and renaming some properties.

Following this, it updates the `favoriteItems` key in `localStorage` with a stringified array containing `newItem` at the beginning, followed by the previously stored items.

Outside of `setTimeout`, it calls `fetchCityWeather` with the item argument, fetching weather data for the clicked city, and returns the result of this call from `onItemClick`.

Now, when we inspect `localStorage` in our browser, we will see that the objects are listed in JSON format and that the data will persist until users explicitly clean it:

Figure 12.8: Using data from local storage

Excellent job! Everything is now functioning well, and the code is in a robust shape that's easy to build upon. Moreover, the project structure is intuitive, facilitating easy navigation and file location whenever we need to implement changes.

This chapter was quite extensive and was packed with insightful information, serving as a great recapitulation of the knowledge you've acquired thus far. While it would be engaging to continue adding more features together, I believe now is an opportune time for you to dive in and apply the concepts and techniques you've gleaned from this book. I'll entrust the enhancement task to you, confident that you'll make commendable adjustments as you introduce more features.

Summary

In this chapter, we embarked on creating a weather application from scratch, adhering to the TDD methodology. We employed Cypress for user acceptance tests and Jest for unit tests, progressively building out the application's features. Key practices such as modeling domain objects, stubbing network requests, and applying the single responsibility principle during refactoring were also explored.

While not exhaustive in covering all the techniques from previous chapters, this chapter underscored the importance of maintaining a disciplined pace during the development phase. It highlighted the value of being able to identify code "smells" and address them effectively, all while ensuring a solid test coverage to foster a robust and maintainable codebase. This chapter served as a practical synthesis, urging you to apply the acquired knowledge and techniques to enhance the application further.

In the upcoming and concluding chapter, we'll recap the anti-patterns we've explored, revisiting the design principles and practices we've examined, and also provide additional resources for further learning.

13
Recapping Anti-Pattern Principles

In this short final chapter, we'll briefly revisit the crucial insights from the book and furnish additional resources for you to delve deeper into the realm of React and software design.

The primary objective of this book was to unearth common anti-patterns often encountered in React code bases, especially within large-scale React applications. We delved into potential remedies and techniques to rectify these issues. The examples throughout the narrative were drawn either from my prior projects or are related to domains with which developers are likely to be familiar – such as shopping carts, user profiles, and network requests, to name a few.

I championed a step-by-step and incremental delivery approach, guiding you from an initial, less-than-ideal implementation toward a polished version, making one small improvement at a time. We embarked on organizing a typical React application, ventured into the realm of frontend testing through **test-driven development** (**TDD**), and initiated our journey with common refactoring techniques. Thereafter, we navigated the challenging waters of data/state management in React, elucidated common design principles, and explored compositional strategies. A slew of chapters were dedicated to constructing full examples from scratch, including a drop-down list, a shopping cart, and a weather application.

During this expedition, we discovered numerous handy tips, such as how to stub network requests in both Cypress and Jest, apply the strategy design pattern to a JavaScript model, and employ **Anti-Corruption Layers** (**ACLs**) in real-world code scenarios.

The techniques discussed in this book may not be groundbreaking or novel; indeed, many are well established. However, their application in the React ecosystem has remained underexplored. I earnestly hope that this book has adeptly bridged that gap, reintroducing these invaluable design principles and patterns to the React community, thereby facilitating a smoother coding experience for developers in the long term.

In this chapter, we'll revisit the following topics:

- Revisiting common anti-patterns
- Skimming through design patterns
- Revisiting foundational design principles
- Recapping techniques and practices

Revisiting common anti-patterns

We explored numerous anti-patterns in the preceding chapters. Recognizing an anti-pattern is the initial step toward rectifying it. Let's briefly recap what we've learned thus far.

Props drilling

Props drilling emerges when a prop traverses through multiple component levels, only to be employed in a deeper-level component, rendering intermediate components unnecessarily privy to this prop. This practice can lead to convoluted and hard-to-maintain code.

Solution: Employing the Context API to create a central store and functions to access this store allows the component tree to access props when needed without prop-drilling.

Long props list/big component

A component that accepts an extensive list of props or harbors a large amount of logic can become a behemoth, hard to understand, reuse, or maintain. This anti-pattern infringes upon the **Single Responsibility Principle** (**SRP**), which advocates that a component or module should only have one reason to change.

Solution: Dismantling the component into smaller, more digestible components and segregating concerns can ameliorate this issue. Each component should embody a clear, singular responsibility. Custom Hooks also serve as a potent means to simplify the code within a component and reduce its size.

Business leakage

Business leakage transpires when business logic is implanted within components that should remain purely presentational, which can complicate application management and reduce component reusability.

Solution: Extricating business logic from presentation logic using custom Hooks or relocating the business logic to a separate module or layer can address this issue. Employing an ACL can be an effective technique to rectify this issue.

Complicated logic in views

The embedding of complex logic within view components can muddle the code, making it arduous to read, comprehend, and maintain. Views should remain as uncluttered as possible, solely responsible for rendering data.

Solution: Relocating complex logic to custom Hooks, utility functions, or a separate business logic layer can help keep view components clean and manageable. Initially, breaking down components into smaller ones, and then gradually segregating the logic into appropriate places can be beneficial.

Lack of tests (at each level)

The absence of adequate unit, integration, or end-to-end tests to ascertain application functions, as anticipated, can usher in bugs, regressions, and code that's challenging to refactor or extend.

Solution: Adopting a robust testing strategy encompassing unit testing, integration testing, and end-to-end testing, coupled with practices such as TDD, can ensure code correctness and ease of maintenance.

Code duplications

Reiterating similar code across multiple components or sections of the application can complicate code-base maintenance and augment the likelihood of bugs.

Solution: Adhering to the **Don't Repeat Yourself** (**DRY**) principle and abstracting common functionality into shared utility functions, components, or Hooks can help curtail code duplication and enhance code maintainability.

Having dissected common anti-patterns, it's now imperative to delve into the design principles that act as antidotes to these prevalent issues. These principles not only provide solutions but also guide you toward writing cleaner, more efficient code.

Skimming through design patterns

There are effective patterns to counter anti-patterns in React, and interestingly, some of these patterns extend beyond the React context, being useful in broader scenarios. Let's swiftly revisit these patterns.

Higher-order components

Higher-order components (**HOCs**) are a potent pattern in React for reusing component logic. HOCs are functions that accept a component and return a new component augmented with additional properties or behaviors. By leveraging HOCs, you can extract and share common behaviors across your components, aiding in mitigating issues such as props drilling and code duplications.

Render props

The **render props** pattern encompasses a technique for sharing code between React components using a prop whose value is a function. It's a method to pass a function as a prop to a component, and that function returns a React element. This pattern can be instrumental in alleviating issues such as long props lists and big components by promoting reuse and composition.

Headless components

Headless components are those that manage behavior and logic but do not render the UI, bestowing the consumer with control over the rendering. They separate behavior logic from presentation logic, which can be a viable solution to business leakage and complicated logic in views, making components more flexible and maintainable.

Data modeling

Data modeling entails organizing and defining your data, which aids in understanding and managing the data within your application, thereby simplifying the logic within your components. This principle can be employed to tackle complicated logic in views and business logic leakage.

Layered architecture

Layered architecture involves segregating concerns and organizing code such that each layer has a specific responsibility. This separation can lead to a more organized and manageable code base, addressing issues such as business leakage and complicated logic in views.

As a reminder, *Figure 13.1* depicts this layered architecture. In a layered architecture, each layer contains numerous modules, each dedicated to specific tasks within the overall application. This includes modules for data retrieval (the **Fetcher** module, shown in *Figure 13.1*), adapters to interface with external services such as social media logins and payment gateways (the **Adaptor** gateway, shown in *Figure 13.1*), as well as components for analytics and security-related functions:

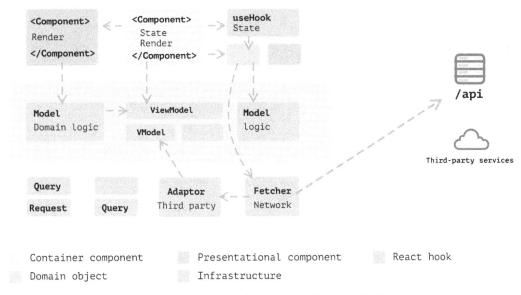

Figure 13.1: Layered architecture in a React application

We conducted a comprehensive case study on this topic in *Chapter 11*, delving deeply into the evolution of the system and pinpointing the appropriate circumstances for applying such an architectural style.

Context as an interface

Utilizing context as an interface allows components to interact with data without the need to pass props down multiple levels. This strategy can alleviate props drilling and long props lists, rendering the component tree more readable and maintainable.

With a solid grasp of foundational and design principles, it's time to explore techniques that will arm you with the practical knowledge to implement these principles in your daily coding endeavors.

Revisiting foundational design principles

Besides React-specific patterns, we've discussed several higher-level design principles throughout various chapters. These principles serve as guidelines applicable to various aspects of your work, be it React, data modeling, event testing, or scripts that facilitate integration. They are not confined to a particular context, and embracing them can significantly enhance your coding approach across different domains.

Single Responsibility Principle

The SRP advocates that a class or component should only harbor one reason to change. Adhering to the SRP can lead to more maintainable and understandable code, mitigating issues such as big components and complicated logic in views.

We've explored this principle at various levels, from carving out a smaller component from a larger one, to creating a new Hook, and up to significant refactoring such as integrating an ACL into a weather application. It's worth noting that whenever you find yourself entangled within a large component, the SRP remains your most trustworthy ally.

Dependency Inversion Principle

The **Dependency Inversion Principle** (DIP) emphasizes depending on abstractions, not concretions, which leads to a decoupling of high-level and low-level structures. This principle can be utilized to manage business logic leakage and promote a clean **separation of concerns** (SoC).

Don't Repeat Yourself

The DRY principle is about minimizing repetition within code. By adhering to the DRY principle, you can minimize code duplication, making your code base easier to maintain and extend.

Anti-Corruption Layers

An ACL serves as a barrier between different parts or layers of an application, creating a stable interface. Implementing an ACL can be a potent strategy to manage business leakage and ensure a clean SoC.

An ACL proves to be especially beneficial when your code needs to interact with other systems in any capacity, a scenario that often arises when collaborating with different teams—a common occurrence in many setups. By establishing a clear system boundary through ACL, we can mitigate the impact of changes in other systems on our own, thereby maintaining better control over our application and alleviating potential integration challenges. *Figure 13.2* illustrates how an ACL is applied in React:

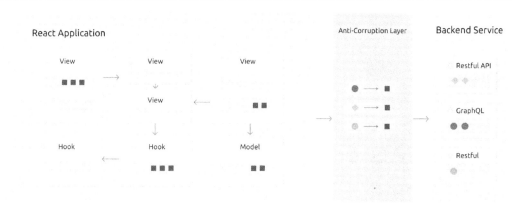

Figure 13.2: Applying an ACL in React

Using composition

Composition is a core principle in React that empowers developers to build components from other components, promoting reuse and simplicity. Employing composition can alleviate various issues, including long props lists, big components, and code duplications, leading to a more maintainable and organized code base.

Understanding these anti-patterns, design patterns, and principles is crucial for managing the complexity of a frontend code base. However, the techniques and practices are equally important as they represent the hands-on work developers engage in on a daily basis.

Recapping techniques and practices

We have placed significant emphasis on the importance of testing and making incremental improvements. This approach not only maintains high code quality but also cultivates a well-rounded developer – honing critical thinking skills and the ability to focus on solving one problem at a time.

Writing user acceptance tests

User acceptance testing (**UAT**) is a pivotal part of the development process that ensures your application aligns with its specifications and functions as desired. Implementing UAT can aid in identifying issues early in the development process, ensuring your application is on the right trajectory.

As depicted in *Figure 13.3*, we emphasize that tests should be written from the end user's perspective, focusing on delivering customer value rather than on implementation details. This is especially pertinent when you commence the implementation of a feature at a higher level:

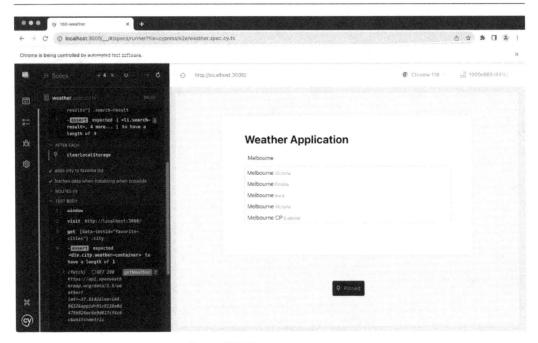

Figure 13.3: User acceptance tests

Test-Driven Development

TDD is a software engineering technique where tests are penned before code that needs to be tested. The process is primarily segmented into the following iterative development cycles: write a test, make the test pass, and then refactor. TDD can significantly help in ensuring that your code base is functional and bug-free, addressing the lack of tests at each level.

Refactoring and common code smells

Refactoring entails enhancing the design of existing code without altering its external behavior. Being cognizant of common code smells and continuously refactoring your code can lead to a healthier, more maintainable code base. This technique can be instrumental in tackling issues such as code duplication, complicated logic in views, and business leakage, among others.

Now that we've navigated through common anti-patterns, elucidated design principles, and explored techniques, it's time to look beyond this book. The following section provides a list of recommended readings that will further deepen your understanding and hone your skills in the domain of React, TypeScript, and software design principles.

Additional resources

As we draw the curtains on the contents of this book, the journey toward mastering React and avoiding common pitfalls is far from over. The landscape of web development, particularly with frameworks such as React, is ever-evolving. Continuous learning and adaptation are the keystones of staying relevant and proficient.

The following section is crafted to provide you with additional avenues for learning and exploration. These books are meticulously chosen to extend your understanding and introduce you to broader or complementary concepts in software development. Each book opens up a new dimension of knowledge, ensuring your growth trajectory remains steep and rewarding. So, as you step forward from here, let these resources be your companions in the continuous journey of learning and mastering the art of web development.

I would like to recommend a few seminal books that can further deepen your understanding and appreciation of good design, architecture, and development practices in the realm of web applications, with a particular focus on React and TypeScript:

*   *Refactoring: Improving the Design of Existing Code* by Martin Fowler

    Martin Fowler's cornerstone work on refactoring is a repository of knowledge on how to enhance the structure of your code while preserving its functionality and bug-free nature. It's a must-read for anyone aspiring to hone their refactoring skills.

*   *Clean Code: A Handbook of Agile Software Craftsmanship* by Robert Martin

    Robert Martin's *Clean Code* is a hallmark in the software development world. It delves into various practices and principles of penning clean, maintainable code, which is crucial for long-term success in complex projects.

*   *Patterns of Enterprise Application Architecture* by Martin Fowler

    Expand your architectural vistas with this book, which dissects various patterns crucial for designing robust and scalable enterprise applications. It's a significant read to grasp the bigger picture of application architecture, extending beyond the frontend realm.

*   *Test-Driven Development with React and TypeScript* by Juntao Qiu

    Immerse yourself in the world of TDD with a focus on React and TypeScript. This book navigates you through the principles of TDD and how it can markedly improve the quality, maintainability, and robustness of your code.

Summary

I want to extend my heartfelt gratitude for your dedication and passion for honing your craft and striving for technical excellence. It's individuals such as you, thirsty for knowledge and improvement, that propel our industry forward. As you turn over this last page, remember that the journey doesn't end here; in fact, it unfolds a new chapter of exploration and application in your real-world projects.

The essence of growth lies in the application and the continuous effort to apply what you've learned to challenge norms and strive for better solutions. This book aims to provide you with a solid foundation, but the real magic happens when you take these concepts, experiment with them, and integrate them into your daily work.

I sincerely appreciate your time spent traversing these pages and engaging with the material. It's my earnest wish that you carry forward this momentum, dive deeper, and continue to enrich the React community with your contributions. As you embark on the next phase of your journey, I wish you the best of luck. May your code be clean, your solutions innovative, and your journey rewarding.

Thank you, and good luck on your onward journey of continuous learning and improvement!

Index

C

City Search feature
  implementing 251
  OpenWeatherMap API 252, 253
  search result list, enhancing 256-258
  search results, stubbing 253-255
class-based model
  benefits 230, 231
code
  refactoring 140-143
Code Oven application 125, 126
  enhancing 223-227
  layered structure 243, 244
  MenuItem, transitioning
    to class-based model 229, 230
  MenuList, refactoring through
    custom hook 227, 228
code smells 292
**Command Query Responsibility Segregation
  (CQRS) 166, 178-180, 185**
commands 178
complicated logic, in views 15, 16
component 22
  creating, with props 23, 24
component-based structure 49
  benefits 50
  drawbacks 50
component design principles
  combining 72-80
  Page component example 72
composition 166, 169, 291
  using, to apply SRP 169-171
composition pattern 187
  ExpandablePanel component,
    implementing 190-195
  through HOCs 188
  UserDashboard component example 69-72
  using 69

Context API 14
  using, to resolve prop drilling issue 161-164
corruption 150
Cucumber 123
Cypress 85, 95
  installing 96, 97
  using, in end-to-end (E2E) testing 95

D

data modeling 288
data transformation 148
Decompose Conditional
  using 115, 116
Decorator design pattern 195
defensive programming 154
**Dependency Inversion Principle
  (DIP) 166, 171, 290**
  applying, in analytics button 174-178
  working 172, 173
describe function 89
design patterns 288
  context, as interface 289
  data modeling 288
  headless components 288
  higher-order components 288
  layered architecture 288
  render props 288
design principles 165
diffing algorithm 29
Document Object Model (DOM) 29
**Don't Repeat Yourself (DRY) principle
  18, 65-69, 151, 287, 290**
Downshift 212
drop-down list component 200
  developing 200-204
  keyboard navigation, implementing 205-208
  simplicity, maintaining 208, 209

www.packtpub.com

Subscribe to our online digital library for full access to over 7,000 books and videos, as well as industry leading tools to help you plan your personal development and advance your career. For more information, please visit our website.

Why subscribe?

- Spend less time learning and more time coding with practical eBooks and Videos from over 4,000 industry professionals

- Improve your learning with Skill Plans built especially for you

- Get a free eBook or video every month

- Fully searchable for easy access to vital information

- Copy and paste, print, and bookmark content

Did you know that Packt offers eBook versions of every book published, with PDF and ePub files available? You can upgrade to the eBook version at packtpub.com and as a print book customer, you are entitled to a discount on the eBook copy. Get in touch with us at customercare@packtpub.com for more details.

At www.packtpub.com, you can also read a collection of free technical articles, sign up for a range of free newsletters, and receive exclusive discounts and offers on Packt books and eBooks.

Other Book You May Enjoy

If you enjoyed this book, you may be interested in these other books by Packt:

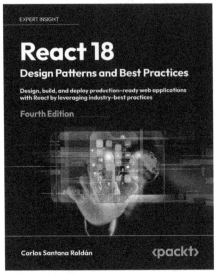

React 18 Design Patterns and Best Practices, 4e

Carlos Santana Roldán

ISBN: 978-1-80323-310-9

- Get familiar with the new React 18 and Node 19 features
- Explore TypeScript's basic and advanced capabilities
- Make components communicate with each other by applying various patterns and techniques
- Dive into MonoRepo architecture
- Use server-side rendering to make applications load faster
- Write a comprehensive set of tests to create robust and maintainable code
- Build high-performing applications by styling and optimizing React components

State Management with React Query.

Daniel Afonso

ISBN: 978-1-80323-134-1

- Learn about state and how it s often managed
- Discover how state splits into server state and Client state
- Solve common challenges with server state using React Query
- Install and configure React Query and its Devtools
- Manage server state data fetching by using the useQuery hook
- Create, update and delete data by using the useMutation hook
- Discover the use of React Query with frameworks like Next.js and Remix
- Explore MSW and the Testing Library to test React Query using hooks

Packt is searching for authors like you

If you're interested in becoming an author for Packt, please visit `authors.packtpub.com` and apply today. We have worked with thousands of developers and tech professionals, just like you, to help them share their insight with the global tech community. You can make a general application, apply for a specific hot topic that we are recruiting an author for, or submit your own idea.

Share Your Thoughts

Now you've finished *React Anti-Patterns*, we'd love to hear your thoughts! Scan the QR code below to go straight to the Amazon review page for this book and share your feedback or leave a review on the site that you purchased it from.

https://packt.link/r/1-805-12397-1

Your review is important to us and the tech community and will help us make sure we're delivering excellent quality content.

Download a free PDF copy of this book

Thanks for purchasing this book!

Do you like to read on the go but are unable to carry your print books everywhere?

Is your eBook purchase not compatible with the device of your choice?

Don't worry, now with every Packt book you get a DRM-free PDF version of that book at no cost.

Read anywhere, any place, on any device. Search, copy, and paste code from your favorite technical books directly into your application.

The perks don't stop there, you can get exclusive access to discounts, newsletters, and great free content in your inbox daily

Follow these simple steps to get the benefits:

1. Scan the QR code or visit the link below

https://packt.link/free-ebook/9781805123972

2. Submit your proof of purchase
3. That's it! We'll send your free PDF and other benefits to your email directly

www.ingramcontent.com/pod-product-compliance
Lightning Source LLC
LaVergne TN
LVHW081516050326
832903LV00025B/1509